CONTENTS

———

INTRODUCTION

"You don't need a mentor."

I met Rahul Rana in December 2019, and I could immediately sense he was bright and ambitious.

It was also clear he was frustrated with his current trajectory.

High school hadn't played out the way the then-freshman at Rutgers had hoped. Rahul had been in the top 5 percent of his class at his high school, an international piano performance winner, and the business program president. He was on the executive board of multiple clubs, well-liked by classmates and teachers, and a dozen other things you could easily brag about in a college essay. His grades and test scores were solid, but his shot at the more elite colleges and universities would depend on his extracurriculars, leadership roles, and ambition.

Rahul applied to fourteen schools, each promising him access to their exclusive networks and a path to lifelong success.

And all fourteen rejected him.

Rahul was devastated. Without a better option—he hadn't even applied to a "safety school"—he scrambled and enrolled at Rutgers, the state school in his home of New Jersey. He planned to take what he could get, work even harder, and transfer to a "better" school.

But his first semester of college didn't start much better. Rahul had his sights on working in venture capital—a dreamer's dream job to discover and invest in the next Facebook, SpaceX, or Amazon. But most of his classmates didn't share his ambition, and he couldn't find many Rutgers alumni currently working in venture capital. Plus, venture capital firms made it clear they only hired MBA graduates, traditionally those at the top of their class at Stanford, Harvard, or a handful of other elite schools. Ambition alone wasn't enough; Rahul just wasn't in these circles.

"I keep getting told I need to find a mentor," he shared.

Rahul's friend introduced us because he knew I had been a venture capitalist and investor, so he told Rahul to reach out to me for some advice. I knew something Rahul didn't; he didn't *need* a mentor or my advice. What Rahul *needed* was an opportunity and an approach to get hired by a venture capitalist.

"You don't need a mentor," I replied.

I allowed a pause on the other end of the phone to let that sink in.

"You need a *meeting*," I continued. "Tell me which venture capitalist you'd like to work for in my network."

"Like, anyone?" he replied.

"Anyone. Aim *high*."

We sat through another long pause. "I mean, anyone... it would have to be Josh Wolfe, the founder of Lux Capital. Yeah, it would have to be Josh."

Josh is a whale in the venture capital and start-up world. This guy founded and runs a four-billion-dollar venture capital firm. I'd met Josh once, and we had a terrific call getting to know one another, but why would Josh want to meet Rahul?

"Would you, like, really introduce me to him?" Rahul asked.

"I'll do you one better. Let's figure out a way where I don't even *need to* introduce you," I replied. "We will do something *together* to get you a meeting and hopefully something more."

Less than a year later, Rahul was an associate for Lux Capital, working for Josh at arguably one of the top five best-known venture capital firms. Lux Capital invests in "deep tech" ventures, and Rahul was now hunting for the next Apple, Google, and Amazon, collaborating with some of the world's best investors. *Business Insider* even named Rahul Rana one of the Top 29 Gen Z Venture Capitalists in 2021.

And all it took was *one* meeting—well, a just *bit* more, as you'll see later in the book.

Rahul shared in a podcast interview, "I found the right mentor." Yes, in case you were wondering, he's referring to me in the interview.

But here's the dirty little secret: Most people would never define *me* as his mentor. We've never met in person; we've only had two short conversations by phone; I didn't make a direct introduction to Josh, the person who hired Rahul, and I can't name a single piece of advice I gave him.

Is *this* mentoring?

You're about to learn the realities of modern mentorship aren't what they always seem.

Rahul got *exactly* what he needed to achieve what most ambitious people seek—his *opportunity*.

***

You are reading this book because you have goals. You're ambitious with your work, your passions, and your life. And ambitious people typically have *big* goals, the sort that are challenging, don't follow a linear path, and come with lots of uncertainty. You want to start a company. You want to get hired in a competitive industry. You want to build or launch something. You want to inspire people. These are big life goals.

These big life goals typically require others to help you achieve them.

That's where mentors come in. They can help you achieve your big life goals.

But, in truth, this is not in the way most people imagine a mentor will help you.

When I talk to people about mentors, they usually describe a mentor as a single wise, experienced person in their life who takes them under their wing and guides them with advice and wisdom toward their success. Rahul had assumed that too. Most ambitious people assume this.

You don't need *that* and neither did Rahul.

Modern mentorship is very different. We need mentors who help us solve our biggest challenges, problems, and struggles.

Great mentors will help you in these ways. This book helps you understand why the most successful people today attract, activate, and leverage great mentors differently to solve their ambitious challenges. You'll learn how to leverage a modern approach to mentorship in an unconventional way that helps ambitious people solve challenging obstacles they face. This book will help you if...

- You are in college or graduate school and feel like you aren't on the track you want in your life or career.
- You are a recent graduate or early in your career, and you don't feel like the job you have (or recent jobs) are helping you live up to your potential.
- You have been working for a bit and have decided it's time to do something different, but thinking about pivoting your career is overwhelming and unclear.
- You have an important project, start-up, business, product, or challenge. You need to expand your network and access beyond your current stage, level, or plateau but don't know how.
- Or some combination of these traits.

If you're ambitious with your career, passions, and life, you'll need mentors to help you realize your potential.

This book itself uses a simple idea.

Aim Higher, Ask Smaller, and Do It Again.

I taught Rahul and thousands of others like him the same idea, but this isn't even my idea.

Successful people have known this for years, even if they couldn't quite put their finger on it. The most successful people I've ever met describe their mentor relationships differently.

I interviewed, researched, and studied executives, entrepreneurs, billionaires, Grammy and Emmy winners, best-selling authors, military generals, award-winning chefs, and countless others like them. They described their mentoring experiences in ways that surprised even me. Very few talked about a single person who took them under their wing over long periods or guided them with their advice or wisdom. Their experiences were driven by what I call "opportunity bursts."

Rahul only needed a short six- to twelve-month period—his opportunity burst—to change his entire trajectory. In this period, he approached mentorship through the lens of aiming higher, asking smaller, and repeating it time and time again.

In hundreds of conversations, successful people usually could pinpoint their period of short, intense, surprising experiences transforming their lives and their trajectory. At the center of their opportunity bursts were people we call Super Mentors, individuals who provided them with their opportunity and helped them solve their problems and challenges.

The pattern is *nonobviously* obvious, which I hadn't considered when I began the research. But once I'd really thought about it and even reflected on my own life, the pattern made perfect sense. Today, I can summarize nearly every mentoring story as the mentee had aimed higher, asked smaller, and did this repeatedly throughout their careers and lives.

This book offers a modern approach to mentorship given today's reality in a more dynamic, more connected, and transparent world. The world is different now. Networks rather than hierarchies drive it. Yes, mentors are still important, but modern mentorship has changed how we make it effective. And you'll need to change with it.

This book will divide mentors into two categories by their role for the mentee:

1. **Inspirational** (advice, role model, motivational)
2. **Problem Solvers** (introductions, shared experiences, connections, direct opportunities)

Inspirational mentors make us feel good, feel heard, and may even offer us an example of what's possible for us. Maybe they offer a picture of who we could be, perhaps giving us some positive words of encouragement. Or maybe they just listen. Most mentorship falls into the 'Inspirational' category.

Problem Solvers are the mentors most of us seek. They help us with specific challenges, obstacles, hurdles, and roadblocks we encounter. Problems are a normal part of our lives, so recognizing them and working to solve them is a hallmark of success. Most people who haven't had transformative mentor experiences have only had inspirational mentors.

You want mentors who can help you solve your problems.

Whether you are doing something new and unknown—like trying to get interviews for your first job or internship, raising money for your start-up or to write a novel, working to break into a new career, or make in-roads into a dream role or company—or trying to accelerate at your current job in your current industry, you will experience problems that are difficult, challenging, and complicated to solve on your own. You'll need the *right* help.

Mentors can help drive tangible outcomes:
- Guidance to solve a specific challenge.
- Opportunities to collaborate or work on something together.
- Connections and access to people.

Problem Solvers (i.e., Super Mentors) provide these outcomes—beyond just advice and inspiration. They help us solve our greatest challenges. For people who currently have a mentor (just 37 percent), I found that nearly two-thirds of those reported receiving a *direct opportunity* from their mentor. Lasting mentor relationships come from people who actively help us solve a challenge or problem in our lives.

Most ambitious people I meet are surprised to learn they already have individuals in their lives who can solve their problems, becoming their Super Mentor. Exceptional mentors usually aren't the most famous, richest, networked, or inspirational people you know. The right person and the right ask can transform your trajectory.

You just need to figure out how to unlock opportunities.

HOW TO USE THE SUPER MENTORS BOOK

If you're anything like Rahul or other ambitious people, you may have picked up this book thinking you needed to find a mentor. And like I told Rahul, you don't need a mentor. You do need an opportunity. And with a focused effort over a few months, you're going to create many new opportunities from mentors. This book's guidance is different from most mentoring advice. Don't worry about the person (a.k.a. finding the perfect mentor); worry about the process (a.k.a. doing the key activities creating opportunities).

You will learn how to create your opportunity burst. You'll be *aiming higher, asking smaller, and doing it over and over again over a short period.* This philosophy is the foundation of a course I've taught to more than two thousand people, which has yielded thousands of unique, surprising, and amazing opportunities much like Rahul experienced.

It will take a series of small, smart actions performed repeatedly over a few months to reap huge rewards. The impact of these actions will compound over time—an effect that Einstein once called the

Eighth Wonder of the World. You're going to learn a process to create opportunities *through* mentors.

More specifically, you'll learn how to leverage the *PAST* framework, the way most hyper-successful people create Super Mentor relationships. This approach is built on the right people, ask, start, and time and will serve as your system to move *past* normal mentors into Super Mentors.

One person who knows a thing or two about Super Mentors is Adam Saven. Adam is the cofounder and CEO of PeopleGrove, the leading mentorship software used by more than 450 colleges, universities, and institutions worldwide. As a result, Saven has a wealth of knowledge on mentorship and how the most effective relationships form. Adam has been my partner and collaborator in building the Super Mentors framework.

"Many people think finding the right mentor is what matters. Find the right person, and everything happens from there," Adam told me. "But we find people who get jobs or opportunities from mentors engage differently. They reach out more, respond faster, ask questions, and are much more active in the process."

We want you as the reader to experience it firsthand. *You* have to drive value from mentors. Modern mentoring doesn't happen by accident.

"Obviously, mentoring matters. We see this in our work every day," Adam told me. "But we're also seeing how mentoring is wildly different today than five years ago. The traditional one-to-one, long-term relationship the word *mentorship* implies still has value. Still, more and more, learners are discovering that cultivating many relationships provides them with a wider range of guidance and, more importantly, greater access to opportunities."

My research into how the most successful people leveraged mentorship—aim higher, ask smaller, and do it again—is what Adam's team finds with its users and customers.

"The more relationships you build, the more ready you feel to tackle your next step," Adam shared. "Learners in our communities who had at least five casual mentor relationships were 78 percent more confident in their ability to succeed in the job market. The world looks so different today, and your ability to leverage casual and formal mentors isn't just a nice-to-have. It's a must-have."

I'd recommend reading the book sequentially from start to finish, as the concepts will build on one another. We built the book around the four laws of Super Mentors designed to get you a meeting with the right person and the right ask at the right time. But if you'd prefer to skip around—or come back to key pieces—here's what's ahead:

- Chapters 2 and 3 lay out some of the foundations of modern mentoring, including your role as the mentee and the "skill" of being mentored.
- Part I—Law of the Right Ask
  - Chapter 4, learn how to leverage the 'seeker' mindset and look for opportunities rather than advice
  - Chapter 5, defining a collaborative project to involve potential mentors in
  - Chapter 6, how to think smaller in what you ask for to build casual mentors
- Part II—Law of the Right People
  - Chapter 7, identify your 'aspirational peers' and expand your targets through their connections
  - Chapter 8, learn how to leverage the "Micro-Request" framework to build a relationship
- Part III—Law of Right Start
  - Chapter 9, understand how to grow and expand relationships through (faster) feedback loops
  - Chapter 10, discover how to embrace the unexpected opportunities and harness those that can transform you
- Part IV—Law of Right Time
  - Chapter 11 through 19 are a series of chapters designed to help you learn more about the right timing for specific mentors and how to best align your needs to the types of mentors who can

be most valuable—whether you are a current student, a seasoned executive, an aspiring entrepreneur, or a changemaker.

The book is full of "One Meeting Away" mini-summaries—look for the One Meeting Away boxes. We designed these to deconstruct how ambitious people like you were able to earn and leverage a single meeting for transformative results.

If you'd like to say hello, you can find me at eric@erickoester.com or @erickoester on Twitter or text me at 703.587.4430. You can find additional resources, interviews, and a community of creators at www.erickoester.com.

As long as you find multiple people rather than one person (covered in chapters 7 and 8) and create engagement with them through targeted engagements via positivity, projects, and micro-requests (covered in chapters 4, 5, and 6) that build relationships over time (covered in chapters 9 and 10), you'll begin to relatively quickly find your way unlocking powerful relationships that can lead to your inflection points.

Let's get started.

1

WHAT MAKES A
MENTOR SUPER?

Few topics create a stark divide between the *haves* and the *have nots* as mentors.

Sit in nearly any conference or college classroom and listen to one of the successful speakers telling their life story about how they "made it." Many of them will wax poetically about all the amazing mentors who helped them.

Now go out in the audience and talk to everyone else "in the trenches" trying to make it. These are the rest of us struggling in our job hunts, hustling to get promoted, starting a new business, raising capital, looking to make a career switch, moving to a new place, c just trying to do something for the first time. Ask them about m tors, and most roll their eyes at the number of times they hear, "ou really should get a mentor."

"Find a mentor," we're told when they should be teaching how to engage with one.

Christina Qi founded a billion-dollar hedge fund in er dorm room, started a data analytics company, serves on the bard at MIT, and is a member of the Forbes 30 under 30 list. She told ae the single most common question she gets from younger peopl is how to find a mentor so others can follow in her footsteps, or even if she would be their mentor. But here's the funny thing. She doesn't have one. She finally had to write a blog post announcing she didn't have a formal mentor to let others know it was okay if they didn't have one. Plenty of people *helped* her, but no "formal mentor."

And quite honestly, she never *needed* a mentor to succeed.

Most people seem to view a mentor like we view a college degree. It's another box you need to check if you're ambitious.

> **Mentor Fallacy:** Mentors give you advice, guidance, and ideas, but it's up to you to put them into action.
>
> **Super Mentor Reality:** Mentors are active in how they help, often providing opportunities and network access to help you solve a specific problem or challenge. Two-thirds of those who have a mentor report receiving a direct opportunity from their mentor.

Entrepreneur and author Rajesh Setty told me if you ask for help, just make sure it's valuable to *you*. And it's even better when it's valuable for you and easy for them.

LASTING MENTOR RELATIONSHIPS COME FROM PEOPLE WHO ACTIVELY HELP US SOLVE A CHALLENGE OR PROBLEM IN OUR LIVES.

Now, I understand if this sounds a little "inspirational" and not "problem-solving" enough. Let's cut to the chase and answer the critical question for this chapter:

What makes a mentor super?

> **Super** Mentors help solve significant problems in your life.

What are significant problems? You probably already know your most significant problems, especially if you sit down and thought about them. For most of us, our "significant problems" stem from the gap between what we want in our career and life and what we currently have.

This gap often ties to careers—a specific role or opportunity we want at a job or a promotion. It might be how to accelerate our career. For others, we're making a career or life transition. Sometimes, it is about an important project, start-up, business, product, or challenge. It could also be the new thing we're hoping to achieve.

The specific problem—how to get hired, funded, connected, or go to the next level—depends entirely on your specific circumstances.

Perhaps no group feels this as acutely as college students. After all, study after study tells us the number one reason someone pursues higher education is to open up opportunities for themselves—specifically career opportunities.

When we're at these critical life stages, it's common for us to look to others simply to guide us through uncertainty. Think of how many times you've gone into a conversation with the hopes of having the answer just magically appear as if the person on the other end can read your mind.

Here's the secret. Don't start with the person; start with the problem.

1. Figure out what help is valuable to you (what specific problem you need to be solved).
2. Figure out who is well-positioned to give you the help (what spe- cific opportunity you need).
3. Figure out how to make it easy for them to help you (what activities are easy for them and valuable for you).

Start with your problem. Find people who can help you. Make ^{y} for them to help.

The best mentors are super not because of what they sa~ what story they might tell but because of their *actions*. We spen~ much of our time hunting for a person to be our mentor rather ~ finding the right person who will actively help solve our proble~ Our job is to identify the right problem and then make it easy fc~ ~em to help.

Super mentors should drive tangible outcomes:
- Guidance to solve a specific challenge.
- Opportunities to collaborate or work on something together.
- Connections and access to people.

The right person with the right ask can transform our trajectory because they help us solve our greatest challenges.

Mentors are Super because of what they *do* not who they are.

AIM HIGHER, ASK SMALLER, AND DO IT AGAIN

Why do only a third of people have a mentor, despite most people admitting mentors are critically important for our success?

I struggled to answer this big question. Part of the problem comes down to storytelling.

> **Men tor Fallacy:** Nearly everyone has a mentor.
>
> **Super Mentor Reality**: Only about a third of people (37 percent) have a mentor.

We love simple, delightful, aspirational stories. I do it too throughout the book as you'll hear the stories from people like Sheryl Sandberg, Bradley Cooper, Warren Buffett, Oprah Winfrey, and many others as well as their mentors. I led off the introduction to the book with a story of how Rahul got hired by Josh Wolfe, one of the most successful venture capitalists on the planet.

But I don't want you to worry about *who* was the mentor. Instead focus on how the mentee was able to get such incredible and transformative opportunities. Who the mentor is doesn't matter. The opportunities the mentor creates for you matter.

Here are the origin stories of the mentoring relationships of some of the world's most successful people:

- Your daughter is my classmate in college. Could we meet? (Mark Zuckerberg)
- Want to come up for coffee? (Oprah Winfrey)
- Want to go to the movie premiere together? (Bradley Cooper)
- Would you be willing to be a speaker for a new student club we're starting? (Sheryl Sandberg)
- Can I come to dinner after class? (Warren Buffett)

These moments don't sound very earth-shattering. They all sound pretty mundane, which is precisely the point. It's not *that* they met or even *how* they met. It's how the mentee leveraged the relationship to solve a key problem. They all form the Super Mentor pattern: aim higher, ask smaller, and do it again.

Most of us have never learned how to *leverage* mentors.

You'll find oodles of mentor-matching events, mentor networking, articles on finding a mentor, and inspirational stories of famous mentor-mentee pairs. But very little out there describes how to engage with a mentor to solve your problems.

Quite frankly, too many people evaluate mentors over *time*. They worry about developing this deep, intimate relationship with someone over a long period. They see a mentor as one person they schedule regular check-ins with, who they turn to regularly and frequently for advice and guidance. Those people are supposed to magically drop into their life at school, work, or in their day-to-day life.

This sounds great on paper, but the people *you* want don't operate this way, nor do they have time for this type of relationship.

And, you don't even need it.

You need to know those small actions to get you the meeting or the opportunity to change your life.

> **Mentor Fallacy:** Time spent matters in developing a deep relationship with your mentors.

> **Super Mentor Reality**: Time and outputs are not the same. Super Mentors can provide 10–100x value in a fraction of the time others may take.

It's *not* about the time spent together. I've researched and studied the mentoring relationships of nearly two hundred of the world's most successful people. I've taught thousands of students these principles. Super mentoring is about the opportunities created together regardless of time.

You create those opportunities with your mentor through small actions done with a bit of enthusiasm.

As Rahul discovered, some people can transform your life with a single meeting. I call them Super Mentors. You can get access to them, get help from them, and create opportunities with them.

I don't want you to worry about who your mentor is, but instead focus on the small actions that most matter to unlock your opportunities from any mentor. You're going to learn how to act, engage, and behave.

I love the quote by Jon Katzenbach: "Start with changing behaviors, not mindsets."

Most of us "in the trenches" won't need a dramatic mindset shift. You already know mentors can be a transformative force for you. You'd love to have a good one. You, maybe, haven't seen value from yours. You want the simple and small actions that matter to make that transformative force for you. You need to change some of your behaviors.

As Katzenbach says, "It is much easier to 'act your way into new thinking' than to 'think your way into new actions.'"

This book is about *acting your way into new thinking* about mentors.

***

You met Rahul Rana already; his story is instructive. He did what most of us do. He was asking people to be his mentor. He was attending mentor-matching events. He was reaching out to alumni to pick their brains.

However, after he did, he kept getting inspiration and advice. He was trying *really* hard and feeling bad about himself because it wasn't working. He wasn't getting help to solve his problems of getting a job or an opportunity in venture capital. He was operating with a very traditional view of mentors.

Rahul had what many people have—a linear idea of mentorship. He was looking for *a* mentor, particularly an exceptional one, his Yoda.

"Don't get me wrong," Adam Saven told me when he first heard Rahul's story. "Mentors in the truest sense of the word are important. But Rahul's story is one we've seen so often at PeopleGrove. College students network with the idea that a perfect mentor is out there for them, and when they don't find that person right away, it can be very deflating."

When I met Rahul, I encouraged him to ratchet down the pressure.

1. Figure out what he *needed* from his mentors.
2. Create *more* casual, natural mentor relationships.
3. Work to turn some of those relationships into Super Mentor relationships.

There is not just one perfect person to help you solve your most pressing challenges and problems.

For Rahul, this meant he needed to narrow his scope and broaden his outreach simultaneously. We discussed scoping out a project. He decided to research and write a book about his interest in "moonshots"—individuals working on big, crazy, audacious ideas and companies trying to change the world.

"I never really thought about writing a book," he admitted. He hadn't realized that even if he never published the book, it would provide him with a critical tool to engage with the people he wanted to meet.

Rahul didn't need a mentor; he needed a project.

Projects are tangible, finite, meaningful things providing us a reason to engage with people. They hopefully feel like fun or at least don't feel like work. Then it's not just, "Will you be my mentor," or, "Can I pick your brain." Your project gives you a *context* or a *tactical reason* for your engagement with someone. It is about matching your interests to the project you are excited about and then making the project more collaborative. It's a way to signal your interests to others.

Rahul's project was the first step for him to *narrow his scope around his project*.

From there, Rahul expanded his outreach. He stopped looking for a mentor. Since he wanted to break into venture capital and was interested in venture capitalists who backed some of the biggest, craziest ideas called moonshots, those people became his targets to speak to for his book. Then he began engaging—much smaller and simpler at first—by following them on social media, engaging with their content, and eventually reaching out to see if they had a few minutes to talk with him about his project.

This was his second step: *broadening his outreach*.

Rahul radically increased the number of potential opportunities he could earn.

Many people he'd reach out to wouldn't reply, many took multiple follow-ups, and a few thought the project was intriguing and loved his ambition and persistence. All of these relationships—me included—became his casual mentors. They never formally agreed to be his mentors, had a conversation about "going steady" as his mentor, or took the time to change their shared LinkedIn statuses.

Rahul began to change his behavior.

He engaged on social media with more people interested in moon-shot ideas. He'd post his thoughts about moonshot companies. He had conversations with his new peers and near-peers. He continued to progress on his project, which required collaboration with these casual mentors he was cultivating.

One of these casual mentors would be Josh Wolfe of Lux Capital. Why would Josh want to meet Rahul?

Remember, Rahul was a sophomore at Rutgers. Lux didn't hire sophomores and didn't hire from Rutgers. But Josh made time for a personal call with Rahul, made time to read Rahul's work, and hired Rahul without an interview.

Rahul had behaviors *aligned* with Josh. More specifically, Rahul narrowed his focus and broadened his outreach.

Rahul created a reason for Josh to engage.

At first, Josh was just one more person in Rahul's expanded out-reach to talk to about his project. In a cold email, Rahul shared details about his book project, the activities he'd done and the people he'd met, and the context of why it was relevant to Josh and his work.

That cold email was enough for Josh to recognize the potential for the meeting to be valuable. Rahul still had to follow up seven times to get his first fifteen-minute call with Josh. But Rahul wasn't waiting on the meeting. He continued to work on the project.

Then in their first phone conversation, Rahul shared his learning about moonshots and the mindset of moonshot founders. He asked Josh if it matched his experience and findings. Four months later, Rahul shared a single chapter he'd written based on insights from Josh and others.

"No résumé, no interview, no application," Rahul said. "I sent him a chapter of my book, I thanked him for his contribution, and he hired me on the spot for an internship."

Rahul put himself in a position to have a few of his new relation-ships create transformative opportunities. Rahul had built a Super Mentor.

Right Person: Josh Wolfe is one of the premier venture capital investors whose firm focuses on deep technology (e.g., biotechnology, nanotechnology, space exploration, and human longevity).

Right Ask: "Can I interview you for my book about moonshots—start-up companies who make big bets and have the potential to change humanity?"

Right Start: Social media engagement followed by a cold email, multiple follow-ups to schedule a call, and then delivery of a book chapter that includes Josh's insights.

Right Time: Rahul connected with Josh at the height of the pandemic, just before the summer, as traditional interviewing for venture capital associates in MBA programs was still being figured out. Following his book interview, Rahul followed up to ask to work for Josh.

"Getting a job at Lux wasn't the end," he said. "It was the beginning for me. Now I'm working with a team to build a frontier biotech moonshot factory called Arcadia Science that makes my book a reality. I'm building a Deeptech venture capital fund and network at the university level. I'm working with a Hollywood producer to create movies and animated short films around optimistic science fiction."

All this while finishing his junior year at Rutgers, which he has no plans to transfer from!

The irony is this. Many brilliant, ambitious people got accepted to those fourteen prestigious schools that rejected Rahul and would gladly trade places with him today.

Rahul Rana credits much of this to mastering the skill of leveraging mentors. He aimed higher, made smaller asks of people, and repeated this process repeatedly until it worked. In Rahul's case, it worked multiple times with multiple people.

"I stopped looking for mentors," he said, "and I began to get help from many people who became mentors."

***

Exceptional mentors don't give you advice. They give you opportunities.

For Rahul, this just meant helping him with a series of small actions to unlock the opportunities, eventually transforming his trajectory and his life.

Like most people, Rahul focused on *who* would mentor him. Once he changed his approach to focus on how he'd leverage a mentor, the results changed. Rahul learned how to act, engage, and behave.

For me, my experience with Super Mentors all started with a walk.

I had several relationships with people I would call mentors in my teens and twenties. Those relationships were fine and kind people, but none of them would lead to a transformative experience in my life. My relationship with mentoring would change in 2013 when Steve Blank invited me to his ranch just south of San Francisco.

Steve is an eight-time entrepreneur turned educator, teaching at Stanford, Berkeley, Columbia, and New York University. He created the National Science Foundation (NSF) Innovation Corps and his last start-up, E.piphany, which was such a big success that he "retired" in 1999. But Steve made much of his broader impact after his start-up journey. He developed the Lean Startup movement, fundamentally changing how founders build start-ups, how professors teach entrepreneurship, how science is commercialized, and how companies and the government innovate.

In the start-up world, everyone knows Steve. I read his books and took his online courses, but we didn't meet until he joined the UP Global nonprofit board with me. UP Global runs events like Startup Weekend and Startup Week. Admittedly, I was a bit starstruck meeting Steve but tried to play it cool. In one of our board meetings, I mentioned to the group my current start-up was based in San Francisco, and Steve replied, "Oh, you should drive down to the ranch someday and say hi. Any of you in the Bay Area are welcome at the ranch."

We continued to see each other at monthly board meetings, but about six months after my start-up had begun to crumble, I realized I should make time to see Steve at his ranch.

It was a long drive to Steve's home in Pescadero, California, longer than I expected, and I arrived late. Steve, gracious despite my tardiness, met me at the car, left my bag in his house, and said, "Let's go on a walk."

He took me on a well-worn walking path leading from the main home. He periodically stopped to point something out or move something out of the path as we meandered. He shared a few stories about the ranch's history and why he and his wife purchased it.

I had yet to publicly share the struggles of our start-up and my as-yet-unannounced departure from it, so when Steve asked me how things were going with the company, I paused before answering.

"We raised too much money," I confided. "We don't have things figured out, and our investors are getting squeamish. My cofounder told me I needed to go about a month ago, so I'm unsure what's ahead."

"Totally normal," he replied matter-of-factly. "Happened to me. Have you processed what went wrong?"

In truth, I hadn't. I was focused on the shot to my pride, my anger at my business partner, and my overall frustration at the situation. I hadn't even stopped to process why the company was at this point. I was embarrassed, and this was one of the first conversations I'd had about it.

"Not really," I replied.

"Then I've got an idea for you," Steve continued. "You should teach. I've found that the only way to learn is to force yourself to teach others. If you want, maybe we can do something together. I've got this new project that might be good."

In some ways, I'd imagined Steve would suggest another start-up to consider or recommend I go into investing. I'd anticipated and expected these opportunities. But as a Super Mentor, Steve had access to and awareness of opportunities that I'd never even considered. What I received that day was impactful. He knew what I couldn't see (yet).

"Let's keep talking about it," he said.

I looked up and realized we were back at my car. Steve grabbed my bag he'd stashed in the doorway when I arrived and handed it to me, saying, "This project could be good for you. Let's follow up when you're back."

I wasn't sure what had happened during those thirty minutes, but it kicked off something unexpected. The next day, I followed up and told Steve I thought teaching sounded fun, and I'd be open to whatever he thought.

Over the next six months, I went through a transformative whirlwind. Steve knew what I needed and took it upon himself to volunteer me to help him launch a new course. I went on to teach with Steve in more than a dozen places across the country and expanded the course to more than sixty accelerator and incubator programs around the globe. It was hard work, but it was enjoyable and something I speak about to others nearly ten years later. As I learned later, Steve was a Super Mentor of the highest order. To help find their footing, he worked with other failed founders like me, including Eric Ries (author of *The Lean Startup*) and Derek Andersen (cofounder of Startup Grind & Bevy).

I realized later that Steve had done something very unique with each of us.

One Meeting Away: Eric Koester

Right Person: Steve Blank had experienced start-up successes and failures. He'd been able to learn about me over the prior six months we casually shared on a nonprofit board.

Right Ask: What's ahead for me after getting fired from my start-up?

Right Start: Asking to visit Steve's ranch, a walk, an offer to teach together, and six months of collaboration to launch a course together worldwide.

Right Time: Steve wanted to launch something new and was looking for someone looking for a project to help do it well, leading to the opportunity to launch programs in thirty countries at more than seventy-five start-up accelerators, incubators, and laboratories.

I wondered if I could do the same thing Steve did for us for others. I first tried teaching a class at Georgetown. It was fine, but I quickly realized I wasn't having any lasting or transformative impact on my students—certainly, nothing even close to Steve's impact on me.

So I asked myself a straightforward question, "What would Steve do?"

Steve was a transformative force in my life, not because of the amount of time or individual support or coaching I received from him. He created opportunities and access for me. We had a project to engage in. Could I create something similar for others? I continued down the rabbit hole and studied other successful people and their mentors.

I realized I had something here, so I decided to take what I'd learned and bring a new course to Georgetown to help my students create Super Mentor relationships. That course has become one of Georgetown's most popular elective courses, and now I teach versions of it to nearly two thousand people. Just two years after the first time it was offered, the course would be named the most innovative course of the year, and soon I was named the Entrepreneurial Educator of the Year by USASBE.

I was more than a little surprised by the reaction. But maybe it makes sense. We all know that we need help from others to succeed. We don't necessarily know *how* to get the right help. Some incredible people are willing to help us, and we just need to make it easier for them.

Steve offered me a playbook that became the core of the course: **Help someone work on a meaningful project that lets them engage with people they admire.** While my project with Steve was a new course, I've learned how to help anyone develop a project, including novels, audio shows, TEDx talks, an album, a YouTube channel, coaching businesses, and nonfiction books. Then, we work on leveraging that project to create potentially transformative relationships with others.

This approach leverages everything I've learned about Super Mentors. You create them by aiming higher, asking smaller, and repeating the process. This process works because you are building a collection of casual mentors, some of whom will ultimately become your Super Mentors.

When I tell people about what I teach at Georgetown, almost everyone says, "Oh, can I take the class?" For years, I've had to answer no to that question, at least to everyone who didn't happen to be one of the ten thousand students at Georgetown. But that is no longer the case. I've begun offering workshops to everyone, and I've written this book, so you don't have to go to Georgetown to learn how to create Super Mentor relationships.

You will have to stop waiting. You'll have to stop asking for advice. You have to have fun with the process. And you're going to have to ask for opportunities and access.

***

If you've read this far, now is a good moment to take stock of your problems. Remember, it's not bad to have problems—quite the opposite. Ambitious people have big dreams, and their problem is how to realize them. Achieving big, hard, challenging goals rarely happens by ourselves.

I've used this framing question to help thousands of my students:

Ask yourself that very question. What would you love to do more of? Not tomorrow, but in the future. Dream a bit, and push the envelope. Ten years is quite a while, so you've got quite a bit of time, even if you're nowhere near it.

Take that longer-term goal of what you'd like to do more of and examine where you are today as far as a path there—job, industry, role, start-up, profession, skill, finances, time, etc.

The specificity of your ten-year ambitions isn't important. You don't necessarily want to be in a specific role, industry, or place. Think about activities you'd like to do more of:

- I enjoy coaching and collaborating, so I'd love to be able to do more building and managing of a team.
- I enjoy writing, so I'd love to have the freedom and flexibility to write more books.
- I enjoy traveling, so I'd like to work for a company that lets me work from anywhere or have a travel job.

That space between the activities you're doing today and where you'd like to be is where Super Mentors come in.

This gap may seem daunting or overwhelming. And it probably is when you start. You want to start by simplifying the gap down to a problem statement. Then you'll identify people who can help you, some you may already know and many you'll meet. Finally, you will make it easy for them to help you. It seems simple when you write it out... because it is. The best part about modern mentorship is there is a repeatable, reliable process anyone can leverage. You just have to leverage it.

MENTORS ARE SUPER BECAUSE OF WHAT THEY DO NOT WHO THEY ARE.

You have or can get access to plenty of incredible people to help you solve your problems and become your Super Mentors. We will teach you the framework behind it: aim higher, ask smaller, and do it again.

Here are a few words of encouragement as you begin your journey.

First, people are kind. When I've taught this class in the past, my students were blown away at the kindness of busy people. They genuinely want to help ambitious people.

Second, even the most unkind people are too busy to be unkind. Many of us worry about engaging busy, successful people who are asked for things all the time. The good news is that even the most unkind people will just ignore you. In all my years of doing this— where my students have probably sent hundreds of thousands of emails and messages to people they didn't know—I've never had one receive any mean or hurtful replies. The responses are either positive or nothing.

Third, warm networks exist all around us. *Everyone* has access to a whole range of networks. The internet and social media allow us to access a host of these communities that can open the doors to opportunities. While leveraging those networks is important, it can be very easy to fall into the complacency trap—as if just being a member of that community will get you where you want to go with little effort on your part. What matters in mentorship is how you act and behave, and the great news is that those are things you can learn.

Fourth, although building and harnessing Super Mentor relationships takes time, you'll be amazed at how quickly you can begin seeing the benefits of this approach. Researching people, engaging with them in public and social ways, and working on something creates rapid personal growth and value. What's been most personally fulfilling for me is the level of agency, autonomy, and control it's created for me. I'm not waiting around hoping to be plucked from obscurity; I'm the one doing the plucking. No matter the time it takes to create, cultivate, and unlock the relationships, you'll find yourself motivated in new ways than before.

***

SUPER MENTORS HELP SOLVE IMPORTANT PROBLEMS IN YOUR LIFE. IT'S YOUR JOB TO MAKE IT EASY.

- What help is valuable to you at this moment? What specific problem you need to be solved with your career, your passion projects, your education, or your life?
- Who is well-positioned to give you the help you? Do you know them already? What specific opportunity do you need—an introduction, a chance to share your work or ideas, a job, or something else?
- How to make it easy for them to help you? What activities would be easy for them, and valuable for you? Force yourself to thing very small: What could they do for you in fifteen minutes or less? What guidance, advice, or help could they give that was simple?

'Who are you?

2

YOU WILL MAKE YOUR OWN MENTORS

Many unique and inspiring stories tell about the mentors of super successful people. And those stories are correct that mentors matter.

But mentors do *not* make the mentee.

Yes, Steve Jobs mentored Mark Zuckerberg. Maya Angelou mentored Oprah Winfrey. Benjamin Graham mentored Warren Buffett. Larry Summer mentored Sheryl Sandberg. Steven Spielberg mentored J.J. Abrams. Sir Freddie Laker mentored Richard Branson. Larry Ellison mentored Marc Benioff. Even Professor Dumbledore mentored Harry Potter, and Yoda mentored Luke.

And yes, these all make for great stories that fit an easy-to-follow narrative. Author Joseph Campbell documented our fascination with mentors in stories through the "Hero's Journey" where a mentor guides us—the hero—through a challenging period. That approach of a single figure taking us under their wing and guiding us to success has stuck. Most people view mentors this way, as a single figure who advises and guides us through a challenge.

But it's not true.

What *actually* happens in these real-world, heroic mentor stories? I decided to look deeper into high-profile mentor-mentee pairs and their relationships. I wanted to see *how* the relationship formed and continued over time, studying what I could reconstruct about the early encounters. And after thousands of hours of extensive analysis into 142 highly successful individuals and their actions, activities, and experiences with their mentors, it was pretty obvious.

The mentee *made* their mentor relationship successful.

Did Steve Jobs, Maya Angelou, and Steven Spielberg make a difference in the lives of their famous mentees? Most definitely. But were Mark Zuckerberg, Oprah Winfrey, or J.J. Abrams plucked from obscurity and *made* successful because of these mentors' advice, guidance, force, and will? No way.

Of course, we can't replay history, but I'd wager if Jobs, Angelou, or Spielberg weren't their mentors, Zuck, Oprah, and J.J. would have found other people and other ways to get the help they needed on their paths. They each had a skill at cultivating mentorship.

Mentor Fallacy: Mentors decide who they mentor.

Super Mentor Reality: Mentees drive mentor relationships. Most people won't have a formal or even informal process to define the relationship as mentorship. Instead, they let actions guide the relationship (a.k.a., mentorship is action-based, not agreement-based).

Successful mentees leverage mentors differently. I found that skill across nearly every successful mentor-mentee story.

And even better, you can learn this skill.

What you see is that those hyper-successful mentees identify those individuals who can help them. Then they cultivate their mentor relationships. They create opportunities *with* their mentors, and they repeat that simple process over and over again throughout their careers.

The most successful people have learned to master the skill of leveraging mentors.

This isn't to say that people don't have advantages when it comes to mentors. Being part of a college network, the General Electric alumni community, or whatever group *can* give you an edge or perhaps easier access to potential mentors to help you.

But simply being in those communities, having that access, or even being matched to a mentor isn't enough to make you. According to a Strada-Gallup Alumni Survey, only 9 percent of alumni rate their network as "helpful" or "very helpful." Mentees expect the alumni mentors to make the relationship, not the other way around.

Then why isn't that story being told? For one, it's a little less sexy than the "without this mentor, I wouldn't have been a success" story. But an entire cultural narrative also screws up our perceptions of how mentoring happens.

We are force-fed hero's journey, and then we are informed that *we* are the hero. (Yipee!) Much like the "made-for-television" stories of our most successful members of society, the success stories reinforce a hero's journey and will go something like this:

1. Be Ambitious
2. Meet Your Mentor
3. Become a Success

All the good things about hard work, passion, and a little bit of luck are sprinkled in too, but the tales of our heroes often lack a lot of the nuance that matters here.

Today's arranged mentorship focus reinforces the overall perception of mentorship as a "thing you try to get." Most people who are cynical about mentoring will describe their failed mentor-matching experience, often created as part of a "speed-dating" style experience.

Today colleges and universities work hard to create mentor-matching programs with their successful alums. Companies make mentorship programs for new hires with their peers and their managers. Professional organizations and trade associations pair new members with mentors when they join.

But in my study of uber-successful people, I asked them about how they met mentors. I can't point to a single example of anyone meeting through a structured program.

Then why is it so common? You're probably wondering why all these organizations focus on mentorship?

My theory is mentorship is good for business.

All these institutions and companies want you to feel connected. They want you to feel supported. They hope you feel welcomed. You remain in the group, contribute, and help others behind you if you do. All that's good for their businesses.

But that's okay. Just because it's good for their company doesn't necessarily mean it's bad for you. It can speed along the process *if* you know how to take advantage of it.

That's where these programs fall short. Organizations design these programs with a flawed definition of mentoring and fail to set the right expectations for mentees. Learners enter into a program with such structure that they wait for some kind of Deus Ex Machina, where their unsolvable mentorship problem is suddenly resolved by the "machine" of the program.

The programs often fail to remember that mentorship depends on the mentee.

***

This is all one of those good-news-bad-news things.

On the one hand, it's great to know that I don't need to wait around for some mentor to save me or someone to match me with a mentor speed-dating style.

But on the other hand, what in the world do I do instead? An entire industrial complex has been created to let me—the hero that I am—search for this savior of a mentor I'm told I get when I'm admitted to whatever version of cool kids group I'm waiting on.

We create a pressure cooker experience where the perfect mentor will unlock our goals, dreams, and aspirations. You can blame Yoda,

Dumbledore, Morpheus, and Glinda the Good Witch for ratcheting up our expectations of mentors as kids. The truth is we first need to *stop trying so darn hard.*

AIM TO HAVE MANY MENTORS

Successful people celebrate the vast number of mentors they've had. Everyone from Dell Founder and CEO Michael Dell, Virgin CEO Richard Branson, Facebook COO Sheryl Sandberg, director Steven Spielberg, GE CMO Beth Comstock, and others all publicly share they had multiple mentors throughout their careers. While they also admit that one or more may have been more impactful than others, this didn't lessen the impact of any of the others.

> **'I'VE HAD MANY MENTORS THROUGHOUT MY CAREER.'**

Initially, I was surprised at the number of casual and formal mentor relationships mentioned by the 142 highly successful individuals we studied for the book. But once you think about it more, having many helpful mentors in your life makes perfect sense: you'll need different help at different points in your life, and you'll need help from multiple different people to solve some of your biggest challenges.

If you've ever played a video game, you're probably familiar with the idea of the 'power up,' an object you obtain that adds a temporary ability or benefit to the player. You might jump higher, have extra lives, skip by a challenging monster, etc. You need different 'power ups' at different times, places, and levels of any game. Mentors are like modern 'power ups' in the game of life… the right person, ask, start, and time with your mentors can be extremely powerful to navigate a challenging situation or take advantage of a unique opportunity. And like video game 'power ups' that give you extra lives, powers, or shortcuts, you'll need lots of different ones depending on the challenge in front of you.

Successful individuals report having many mentors over their careers and even have multiple at one time. One of the most common fallacies I see among ambitious individuals is a belief that you're looking for a single mentor to drive value.

You are likely to create more opportunities for yourself if you build multiple casual mentors and create smaller, effective engagements with them.

> **Mentor Fallacy:** Successful people have a single mentor throughout their lives and careers.
>
> **Super Mentor Reality:** Successful people have many mentors, some of whom might be more impactful than others.

Author and entrepreneur Arvid Kahl says successful people build a community of people around them. That community increases our "opportunity surface area," he says. The more people around us in our community who feel connected to us, know what we are capable of, and are incentivized to help us will increase the chances they do.

My conversations with Adam Saven amplify this point. "A big trend we've seen in mentorship over the last few years is the growing importance of what sociologists call 'weak ties,'" Adam shared. "They are not 'weak' in terms of their power (in fact, quite the opposite), but they require much less maintenance—think a parent's friend that you want to run a real quick question by. And since those ties are more plentiful, there is a greater chance that the opportunity a mentee is looking for lies in that network."

Heroes don't need a single guide for their journey. Heck, if you're on a journey, don't you want the best guide for that challenge? When you come to a mountain, get the guide who has climbed the mountain. When you are about to jump out of a plane, best to call on the guide who is good at packing a parachute. You need the right 'power up' for the level you are playing.

That's why it's important to design an enjoyable process that lets you aim higher, ask smaller, and do it again (until it works... and then do it when you need it again). Call all these helpful people you are working with to solve your problems a mentor. Know they are your secret 'power ups.' Treat them as mentors, and they'll often find ways to help you beyond what you expect.

Instantly you will increase your opportunity surface area.

START WITH THE MENTORS YOU ALREADY HAVE.

Once you realize you make your mentors, you'll begin to see the people you already have around you differently.

Most of us have mentors already, whether we currently call them our mentors or not.

Start with this simple change.

Tell yourself the helpful people in your life are mentors.

Remember, *you* are on a hero's journey. And that makes you the hero of this amazing journey you're on. Those who will provide help and assistance on that journey are your mentors.

Own it.

Once you call someone your mentor—even just in your mind— you will automatically change how you engage with them.

We treat mentors differently.

Then why are we often so afraid to call someone our mentor?

I believe this happens for two reasons.

First, we feel like we need to have a DTR talk first—*define the relationship*. We have to talk about it and ask the person if it's okay. That means we put ourselves out there for rejection, asking this prospective mentor if they agree we are in a mentoring relationship.

Second, we often feel like we should only have one primary mentor, so we're holding out on labeling someone our mentor in case someone better comes along.

Neither of these is true.

The first step to change your relationship with mentoring is thinking of helpful people as mentors. You don't need to ask their permission or change how you speak to them.

Act as if helpful people in your life were mentors.

Create more casual, natural mentor relationships. Remember, calling someone your mentor isn't offensive to them; it's usually quite flattering. Plus, much like how Facebook has redefined the term "friend" for us, it's okay to describe informal, casual, helpful relationships as mentors. I've had dozens of people in my career say, "I spoke to one of your mentees..." Never once did I say, "Well, they aren't really my mentee..."

> **Mentor Fallacy:** You need to confirm with your mentor that they *are* your mentor.
>
> **Super Mentor Reality:** Mentor is not a title. It's an activity. If someone provides you advice, guidance, access, or opportunities, they are mentoring you. That person is—by definition—a mentor. Modern mentorship isn't an exclusive, limited relationship.

And once you realize you can and should have more casual mentors, take a look at the people you currently have around you.

Most likely, you've already got casual mentors in your life. And that's terrific. Your decision to label someone as your mentor will immediately change your relationship with them... for the better. Rahul Rana called me his mentor, but we never discussed it, never agreed on it, and never shook the label. But he decided to treat me as his mentor. That decision changed the way he engaged with me... for the better.

And there's no better way to start that process by inventorying who you already have in your life who is already or could quickly provide you a *free* transfer of "assets." Here's how you can begin a process to identify who has already been a helpful resource to you:

- Who have I spoken with for career or educational advice?
- Who has done informal or informational interviews with me?
- Who welcomed me into a new school, group, organization, or job?
- Who have I engaged with in organizations I'm a part of—volunteering, hobbies, sports, groups, associations, etc.?
- Who have I met who was a speaker, professor, teacher, or facilitator and helped me learn something new?

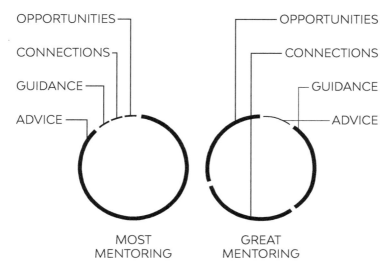

OPPORTUNITIES	OPPORTUNITIES
CONNECTIONS	CONNECTIONS
GUIDANCE	GUIDANCE
ADVICE	ADVICE

MOST
MENTORING

GREAT
MENTORING

WHY MOST MENTOR RELATIONSHIPS FAIL

HOW TO REDTR (REDEFINE THE RELATIONSHIP)?

Many of these individuals you identify are likely to have played a role in your life as more of an inspirational mentor, offering you advice, serving as a role model, or perhaps more. We want to start by moving them from inspiration to Problem Solver.

Chapter 5 will discuss the importance of defining a project to engage prospective mentors, as you saw with Rahul.

If you already have a project, one of the simplest and easiest things you can do is reach out to the current individuals who have already been helpful and engage them on the potential project you're considering. Make the outreach or conversation around something important to you but easy for them.

Review the list of common projects that are meaningful and collaborative: an article series, a book, a concert or art demonstration, a student club, conference or event series, a course or workshop, a new design or product idea, a podcast season/series, some research you'd like to do and publish, or a video show/series. Identify any that could be interesting and schedule a conversation to discuss how to select a project.

Remember, you don't have to know what the project is yet but just begin around identifying a project category as a reason to engage with people who have already been helpful.

SAMPLE EMAIL REDTR MESSAGE

Hi [Name],

Hope you are doing well. [Reference a recent event or activity in their life—something you observed on their social media feed.] I am planning to tackle a new project. Right now I'm considering working on [list 2+ project types]. I don't yet have the topic or direction laid out, but I wanted to talk through the project types with you first. I thought your insights could be really valuable. Would you be available to do a short twenty-minute phone interview in the next couple of weeks? I'm early in the process and would appreciate your thoughts.

[Your Name]

In part IV of the book, we'll discuss some of the most common Super Mentors to help more closely match periods in our lives when we seek or leverage mentorship.

COMMON INFORMAL MENTORS

- Professors and school administrators.
- Advisors or speakers in your organizations, groups, and clubs.
- Peers or near-peers (individuals with more experience in something but at or around the same age as you).
- Alumni of your school/college.
- Internship or job managers.

***

You make your mentors.

Mentors do not make you. No one makes you but you.

However, mastery of the skill to leverage mentors has the power to alter your trajectory in some remarkable ways. You'll just need to change behaviors and actions first.

3

THE SKILL OF BEING MENTORED

Let's start with an essential rule:

STOP USING THE WORD "MENTOR."

Do you want to know the fastest way to get a *potential* mentor to decline to meet with you? That's right, use the word mentor.

First Round Capital launched a program pairing the founders of companies it invests in with successful and established people in business. They spoke to the one hundred most favorably reviewed "mentors" matched to founders in their program. The number one reason these successful mentors were dissuaded or disinclined to talk to someone was they used the word mentor.

They reported the word mentor felt like more *work*. It implies a long-term relationship, lots of time, and developing this deep relationship with someone you barely know. It isn't how modern, effective mentorship works.

"If you seek help from someone, make sure that it is easy for them, valuable for you. And if you want to help someone, it should be easy for you, valuable for them."

—RAJESH SETTY

Remember, you don't need a mentor. This book is designed for any ambitious person who wants to create transformative opportunities—inflection points—in their lives. You know or can get to the people who will help you make those opportunities.

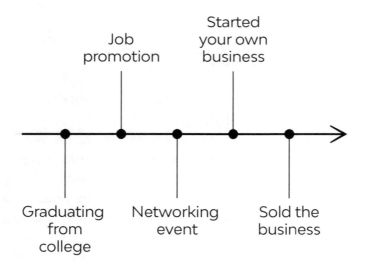

But here's a little secret. It doesn't matter if *they* call themselves your mentor or not. Your goal is to be able to call them *helpful*.

Shark Tank's Robert Herjavec identifies his most important mentor as his then-boss, Warner Avis, Avis Rent a Car founder. While Warner was never a formal mentor to Herjavec, he still impacted his career and life immensely. Herjavec writes in Entrepreneur magazine,

"Stop the 'will you be my mentor?' emails and start being present to embrace the learning opportunities all around you. Ask your colleagues and executive team members for their points of view. Seek advice from your direct leader or leader once removed. Start having conversations and soaking in the mentorship moments."

Adam Saven admits to a complicated relationship with the word *mentor*. "We've facilitated all sorts of meaningful relationships at PeopleGrove," he told me. "But time and time again, the most successful are the ones where the mentee gets some sort of the desired outcome. In almost all of these cases, the mentor wouldn't even use that word to describe themselves."

Treat important people in your life as mentors—whether or not they give themselves that title for you. Surround yourself with many people who could transform your life and engage with them as if they are a mentor today.

Focus on building casual relationships with exceptional people. This puts you in a position to have a few of them help you create transformative opportunities.

Opportunities & access

SUPER MENTORS PROVIDE YOU OPPORTUNITIES AND ACCESS NOT ADVICE.

Mentors *want* to help. Your job is to make it easier for them to help you.

There's a skill to being mentored. Learning to leverage your mentors is one of today's most powerful and misunderstood skills. Many people with power, influence, prestige, connections, and knowledge want to lend them to you to help you succeed faster.

You just have to know how to leverage them.

You quickly observe a pattern when you study how many of the most successful people leverage mentors:

1. You will drive mentors. You won't wait for permission.
2. Be more ambitious in who you want to help you and less ambitious about what you need from them.
3. You are closer than you think. Most of us are just one or two moves away from a transformative mentor in our current life.

I told you all this having just said to treat the word "mentor" like Fight Club: The one rule of mentors is we don't talk about mentors.

It's an unfortunate reality. The word mentor has all these negative connotations while the actions of mentoring simultaneously have so many positive ones. We conflate mentorship with coaching, advising, role modeling, and sponsorship, so it's hard to pin down why you need it.

Let me offer my definition: Mentorship is a free transfer of "assets" from one person to another.

So many successful people cite mentors as adding tremendous value to their lives because they get that value for free. You get a meeting, an introduction, a project, or a collaborator that can potentially change your life without being asked to pay for it. That's amazing. You will become the master at extracting free value and assets from people in your life.

It's important to know that mentoring is less about the specific person. Mentoring is about a free transfer of opportunities, connections, knowledge, and potentially life-transforming experiences.

So, yeah, you want that. You'll learn there's a skill in being mentored to unlock these transfers.

The "free" part of the mentoring relationship is an essential element. As you'll see later in the chapter, other types of connections may involve money. First, 'free' means that anyone can get access—regardless of the starting size of your network. Second, the giver may offer you things that you didn't expect, want, need, or realize would benefit you. Mentors are generous but want to know that their contributions are valued to the point that when you create feedback loops as to the impact of their contributions, they often provide you with greater and greater levels of value.

These "assets" are crucial to understanding and leveraging Super Mentors. Mentors provide you with something of value—critical assets you need to succeed. Those assets can include advice, skills, guidance, opportunities, or network access assets. Why are they providing these assets to you? Many people are wired that way, some feel a sense of duty, and others recognize the positive emotional feelings they receive by giving value to others. But at the end of the day, mentors are an incredible opportunity to get these free assets to help you on your journey.

But a second and equally excellent reason this approach to mentoring is transformative is because Super Mentors have a set of opportunities at their fingertips that you may not have even imagined. These opportunities have been earned through their experiences, connections, and lessons.

Remember this common adage: "No such thing as a *free* lunch." You have work to do on your end to ensure you get the "free lunch" you need—not just the lunch that you are used to eating.

You need to figure out *what assets you need*.

YOU DON'T NEED *MORE* ADVICE. • More knowledge and experience first

Of all the assets you can get from a mentor, advice is the easiest to provide and the least valuable to receive. And it's probably why so few people have mentors. They've figured out that they can get *better* and *faster* advice by looking online. When I ask people about their negative mentoring experiences, they almost always discuss the fact that they were hoping their mentor might help them find a job or introduce or provide them with an opportunity. Instead, they just got unwanted advice. True story: One of my graduate students shared that at a "mentor mixer" she had three people give her advice that... she should find a mentor!

OF ALL THE ASSETS YOU CAN GET FROM A MENTOR, ADVICE IS THE EASIEST TO PROVIDE AND THE LEAST VALUABLE TO RECEIVE.

I was right there with you. I can trace my first major career failure—I was pretty much fired from my first real job—back to bad advice I received from my assigned mentor in college (a.k.a. the business of mentorship). My first mentor in college urged me to "follow his path" into the financial services industry, recommending I shut down an entrepreneurial venture—a small consulting company I'd run—to pursue something more "professional" like financial services. And I listened. I shut down a small business I enjoyed working on, took a job that paid me less than I was making working for myself in a field I wasn't that interested in, and eventually left on less than stellar terms with my boss. I got advice from a mentor, and then I took it because I thought that's what mentees did. We were supposed to listen to advice from our mentors.

When you study or interview the most successful people and their mentors, they rarely mention "advice I received." Why? Because that's not the value or the key asset they received. Instead, they'll mention "the opportunity" or "the access to someone in their network."

YOU DON'T WANT ADVICE; YOU WANT OPPORTUNITIES.

However, if you don't ask or don't know how to ask for the opportunities or network access you want, you won't get it. Opportunities may be a job, a project, or a connection to someone who has one of the above. This could be their time or involvement in a project, offering their name on something like your book or podcast, or possibly helping you develop a list of potential investors or distribution partners and making connections. These things lead to inflection points.

Advice is the easiest "asset" to transfer and is the default "asset" transferred if you don't ask for what you want. Sadly, you probably could have used Google and gotten better advice anyway!

Mentor Fallacy: Mentor relationships will happen naturally.

Super Mentor Reality: Only 22 percent of people have mentor relationships that happen naturally; 15 percent of people formally ask their mentor to mentor them, and the remainder (63 percent) don't have a mentor, according to research from Olivet Nazarene University.

Now, to the good news. As I shared earlier, Super Mentors are easier to find and engage with than ever. They are more willing and able to provide you with opportunities and network access than ever. Their opportunities and network access have also never been more valuable to ambitious people. They want to help, and you'll want to make it easier for them to do so.

We'll detail four laws of Super Mentors throughout the book:

- Law of Right **People**
- Law of Right **Ask**
- Law of Right **Start**
- Law of Right **Time**

PAST.

It is important to note that each of these laws relies on *you*. There's a fundamental trait in Super Mentors. They are *not* actively looking for a mentee or a protégé. Most of them are happy to be helpful, most love seeing their impact on others, and most have extensive things to offer you. But Super Mentorship is driven by you—the mentee or the protégé. We will use the terms mentee and protégé to refer to the person seeking mentorship throughout the book.

Since you're no longer waiting around for this person to pluck you from obscurity and mentor you, the traditional process of mentorship flips. You can aim much higher in who you're looking to engage. Remember, just because someone is more easily accessible doesn't mean they are a desirable mentor.

Remember, signing up for a mentoring pairing program isn't likely to create your desired inflection point. But if you remember that *you* drive the mentorship—not the mentor or even the program itself—you can see amazing results. You're aiming higher, and you're open to the fact that multiple people are likely able to deliver transformative moments to you. You need to find one—not the only one, which will make this process is much more effective and enjoyable.

PAST gives you agency and autonomy over cultivating these transformative relationships. As you'll read throughout the book, successful mentees *pursue* their Super Mentors.

When you aim higher, you'll want to ask smaller. Super Mentors are excellent sources of opportunities and network access. That's where we want to focus. The other things we had associated with mentors—advice, information, coaching, and training—are more accessible than ever. So you probably won't need to burden a Super Mentor for those things. We'll discuss the importance of a project in cultivating these relationships and how to be much more targeted in what you ask.

Becoming more focused on your ask—perhaps even said another way, what not to ask—will also change how you start the relationship: the right start. You'll see that first impressions matter, and focusing on a single meeting and building from there is the key.

Lastly, but perhaps most importantly, is the right time. Your goal isn't to have a single person as your only Super Mentor for your entire life. Phases of life correspond to phases of mentors. Understanding your phase and the appropriate relationship is critical.

> **Mentor Fallacy:** Mentorship is only valuable when you are young (in college or early in your career).
>
> **Super Mentor Reality:** Mentoring becomes more valuable to successful people the further they progress in their career as opportunities and network access are less transparent.

The core insight is understanding mentorship as a free "asset" transfer. That's why mentorship is so powerful. People are willing to give you these assets. If you help make it easy, mentorship will pay off exponentially. However, it may not pay off directly, right away, or how you thought. That's why the delight and surprise of these opportunities are part of the magic.

You may be asking yourself, "Doesn't this make things very transactional?"

I'd suggest thinking about this approach around "transparency." You're building a relationship with someone, but you're better able to signal your aims and your needs to help everyone create value from the relationship. While some of your Super Mentor relationships could be very brief—perhaps a single phone call or an introduction to someone else—leveraging the power of feedback loops can create long-term, deep relationships.

THE PROCESS HAS TO BE FUN (SERIOUSLY).

Mentorship feels important. Nearly all of us know it's critical to success. And then it becomes one more big box to check. It's work. It's about our future.

Now it's this big, heavy, scary, critical-to-the-future-of-our-lives thing.

And that's a big part of the problem. Once it feels like a big, weighty thing, we don't know how to get started. I have good news. When you listen to the stories of Super Mentors, they describe the beginning of their relationships quite differently.

We went to a movie. He spoke at my event. I invited her to coffee. We went to dinner with my classmates after class.

Why does that matter? We *do* enjoyable things. And mentoring done well is fun.

This is also why asking someone to be your mentor rarely works—because it doesn't feel enjoyable. It sounds like a lot of work.

How do you create experiences for you and others that feel enjoyable?

AIM HIGHER.

Try to engage people who are a bit of a reach. Aim higher... and I don't just mean higher in terms of fame, celebrity, or success. I mean the aim for the activities that feel *worth* doing.

Part of the reason my walk with Steve Blank was so powerful for me was because he was a personal hero. He was working in a world I enjoyed and wanted to be more involved with. Plus, I was already working in this realm. I was excited to be spending a half-hour with him. It was a win for me just to engage. Rahul was thrilled at the idea of engaging with people like Josh Wolfe, cryptocurrency expert Anthony Pompliano, the founder of a space exploration company, and others. That's it.

Mentoring isn't something you have to do to succeed; it's something you get to do, *and* it will help you succeed.

I encourage you to reach out to several circles beyond yours. Why? Why not? It's fun to reach out to someone you admire, who you don't think would ever even respond.

I want you to reach out to some total longshots and throw some Hail Mary passes. I used to believe a lack of motivation often held people back from finding a mentor. I was wrong. Things changed when I changed my approach and added more fun to the process. This process of engaging, connecting, and working with mentors should make you feel better not worse. It should create stories you share and reinforce the positive actions and behaviors you do.

Katy Milkman is a professor at Wharton and the author of *How to Change: The Science of Getting from Where You Are to Where You Want to Be*. It's a terrific book, and I can't recommend it highly enough. One of my favorite insights is the importance of fun in behavior change. Leveraging mentors or leveraging them differently is a behavior change for most. In life, we do things that are just painful to do no matter how you look at it—eating right, exercising, preparing our taxes. Other activities are enjoyable indulgences—watching reality television, eating truffles, playing Words with Friends. It's great when things are naturally enjoyable to you, but not everything is. For Milkman, going to the gym was painful, especially at the start. So she began trying to pair the painful with the pleasurable—combining her gym visit with listening to the Harry Potter audiobooks. The technique is called "temptation bundling."

First, lean into the parts of the process that feel naturally indulgent to you. Perhaps you'll love listening to TEDx Talks or podcasts or YouTube interviews of inspiring people. Maybe you like engaging in social media debates on Twitter. You might like the thrill of cold emailing, or perhaps you love making video or audio content. Recognize that these actions are enjoyable indulgences for you. They are easy for you (hopefully) and, when done in the context of Super Mentoring activities, won't feel hard or challenging at all.

Other things may not feel like fun. Instead, they might feel painful or intimidating. Maybe you don't like sending cold outreach emails or direct messages. You're not an avid social media user. It feels like work to research someone's connections. You've never been one for creating content for social media (other than viral TikTok dances). Recognize what you don't enjoy and what's painful.

How can you bundle the activities? How can you blend pleasure with pain? Maybe you force yourself to send a cold email out to the speaker of every TEDx Talk you watch or every podcast guest you listen to. Or you might push yourself to send a DM to the writer of every Twitter thread you retweet. Or you might create video or audio content to share with someone you're looking to meet.

This work takes time, but I'd encourage you to make time for it. One of the easiest ways to prioritize this is to carve off one to three hours a week for these activities. We'll encourage you to do them in the context of a project, so you may find that simply by tying it to your existing project timeline, you'll have that time.

One of the easiest things I've discovered to make this fun is to focus on aiming higher in our mentorship targets. That simple shift will add an element of delight to this—almost gamify your experience. We design a process and an experience that may lead you to speak to Taylor Swift's manager, interview Deepak Chopra, share your work with a producer for *The Bachelor*, or talk to an executive after her speech at a conference. That's just pretty cool... and pretty cool is a lot more fun to do than something that feels like a lot of work.

This process is a positive behavior change, but it's a change nevertheless. Make it fun. That's an order.

YOU'RE READY (EVEN IF YOU DON'T THINK YOU ARE).

If you don't have a mentor, or even if you do, just get started.

Remember, one of the keys to getting started is to make it fun. Here's how you can start now in a fun, low-pressure way. It's called the five-minute favor, inspired Adam Grant's insights about the power of simple acts of generosity in his 2017 TEDx Talk "Are You a Giver or a Taker?":

- Identify five people you'd love to meet, people you think could be helpful to you if you had fifteen minutes with them.
- Pick your favorite social media platform, and connect with all five.
- Scroll through their posts from the past week, and identify two posts from each person that resonates with you. If you can't find any, replace them with another person until you have five.
- Leave an insightful comment—something that thanks them for their post and offers your thoughtful response or reply.

FIVE MINUTE FAVOR EXAMPLES

Like the post	Leave a comment	Share the post

There you go. You've started already. Eventually, you'll see how to use the five-minute favor to leverage generosity and increase the chances of these encounters turning into more. You aimed higher; you asked smaller (in this case... you asked nothing), and you will do it again (hopefully soon).

You don't need to have all the answers before you get started. One of the big reasons people are hesitant to engage with prospective mentors is that they feel like they *don't* have things figured out yet.

None of us have it figured out, and thankfully the people you're about to meet will help you figure it out.

LEVERAGE THE "BUSINESS" OF MENTORING

We have a particular goal in this book—to help you develop Super Mentor relationships. We want you to get the "assets," opportunities and network access, transferred to you from exceptional people.

You'll get great value from casual mentor relationships through your schools, workplaces, and organizations. It's important to view these as casual mentor relationships you'll build, not a ready-made Super Mentor relationship. It's equally important to know that matching programs are often not specific enough for what you'll need, so you may see you'll need to use these approaches to make the most of every relationship.

Not every asset transfer has to be free. You may find a career coach beneficial. You may want to offer an advisor equity in your company for strategic support. You might find that your company mentor program builds good relationships with senior managers. You may find that your university offers a peer mentor that helps navigate certain choices.

You can and should take advantage of more in the business of mentorship to help you in your life and career. While this book focuses on mentorship as a *free* transfer of assets, mentorship has coaching, consulting, counseling, advising, guidance, role modeling, and sponsorship, all of which can sometimes cost money depending on the circumstances. Mentorship carries key aspects for our emotional well-being and the connectedness of our communities. All of these are important aspects of our success. People sometimes scoff at paying a mentor, but that's more of a case of misunderstanding the relationship rather than something nefarious or inappropriate.

Mentor Fallacy: You should never pay a mentor; otherwise, it's not mentorship.

Super Mentor Reality: Modern mentorship is more dynamic, and at times a mentoring relationship could become a coaching relationship, an employee relationship, or an investor relationship. Certain relationships for things like coaching, advising, and guidance are beyond the scope of typical mentorship relationships and may require payment. Understand what you need and evolve the relationship into a mutual exchange of value rather than simply receiving value.

Therefore, it's important to understand what you most need as you look to understand and leverage the broader concepts behind mentors:

- **Advising**. While I've made it clear that advice is a low-value asset in the mentoring context, this is not to discount its importance. Advising is to "give advice or recommend particular actions, conduct, etc." The keyword here is "particular." Advising is usually done in the context of a single decision. Should I go to Michigan or Ohio State? Should I work for Google or McKinsey? Should I get a law degree or an MBA? Should we open our next office in Shanghai or Beijing? Advising can be very helpful when the advisor has particular advice that is otherwise difficult to find. The reality for advising is the internet has become quite exceptional at providing certain information. However, if you've combed the internet and been unable to find what you're looking for, advising can be valuable when the advisor has relevant data for you.
- **Guidance**. Guidance is an extension of advising but often in an area with a less discrete decision. This situation occurs more often when someone's "decision framework" can be helpful in a

specific situation. How should I negotiate my salary for this job? How should I choose a major or decide which graduate schools to apply to? In these cases, you want to work through specific fact patterns with someone. Guidance is ineffective when you consider: What should I do with my life? How do I become a better manager? These are more likely extended coaching or counseling relationships.

- **Coaching**. Accepting coaching as a fundamental learning tool for professionals is one of the most exciting developments in the past two decades. While ambiguity can occur across these categories, I define coaching as a relationship not designed with an "end" in mind. You can have a fitness or life coach that helps you regardless of whether you are at a good point or low point. Today, corporate executives nearly all have business coaches. Career and life coaching has become an important service for individuals making substantive transitions where aspects of wellness, including body, mind, spirit, and performance coaching have become well understood. Coaching relationships are most often paid relationships over extended periods that may or may not have a specific endpoint, and they can evolve from a mentoring relationship into coaching and back to mentorship. This can sometimes be called consulting or counseling as well, with consulting and counseling relationships more likely to be fixed to more specific situations or specific time periods.

- **Role Modeling**. Role models are often people we look up to in order to learn from an individual who is ahead of us in experience or age. Universities and colleges have made a strong push into mentoring programs, and students often have ample ways to engage with alumni or more senior students in formal or informal mentoring programs. These programs are good to meet interesting people, learn about their paths and experiences, and build connections to your school, organization, or workplace. It's important to be aware that role modeling isn't designed to create opportunities or network access. Students or early career professionals often engage in these role-modeling programs—called mentoring—expecting their role models to help them get a job or get promoted, respectively. Still, the objective of these relationships is centered more around connection than tactical outputs for the mentee. But, as discussed earlier, if you approach these programs with that knowledge and use the tactics in this book, you are opening yourself up to what could be the best of both worlds.

- **Sponsorship**. Companies and organizations are providing mentoring programs to their workforce, in large part because younger workers are demanding it. While these are often called mentorship programs, it's probably easier to think of them as sponsorship wherein the company has "sponsored" someone to engage with you. As we defined, mentorship is the "free transfer" of assets, and while to you, the mentee, it's free, you should view these as more of a sponsorship experience where the company has decided to sponsor your mentor since they are paying them. This is the same in many of the organization or association mentor programs where the programs are also sponsored.

These concepts that are sometimes called or touch on mentorship are valuable in their own right. Understand the financial considerations, the engagement limitations, and the expected outcomes of each before you participate in any of them. I encourage you to leverage role-modeling, sponsorship, coaching, and guidance, which are critical components of success.

This book will focus on maximizing value from the free transfer of assets from one person to another, specifically through the cultivation of Super Mentor relationships.

PART I

THE LAW OF
RIGHT ASK

Make it specific. Make it simple. Make it schedulable. Explain the opportunity. Acknowledge their capacity. Learn how to make the right ask to get opportunities.

4

DESIGN MENTORING TO MAXIMIZE OPPORTUNITIES

A former student named Melissa came into my office, clearly frustrated. Many of my best-performing students come back for a meeting around two to three years after graduation. I call this period the "real-world reality check" stage.

"This job isn't what I want to do long-term," Melissa shared. "It's just a job. I'm not excited about it."

"Are you applying to new jobs?"

"No," she said with a shrug. "I don't know what I want to do instead. I'm more trying to meet people, but that's more frustrating than applying for jobs."

"Why?"

"Because I met with four people last week, and all of them asked me if I had a mentor."

Gulp. Now, it's frustrating enough to have a meeting with someone where you get the advice you could have Googled. It's worse when that advice is that you should get a mentor.

Why do many initial mentor-like meetings end after a single, mediocre encounter? The four people telling Melissa she needed a mentor formed a pattern that something was off with the encounter. Adam Saven sees the data in PeopleGrove when people have a single meeting that doesn't progress beyond it. I asked him why so many first meetings with a potential mentor don't lead to second or third meetings.

"We don't know. It's a lot like dating," Adam offered. "Most times when that first call or meeting doesn't go well, participants tell us there wasn't chemistry or a good fit or a reason for a follow-up. Usually, they both know it didn't go that well but can't quite put their finger on why."

I'm convinced first meetings go poorly because they aren't well-designed encounters. Designing a productive first encounter for both the mentor and the mentee is key to a second meeting, and the mentee bears most of that responsibility for developing an excellent first encounter. Much like Adam suggests, a bad date could be a lack of chemistry or it could be the fact that the shared experience wasn't well-planned or well-thought-out. Imagine meeting a blind date for the first time and each of you asking "well, what do you want to do?" It's difficult to develop your relationship when there is uncertainty. That's why designing that first encounter is critical. First mentor meetings often have that same lack of structure, blowing any chance at developing chemistry.

Melissa didn't prepare for an excellent first encounter because she didn't know what she needed. Much like having a work meeting without an agenda, it's hard to accomplish much, and when it's over, you don't know if it was a good meeting or not. Those types of arrangements aren't well-designed.

If you don't get what you need out of a meeting, you haven't designed the meeting or the experience well.

Do you know what *you* need?

It's a relatively straightforward line of questioning, and while researchers find that most of us *believe* we know what we want and need, the truth is quite surprising. In her study of more than five thousand people, organizational psychologist Tasha Eurich determined that only 10–15 percent of us are self-aware in all aspects of our lives.

And unless you go into a meeting with a potential mentor knowing what you need out of the meeting, *don't take the meeting*.

Odds are you'll just get some advice you didn't need or, worse yet, be told that you should get a mentor.

DESIGN YOUR FIRST ENCOUNTER.

What would you do if you had fifteen minutes with _____?

Zain Sandhu was an ambitious nineteen-year-old when we first met. He loved music and writing. He thought a career in music or entertainment could be exciting. But was that his passion, his purpose, or his mission? He had a hard time knowing at that early moment.

"Who do you admire in the music industry?" I asked him.

He replied, "Chance the Rapper, Kanye West, Lil Tay, Frank Ocean, and Taylor Swift."

I smiled at him. "I didn't peg you as a Swiftie."

"Taylor is the best I've ever seen in engaging her fans. Hands down. She's the best."

I nodded. "What would you do if you had fifteen minutes to talk with Taylor Swift?"

He smiled uncomfortably. "For real?" he asked.

"Yes, what would you do, what would you say, what would you ask if you had fifteen minutes with her?"

Without hesitation: "I'd ask to be her manager," he said with a smile.

"That's good. So what would you do for her as her manager?"

"Uh, I don't know. Maybe I'd help her figure out how to grow into new industries like fashion, cosmetics, and makeup," he said, obviously making it up as he was going.

"I like that. Okay, now how would you show her you *could* do that?"

"I'd probably need a plan or see what other people do or how the Kardashians do it. I mean, I don't know," he said, raising his shoulders.

But he *did* know. Zain would arrange to meet and interview Taylor Swift's first manager Rick Barker a few months later. He would also cultivate a relationship with one of Steven Spielberg's writing partners.

Zain admitted he'd never even considered music and entertainment management until that moment. He didn't even realize it at that time, but he knew what he'd do with his fifteen minutes with Taylor. He just had to verbalize it to make it *real* and ultimately create it.

If I have fifteen minutes with Taylor Swift, I'm going to show her a plan to expand into fashion and cosmetics so she can grow her platform even further. Then, I will ask to help her manage it.

Most ambitious people I meet are much more self-aware than they communicate. They know what they like, what they want, what would be great, and what they enjoy. Zain knew.

He just needed help framing this self-awareness into something actionable.

Our conversation and discussion exercise led Zain down a path well beyond what he'd imagined. He knew what he needed but had to conceptualize the *specific* opportunities he wanted. From there, he worked backward. What is the opportunity I'd want, and how can I connect with people who can enable that?

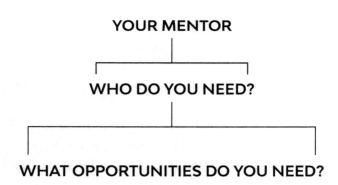

YOUR MENTOR
WHO DO YOU NEED?
WHAT OPPORTUNITIES DO YOU NEED?

One Meeting Away: Zain Sandhu

Right Person. Rick Barker, Taylor Swift's first manager.

Right Ask. What was the most important guidance or advice you gave to Taylor Swift?

• Do deny the research into people and groups!

Right Start. Research into multiple people who had worked with Taylor, outreach for a first conversation, and follow up with the write-up of the meeting.

Right Time. Zain wasn't necessarily sure he wanted to work as an aspiring entertainment professional. He focused on understanding how he—as her first manager—was most impactful. Zain discovered that Barker encouraged Swift to lean into one-on-one relationships with her fans in that conversation. This strategy led Swift to perform at any small venue—from a county fair, a shopping mall, or a school event. Barker credits her work and relentless focus on those engagements as the secret to her album going platinum.

• Relentless focus in a few particular areas

Here are the three elements to conceptualizing the opportunities you want:
What would you do if you had fifteen minutes with _____?
I'm going to _____
so s/he can _____
then I will _____.

The modern mentor solves specific problems for us. These don't need to be these big, life's purpose type problems, but you want them to help you with real, tangible problems and challenges.

What problem could be solved, refined, or narrowed down in a fifteen-minute conversation?

HARNESSING HIDDEN SELF-AWARENESS.

This can all feel like the ultimate paradox:

Don't take a meeting unless you know what you need. Yet, I want the meeting to figure out what I need.

Seekers don't design encounters that create opportunities for themselves for many reasons:

- We don't know what we want to do with our lives.
- We have so many choices that we don't want to pick one and close other doors.
- What we actually want to do may not pay the bills.
- We have external pressures from parents, friends, and family.
- We don't have enough information to get specific about the needs.

Commitment and awareness are very different things.

Zain wasn't *committed* to the music industry because he didn't know much about it, hadn't worked in it, didn't know its specifics, and wasn't sure it paid the bills. Zain was *aware* that he liked the industry, knew what he admired about certain musicians, wanted to learn more about it, and thought it had the potential for his future.

> **Mentor Fallacy:** We know what we need from a mentor.
>
> **Super Mentor Reality:** Only 10–15 percent of us are self-aware about what we need from our mentors.

Don't mistake self-awareness for commitment.

In their groundbreaking research in the early 1970s, Shelley Duval and Robert Wicklund introduced the concept of self-awareness. According to Duval and Wicklund, "When we focus our attention on ourselves, we evaluate and compare our current behavior to our internal standards and values. We become self-conscious as objective evaluators of ourselves."

Said another way, most of us are pretty harsh critics of ourselves.

In her article for the *Harvard Business Review* entitled "What Self-Awareness Really Is (and How to Cultivate It)," Tasha Eurich summarizes two major categories of self-awareness based on her research: (a) internal self-awareness; and (b) external self-awareness. She found virtually no relationship between the two as she studied each component. Eurich writes,

[I]nternal self-awareness, represents how clearly we see our own values, passions, aspirations, fit with our environment, reactions (including thoughts, feelings, behaviors, strengths, and weaknesses), and impact on others. We've found that internal self-awareness is associated with higher job and relationship satisfaction, personal and social control, and happiness; it is negatively related to anxiety, stress, and depression.

• This might be a part for your consideration

Of equal importance to our internal self-awareness is our awareness of how others view us—our external self-awareness. Eurich continues, "Our research shows that people who know how others see them are more skilled at showing empathy and taking others' perspectives. Leaders who see themselves as their employees do tend to have a better relationship with them, feel more satisfied with them, and see them as more effective."

In Eurich's study, less than 15 percent of individuals were strong in both aspects of awareness—internal and external. If you're curious about your performance, Eurich offers a free shortened version of her assessment at http://www.insight-quiz.com/. Eurich's research lays out four personas based on our internal and external self-awareness.

	A	B	C
1		**Low external self-awareness**	**High external self-awareness**
2	**High internal self-awareness**	**INTROSPECTORS.** They're clear on who they are but don't challenge their own views or search for blind spots by getting feedback from others. This can harm their relationships and limit their success.	**AWARE.** They know who they are, what they want to accomplish, and seek out and value others' opinions. This is where individuals begin to fully realize the true benefits of self-awareness.
3	**Low internal self-awareness**	**SEEKERS.** They don't yet know who they are, what they stand for, or how others see them. As a result, they might feel stuck or frustrated with their performance and relationships.	**PLEASERS.** They can be so focused on appearing a certain way to others that they could be overlooking what matters to them. Over time, they tend to make choices that aren't in service of their own success and fulfillment.

As Eurich concludes, "[F]ocus on building both internal and external self-awareness… seek honest feedback from loving critics… and ask *what* instead of *why* can learn to see themselves more clearly—and reap the many rewards that increased self-knowledge delivers."

It's okay and completely normal to be a seeker. In fact, most people find themselves as seekers at one point or another in our lives and careers. And it's probably at these 'seeker' points where we truly need help with our problems.

Most of us are drawn toward mentors when we find ourselves *seeking*.

A good analogy is to think about buying a car. Imagine you're not sold on whether you even need a car. In fact, a lot is changing in your life and you may be moving to a new city or a new part of town. You've been considering whether a bike might be a better option or perhaps one of those new electric scooters. You're got lots to figure out. What's a really bad idea at this point in your own discovery? To head to a used car lot and test drive cars. You're going to get lots of advice

This is you

from the car salesman about cars, which you haven't really addressed the biggest question: does a car best solve your transportation needs?

Mentors aren't quite used car salesmen, but if you go to them asking for advice about your life, you'll probably get advice, often in the context of that person's own experiences. Seekers don't need advice. If you find yourself in this seeker stage, you need to look *inward* before involving a potential mentor.

SEEKERS SHOULDN'T SEEK A *MENTOR*.
SEEKERS SHOULD SEEK A *PROJECT*.

Imagine a project as a way to explore biking, scooters, walking, cars, and all sorts of options for getting around. It's exploratory, it's non-committal, and it's a way to discover without judgment. If you ask someone which car to buy, they'll help you decide which car.

Projects help seekers with internal self-awareness. "This project I'm working on is tied to things I'm personally interested in." And external self-awareness, "I'd love to talk to you about specific aspects of this project where I think you could help."

Too often, we think effective mentorship starts with a mentor, but in reality, effective mentorship starts with a self-aware mentee. It's perhaps a bit counterintuitive but all too common. I need a mentor to figure out what I need/want.

Here's the good news. The next chapter is all about finding your project.

OPPORTUNITIES WILL REQUIRE MORE SPECIFICITY.

Specificity is intimidating, especially when we are at the seeker stage.

That is why it's essential to aim higher with these activities and exercises. I asked Zain about who he admired in the music industry. He came back with names far removed from his reality today: Chance the Rapper, Kanye West, Lil Tay, Frank Ocean, and Taylor Swift.

Discussing Taylor Swift can be a fun role-playing exercise.

And discussing Taylor Swift can start you on a path that has you speaking with her manager two months later.

Let's look at another example to create specificity without being intimidating.

Imagine you want to break into film, television, or theater, and you have the following opportunities in front of you:

- One fifteen-minute Zoom with Lin-Manuel Miranda, the creator and star of *Hamilton*.
- Weekly meetings for a year with a professor of theatrical arts at your college.

Most of us would take our chances with a fifteen-minute meeting with Lin-Manuel Miranda. Why? It's fun and exciting, and that meeting has the potential to be transformative. I donated one hundred dollars to a charity auction through a company called Prizeo for an opportunity to meet Lin-Manuel. Sadly, I didn't win, but I did get a t-shirt!

Zain picked the musicians he did for this same reason.

And if you want to break into film, television, and theater, one meeting with Lin-Manuel Miranda has the potential to transform your trajectory. Even if that meeting didn't change your trajectory, saying you met the guy who wrote Hamilton would be a story you'd tell all your friends.

When I told you to aim higher, your critical brain likely responded, "But Lin-Manuel Miranda is never going to do a Zoom call with me. I don't even know how to reach him. I don't know what I'd ask, and I can't imagine why someone like him would ever bother to use Zoom anyway." Or some version of this, maybe with more curse words.

Remember, I said aim higher, but I didn't say *shoot* higher. I didn't tell Zain to reach out to Taylor Swift. That's not the point of this exercise.

The aim higher rule helps us because when we aim to the extreme edges of what's possible, it often feels so far away that we are less apt to censor ourselves. We shut up that inner critic because it's just a made-up exercise. You'll learn how aiming higher helps frame the people who will become your mentors. We aim high, and then we shoot broadly.

It's essential to understand what you need and what you don't. Zain Sandhu didn't need to speak to Taylor Swift, Chance the Rapper, or Kanye West. But they offered him a way to visualize what he required from them: their managers, producers, and brand partner.

WHAT WOULD YOU DO WITH YOUR SHOT?

It's not accidental that I chose Lin-Manuel Miranda as my example above. Maximizing opportunity defines Lin-Manuel and his characters.

Both in musical and biography, Alexander Hamilton has become a phenomenon, selling out show after show in its flagship Broadway production in cities like Chicago, San Francisco, and Los Angeles. Lin-Manuel was initially smitten with the story of Hamilton as he contemplated his next project and knew school groups would love it, but he wasn't sure it would gain mass appeal.

He underestimated himself and *Hamilton*.

Before the show was ever a phenomenon, Lin-Manuel took a big risk to share the vision for a musical he described as a "hip-hop battle among the founding fathers."

In 2009, President Obama invited Lin-Manuel to perform at an event at the White House—an evening of poetry and spoken word. The organizers suggested he do something from his first show, *In the Heights*, but Lin-Manuel had a better idea.

Although he admits he had yet to finish even one song of his new show and only had "sixteen hot bars about Hamilton," he took a risk—something few might have done—and decided to "workshop" his new material in front of the president and first lady. He felt compelled and called to show the work he was doing, which he thought would best connect with the people in the room at that moment. He set out to maximize his opportunities *from that moment* with some of the world's most influential and powerful people.

As he describes it, "That was a very strange, early lab we did at the White House."

But the showcase was a hit, it resonated with everyone in attendance, and then when the White House put the video online, his performance went viral.

The rest is history.

One Meeting Away: Lin-Manuel Miranda

Right Person. President and First Lady Obama were cultural icons who transcended politics and regularly brought together unique and diverse entertainers and artists, including this night with American spoken word poets at the White House.

Right Ask. Can I perform something new and incomplete?

Right Start. Lin-Manuel let his performance be filmed, recorded, and shared. Once the clip went viral, it didn't lose momentum. He continued to engage the White House and invited administration members to the show.

Right Time. Lin-Manuel Miranda had already produced a Tony-award-winning musical *In the Heights. He* was looking to expand his creative pursuits but had doubts whether a "rap battle between the founding fathers" would appeal beyond a small audience.

Today, I usually start my courses by playing two songs from Hamilton for the class, including "My Shot." Alexander Hamilton and Lin-Manuel Miranda share a kinship in how they maximize opportunities.

As I do with my students, I'd like you to imagine you've got that fifteen-minute Zoom call with Lin-Manuel Miranda—or insert someone you believe is the ultimate individual who has the potential to transform your life. Anyone. Remember, aim *higher.*

Now ask yourself: what will I do with my fifteen minutes (a.k.a. my *shot*)? What would I do to maximize my opportunity with Lin-Manuel Miranda?

- *I'm going to sing sixteen "hot bars" from a musical I'm writing so he can see my work, and then I will ask him to do a cameo.*
- *I'm going to share what our nonprofit does to understand our impact, and then I will ask him to collaborate.*
- *I will tell him my story to know why it is important, and then I will ask him to write the book foreword.*
- *I'm going to wear my fashion designs so he can visualize the project, and then I will offer to design for his next project.*
- *I'm going to demo my mobile application so he can learn how it could help the theater, and then I will ask him to invest.*

This is your shot. Right? Now, of course, this seems daunting at the moment. What would you do with fifteen minutes with your hero, your muse, and your aspiration?

We want people to provide us opportunities we can't get on our own—an opportunity to work together, collaborate on a project, pitch our idea, be connected to someone, or get feedback on our work. Yet when we get these opportunities from others, we tend to view them through good fortune, the right place and right time, being in high-potential communities or networks, or a series of happy accidents.

Don't *hope* for opportunities; *design* your approach to earn opportunities, whether it's Lin-Manuel or someone with similar opportunities, access, and network.

OPPORTUNITIES ARE SOLUTIONS TO YOUR PROBLEMS
Super Mentors solve problems.

Lin-Manuel Miranda *can* solve your problems: do a cameo, collaborate with a nonprofit, write a book foreword, incorporate your designs in his next show, or invest in your venture.

Will he? That's somewhat out of your control. But most mentors admit they want to help others. Your job is to make it easier for them. As we'll discuss further, don't put all your "I need your help" eggs in a single Miranda-shaped basket. He, or your version of Lin-Manuel, offers you a way to become opportunity-focused. For Zain, it was Rick Barker. For me, it was Steve Blank.

Opportunities are the solutions to your problems. We need to target the people who can help you solve them.

Most often, the issues they help us solve are ones they've solved previously for themselves.

- You want to become a Hollywood director. Your Super Mentor likely figured out how to become a Hollywood director.
- You want to work for an NBA team. Your Super Mentor likely figured out how to work for an NBA team.
- You want to raise venture capital for your start-up. Your Super Mentor likely figured out how to raise venture capital for their start-up.
- You want to publish a successful first novel. Your Super Mentor likely published their book and successfully marketed it.

You can begin to see a pattern. You have a problem, and you need help to solve that problem. Find people who have solved that problem for themselves. It is even better if solving this problem *could* transform your life somehow.

Now to be clear, this doesn't mean you should expect that one Hollywood director to hire you, that one start-up founder to invest in you, or that specific novelist to publish your novel—at least yet.

Your goal is to increase your opportunity surface area and give yourself more chances to get those transformative opportunities:

- Expect to engage with multiple people who fit a profile or persona.
- Expect to learn from people.
- Expect to join the communities they are in.
- Expect to engage with them in public.
- Reimagine the digital and nondigital circles you want to participate in.
- Get embedded in those communities... and you're suddenly one step closer to the people you want to know.

Opportunities, rather than receiving advice, come from the right ask of the right people at the right times. You make it easy for Lin-Manuel Miranda to say yes to your help. And thankfully, this process is a skill you can learn.

VALUE TO THE
MENTEE

ADVICE   OPPORTUNITIES

MENTORSTORMING

Most of us are familiar with brainstorming—a group of people collaborating to develop ideas to solve a problem.

Mentorstorming is a twist on brainstorming: identify the group of people who could solve your problems.

Here's how it works in practice. Imagine you are in the room with this one key aspirational mentor—*your* Lin-Manuel Miranda. But I want you to imagine you *are* Lin-Manuel. Embody your aspirational mentor. Imagine you have their personality, talents, experiences, network, and access, all of it.

Now you're the mentor in a big conference room and in walks you—the real you who has these specific problems you need help with.

Play out the meeting, assuming the mentor only has fifteen minutes with you and wants to be helpful if they can.

What happens from there? Imagine, dream, role-play, and get specific. Mentorstorming involves being specific with the scenario to get to the specifics of the opportunities you're seeking. It's fun because who wouldn't want to role-play with someone they admire?

Some questions to think through:

- How does this person react to your problem?
- What is the best-case scenario?
- What is the worst-case scenario?
- Who would they ask to join the room?
- Who might they call?
- Who would they offer to connect you with?
- How might you evolve the request?

Imagine Zain Sandhu walking into the room with Taylor Swift. He wanted to talk to her about her business aims. How does she offer to help? Who does she invite into the room? What happens next?

This is mentorstorming.

START TO DEFINE WHAT OPPORTUNITIES YOU NEED.
Successful people don't succeed by themselves. They need other people to help them, but it can be challenging to look inward to figure out what they need.

Too often, ambitious people are asked:

- What are you passionate about?
- What is your life's purpose?
- What are your dreams?
- What gets you out of bed in the morning?
- What is your mission?

The challenge with a focus on things like purpose, passion, missions, and dreams is they are intangible. That makes them difficult to pin down and, frankly, very intimidating. For most people, these questions are the opposite of fun. So we avoid even trying to answer them.

People are complex, but they are also tangible. They humanize abstract and intangible things like purpose, passion, mission, and dreams. All of the things we love have people behind them.

So many of us get stuck because we're not sure what we need or what our purpose or passion might be.

Look at the questions above. You'll see that each of the questions above begins with **What**. Designing for exceptional mentoring experiences starts with the word **Who**.

Ask yourself these questions:

- Who has done this already?
- Who do I know working in that industry, company, or field?
- Who already made this choice?
- Who do I admire?
- Who do I listen to or watch when I need to learn something important?
- Who else has the person I admire worked with?
- Who do I know already who has worked on something similar?

What you want to do is so hard. But figuring out *who* you admire and want to be is much easier. This happens in Super Mentoring relationships.

YOU START WITH *WHO*.

Designing mentoring to maximize opportunities begins with self-awareness but is less focused around missions or passions.

Who could provide you with a chance that could fundamentally alter your trajectory?

Now, what are you going to do with your shot?

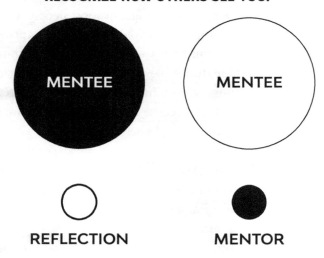

RECOGNIZE HOW OTHERS SEE YOU.

MENTEE   MENTEE

REFLECTION   MENTOR

Don't get hung up on the perfect mentor or the perfect time to engage with a specific person at this moment. It is, however, valuable to recognize how others see you before you begin to engage with prospective mentors.

My research has found three clusters of mentorship periods—educational (college, high school, graduate school), early career (the twenties and thirties), and career transitions (varies). This doesn't necessarily mean the approach to developing Super Mentors will change, but you may find that the more experienced you are, you have greater network access already.

Since I'm a big comic book and superhero nerd, let's look at the spectrum of people most in need of Super Mentors through the lens of three recognizable cultural archetypes from Marvel's *The Avengers*: Peter Parker (Spider-Man), Carol Danvers (Captain Marvel) and Steve Rogers (Captain America). Each is remarkably talented—as you probably are—but they need more to get to those next levels.

PETER PARKER, a.k.a. Spider-Man. *Young, Ambitious and Pretty Lost.* Peter is young, ambitious, and generally very agreeable. He knows how to fight but wants to be more than just the friendly neighborhood Spider-Man. The challenge with Peter is that engaging with him is like engaging with a firehose. He's all over the place, he's needy, and he's a lot to take. Plus, you'll probably get drenched.

Peters are the folks—as well-intentioned and excited as they are—who miss incredible opportunities because of how they engage with potential mentors. They make broad, rambling asks, don't follow up, and engage with people who too often aren't able to help them. Often, a first meeting never turns into a second meeting, or the second meeting is a repeat of the first one. Peters know they want mentorship—and need it—but don't know how to get the value that will unlock their potential. If you are a Peter, you just need to change your approach, and you'll have some incredible opportunities come your way.

CAROL DANVERS, a.k.a. Captain Marvel. *Early Success but Plateaued.* Carol is powerful—maybe one of the most powerful superheroes out there—but she's mostly gotten there independently. She's one of the newest Avengers, and in many ways, she feels a little weird about mentors because she's powerful and she's already made it this far. She's a captain, but she's not *the* captain. She also recognizes that the next level requires more than her talent.

Carols often do all the "right things"—going to good schools, getting good jobs, being accepted to graduate schools and earning great performance reviews. Often Carols may be considering a "bigger leap"—maybe launching their own company, a creative endeavor such as a podcast, a book, or a YouTube channel—but are hesitant because they lack the network. They look at their peers and see themselves behind, whether in reality or imagined. When they ask what they need to get to those next levels, friends and family say, "You need a mentor." So Carols try to find a mentor at work, in their network, or an alum from their school, but typically, that mentor just wants to give advice when Carols don't need more advice. They need access and opportunities. If you are a Carol, you are in luck. You don't need hours of calls, coaching, and advice, but you do need the person who can unlock the right doors and opportunities for you. You just need to figure out your aspirational peers (a.k.a. your "cousins," as we'll cover later in the book) and get more specific opportunities and access.

STEVE ROGERS, a.k.a. Captain America. *Succeeding, but What's Next?* Steve's made it. He's the cap. He's leading the team. But he is also ready for something else. It's tiring saving the world, and he'd love to do something different. He's under a lot of pressure because people expect things from him now; he can't just go back to school or try something independently. He's his own worst enemy.

The good news is that Steves are well-positioned to find and leverage Super Mentors more often than not. The bad news is that Steves often aren't aware of how to leverage mentorship, either because they have a limited view or are somewhat embarrassed to ask. If you are a Steve—and I'll share how I found myself in this place—your path to a Super Mentor is probably the closest to you. Sometimes all you need is a bit of humility to embrace the need for these relationships. But then, with a bit of reflection and self-work to identify where you'd like to go, unlocking learning through peer-like relationships is often nearby.

You want a bigger leap

Listen, these archetypes are superheroes, which was purposeful. Talent is great, and odds are, you are talented. Perhaps you can't spin webs or blast energy from your fists, but still… In nearly every conversation, interview, and story, it's clear that success doesn't happen alone, no matter who we are. Perhaps equally important, you have control in finding those people who will create these opportunities.

Needing a mentor is not an admission of weakness, an indication that you don't have your life together, or a sign your plan isn't mapped out well enough. Those moments when I was able to find the right people to support me through challenges, obstacles, and transitions were when I was at my best. Sometimes we can feel like we *should* have it figured out, but trust me, I've had Super Mentors who are ten years younger than me, Super Mentors who are the same age as me, and others with decades more experience. Now, I know I'm not alone in that sentiment. So, whether you're a Peter, a Carol, or a Steve—and I've had experiences as each in my own life and, more recently, some pretty important Captain America-level help—activating others to help you realize your potential is powerful.

Yes, you're a superhero, but even a superhero could use some help now and again. It's important to recognize how to best leverage it in designing experiences with outcomes.

5

DEFINE A PROJECT THAT REQUIRES COLLABORATION

What you've read and done thus far probably feels very obvious and logical. Identify people we admire, specify the opportunities we want them to create, and expand the list of people who could create them.

As defined already, mentorship is a free transfer of assets from one person to another. But mentorship isn't a pure transaction. It's a relationship. There's an exchange. It's a collaboration. This is where understanding *how* Super Mentors operate is critical.

You need something to collaborate on.

You need something to show, share, and develop.

You need a project.

Why is the project so important?

First, picking your project is an effective way to develop your internal self-awareness. It's a way for you to select something to work on that matters to you, that interests you, and that scratches your curiosity. Picking a project won't be as scary as settling on a career path, picking a major, or starting a company. It's something you'll probably spend four to six hours on each week. But it's fun, it's entirely for you, and it's low pressure. You choose what you're excited to work on.

Second, a project is a powerful way to signal who you are, what you enjoy, and what you'd like to accomplish. You'll leverage this project to seek out and value others' opinions. You'll show who you are to the people you meet.

Third, projects offer a low-risk way to build evidence of your qualifications, skills, and abilities. It gives your mentors a way to know you're awesome. They can recommend you to others based on that evidence. Employers are looking closely at projects as they attempt to weed through potential hires.

If you find yourself struggling with what you want to be when you grow up, what you should do for your next job, whether you should start your own business, or why you're just not satisfied with life at this point, pick a project to help you find out.

Starting your project is the secret to moving from Seeker to Aware. And it's the simplest way to unlock the power of Super Mentors.

PROJECTS MAKE YOU RECOMMENDABLE.

This sounds like extra work, you might be thinking. Not if you pick the right project. The key is identifying a project that doesn't feel like work or like one more thing.

Projects are one of the most efficient ways to stand out today.

"A strong portfolio is essential in today's job market," Adam Saven told me. "Employers want to see that candidates have put themselves out there and worked to build relevant skills and experience. The same is true of mentors. Alumni and others are happy to provide advice but even more eager to contribute to a specific task on a larger project."

But projects are much more than just a useful tool in getting a job. Projects can help set us on the path for long-term career and life success by making us more self-aware and providing us confidence in our trajectory.

In its research, Gallup identified a set of six key experiences that college graduates who had the most early career success had. They called these experiences the Big Six, and college students who had more of these experiences were more likely to feel confident in their preparation for the working world.

"Completing a long-term project was one of the six, and having a mentor was another," Adam offered. "But really all six of the experience can be intertwined into a Super Mentor experience through a project or projects. You can actually architect your own confidence and career success."

Projects make it easier for mentors to provide you with opportunities.

First, let's look at how it can go wrong. Below is an edited version of an actual email I received. The underlined text is modified but representative.

I was reaching out because I have now graduated from _Fancy University_ with a BA in _Relevant Major_ and a minor in _Other Interesting but Not Relevant Thing_. Going into college, I knew it was important for me to find a path that allowed me to go into a career that would pursue more of a creative avenue. I now live in _City, State,_ and am looking for a full-time role in the realm of _Specific Field or Industry Probably Not Directly Aligned to Major_ or in the _Broader Field Maybe More Related_. I am open to in-person, hybrid, and remote work. I would love to stay in touch if you hear of any job openings for entry-level professionals. I have attached my résumé for your convenience.

I applaud this individual for reaching out. But this person put me—or anyone else they reached out to—in a difficult bind. How do I know the person is recommendable? How do I have evidence of their qualifications, skills, and abilities? This approach rarely works, even though people try it all the time.

For many people reading this book, you may be looking for a Super Mentor to accelerate your career somehow—whether it's a job early in your career, switching career, or launching your business or venture. This step of finding a project may feel like an extra step, and it is. But keep in mind an important phrase here: "Ask for a job, and you'll get advice. Ask for advice, and you'll get a job."

If you skip this step and run directly into, "Will you hire me," you're most likely to get advice. Remember, you _don't_ want advice. You want an opportunity, a job, an investment, a shot. That's where projects are critical.

Projects make you _recommendable_.

FIND A PROJECT THAT IS MEANINGFUL.

Projects that require collaboration are a secret weapon for the ambitious individual. This cheat code can get you access to nearly anyone. Why? Because projects feel noble. Think about an artist toiling away nights and weekends in her studio painting, the author writing his memoir at 5 a.m. every morning, or the event organizer working hard to bring people together. These activities feel noble, but they're different from jobs or businesses. We love to support the underdog working on something primarily for its love. That's what projects can be for you.

One of the reasons mentorship is so impactful is that—in most cases—the benefits you're receiving are free. Mentors feel good supporting your noble work on a project. Whereas it can feel "icky" to do substantial work that someone else is getting paid for somehow. Something like referring you to an open job can sometimes feel transactional. Should I be getting a referral for this? Working on someone's start-up or business venture can create financial or equity compensation expectations.

Projects feel meaningful for everyone collaborating. We feel good about supporting an ambitious person working on a project, and that dramatically increases the likelihood of a mentor engaging with you substantially.

Just what do I mean by a meaningful project?

(a) **It's something you care about.** The project connects to a bigger aim/direction/ambition/purpose for you. It's aligned with where you want to go.

(b) **It's finite.** The project is something you can finish and most likely would take six-to-twelve months to complete.

(c) **It's not (primarily) for the money.** You're working on something important where the primary purpose isn't to make money.

Many things in our lives are "shoulds"—things we know we should do. This project is one of those "I get tos"—something you're excited and privileged to do.

I organized a research project to study the career paths of nearly five thousand winners of the *Forbes* "30 under 30" recognition, given annually to the best and the brightest individuals across dozens of fields and industries. My collaborator Adam Saven won this distinction in 2019. In that research, I found that more than 80 percent of them had a substantial project that met the definition of a meaningful project. I found that these projects served as attractive collaborations for them, helping create their individual Super Mentor relationships.

For Adam, his project was the idea that eventually became PeopleGrove. "My cofounder Reilly and I were both at Google together and working on quite a few side projects in the career exploration space," Adam told me. "While putting our thoughts together, we had dozens of conversations with experts. One of those experts was Dr. Farouk Dey at Stanford University, who ran their career services department. Remember, before we even had a business plan, we just had a side project. But Dr. Dey encouraged us to pursue some ideas around networking, and down the road, he became our first higher education partner."

One Meeting Away: Adam Saven and Reilly Davis

Right Person. Dr. Farouk Dey is a highly regarded higher education expert with a passion for helping students design their lives

Right Ask. Can we ask you about the role of technology in your students' lives?

Right Start. Saven and Davis continued to engage with Dey as they developed their project, eventually asking him to sign on as their first education partner.

Right Time. Dr. Dey was hoping to revolutionize how students find their passion and the role of mentors in that process.

Many people already have projects—they might be your hobbies, volunteer activities, side projects, or creative outlets. Part of what's great about already having a project is you can easily find ways to collaborate on it.

In the research, we observed hundreds of different types of projects but were able to bucket them into nine of the most common patterns:

1. Article Series
2. Books
3. Concerts and Art Demonstrations
4. Conferences or Event Series
5. Courses or Workshops
6. Designs or New Products
7. Podcast Season/Series
8. Published Research
9. Video Show/Series

Nearly all of these have a natural collaborative element. Conferences need speakers and panelists. Podcasts need guests to interview. Books need stories from others. It's important to remember that not every project is necessarily collaborative or right for a Super Mentor. You may be producing an online video cooking show, but it's not something you want to be your career or be more than a hobby. Or you may be producing a sports podcast that isn't something you intend to share outside your friends.

How do you choose your meaningful project? You can choose what excites you as the medium to show your work in some senses. Mark Metry found himself listening to many podcasts and decided to start his own that would become his Top-100 podcast Humans 2.0. Jaclyn DiGregorio took courses to learn about nutrition and decided to start her own. Or you may look to your aspirational peers and see what projects they'd undertaken: Ava DuVernay took six thousand dollars and produced a twelve-minute film detailing the struggles of a single mother called *Saturday Night Life*. Victoria Schwab wrote poetry and short stories until she decided to try her hand at a novel project in college that she never intended or intended to publish. Mark Zuckerberg worked on a project for his dad's dental practice to link all the computers in their home and his practice he called "ZuckNet." Projects are usually much less ambitious than you imagined, but they allow us to bring others in to collaborate.

We can start at the end and work backward. What do the people you aspire to do demonstrate? Who do you admire? Are they conference hosts, authors, artists, or writers? What would make them proud?

We call this iterative learning—so start from your interests and evolve as you go.

The smaller, the better. But design a project with "collaborability" in mind: "How would I get others involved?"

MAKE YOUR PROJECT TACTICAL

Sheryl Sandberg has one of the most impressive résumés.

When she joined Facebook in 2008, the company lost $56 million that year. Four years later, the company would go public, reporting revenues of more than $3.7 billion and profits of more than a billion dollars. By 2020, Facebook would be one of the four most valuable companies. While Sandberg is humble regarding her impact, her boss Mark Zuckerberg credited her with the talent influx that followed her hiring in 2008. Within just forty-two months on the job, she was rewarded handsomely for her contributions, earning more than $1.6 billion from stock options and a bonus that totaled more than her base pay.

Sandberg's path to Facebook was unorthodox. Her public sector jobs at the US Treasury Department and the World Bank, under the wing of her former Harvard professor and mentor Larry Summer, led to her first job in tech at Google before joining Facebook. Sandberg wasn't necessarily the obvious fit for Facebook's COO. As the *New York Times* wrote of her in 2012:

Everyone agrees she is wickedly smart. But she has also been lucky and has had powerful mentors along the way. After Harvard and Harvard Business School, she quickly rose from a post as an economist at the World Bank to become the chief of staff for Lawrence H. Summers, then the Treasury secretary. After that, she jumped to Google and, in 2008, to Facebook.

This article points to a key aspect of Sandberg's professional success. Her work with and mentorship by Summers, dating back to her time at Harvard, was critical in setting her up for these next opportunities at Google and then Facebook.

Sandberg first met Summers when she tried to start *Women in Economics and Government,* a new student organization that aimed to inspire more women to study these subjects. Summers took an active role while she spoke with numerous faculty members about the organization's initiative. "He served as our champion and helped rally the support of his fellow professors behind our efforts," Sandberg wrote in her 2008 Huffington Post article. The relationship expanded with Summers offering to serve as her thesis advisor, which provided him with a unique opportunity to see Sandberg's worth ethic, mind, and creativity up close.

This became a meaningful project that allowed her to seek collaborators. While Summers would get involved, Sandberg spoke to numerous faculty members who could have created similar opportunities for her.

She maximized her opportunity for collaborative opportunities.

When asked about Sandberg as a student, Summers shared in *The Guardian* that, "Sheryl always believed that if there were thirty things on her to-do list at the beginning of the day, there would be thirty check marks at the end of the day. If I was making a mistake, she told me. She was totally loyal, but totally in my face."

One Meeting Away: Sheryl Sandberg

Right Person. Larry Summers was a Harvard Professor of Economics.

Right Ask. Can you help us rally other Harvard faculty behind this new student organization—*Women in Economics and Government?*

Right Start. Sandberg engaged Summers in the new organization, began to collaborate on his work and her research, and eventually developed a professional relationship as Summers left Harvard to join the government.

Right Time. In the 1980s, few women were involved in economics. Even today, the American Economic Association finds that just 22 percent of tenured and tenure-track faculty in economics are women. While the cause was important, Sandberg too few women were in the fields alone to cultivate more support for aspiring female students seeking roles in economics and government.

This foundation built on a meaningful project eventually landed Sandberg an opportunity she could not turn down. When Summers was named the chief economist at the World Bank in 1991, he hired her as a research assistant, and when Bill Clinton named Summers the treasury secretary, Sandberg became his chief of staff. Her career acceleration was remarkable, and Sandberg was well aware that her mentorship by Summers was critical in her ascension.

To the *Harvard Business Review,* Sandberg noted, "Those opportunities are ones I wouldn't have had without him." She continued, "[Summers's mentorship] helped tremendously. I've had a lot of mentors over the course of my career, Larry being one of the absolutely most important. And certainly the first."

No matter the level of schooling—from high school through graduate school—you have a distinct advantage as a student in that prospective mentors are more willing to help a student. On the other hand, students are likely to be less self-aware of their own needs or want to make them more likely to fall into inspirational mentoring. The following project styles are uniquely suited to students.

- *Student Organizations and Clubs.* Sheryl Sandberg leveraged the power of a student club as a connection tool, landing Larry Summers as an advocate, advisor, and eventually her Super Mentor. Student clubs offer a terrific opportunity for soliciting individuals as speakers. Find individuals you would personally like to connect with and invite them as a speaker for an organization or club. Offer to interview them or introduce them, and remember the power of the follow-up afterward. Share photos, learnings, write-ups, and more. Ask speakers what would be most useful to them.
- *Group or Class Projects.* Substantive group or individual class projects offer an outstanding opportunity for collaborative projects with individuals.

PROJECTS THAT LEVERAGE BEING AN EMPLOYEE

How do you get time with senior leadership at your company? Find projects to connect and collaborate on. At one of my first jobs, I worked on a project around innovation and asked if I could use the company I was working at as the subject. That project enabled me to get direct, one-on-one time with the CEO. But it doesn't need to be as formal as a project about the company. Look at what the executives do outside of their day job, including nonprofits they work with, hobbies they have, and activities they enjoy.

- *Writing an Article Series.* Content is king in many organizations. Write. Either write insights you're learning in an article series on your platforms or collaborate with your company.
- *Organizing or Supporting Speakers, Events, and Conferences.* Offering to participate, volunteer, or work on projects that involve

external organizations and speakers can get you involved with prospective mentors. Senior leaders may view conferences and events as a great deal of time, allowing you to step in and help them or create value for them. The individuals at conferences and events may see you as an ambitious individual.

- *Create a Research Project.* What would help your company, your team, or your industry uncover or learn a key, shareable insight? Often, offering to do an extensive research project that involves you speaking with, surveying, or gathering data to turn into some type of learning can be an opportunity to engage with people to do the research and then turn and share that research with senior individuals inside and outside your company or organization.

PROJECTS THAT LEVERAGE BEING ENTREPRENEURIAL

If you're starting something—a start-up, a podcast, a book, a video channel, or a side hustle—look for ways to collaborate with others.

- *Gather early customer feedback.* If you are developing a product or a solution, get feedback on it early from people you'd like to establish a relationship with. Don't sell to them, but involve them in the early development process. Keep them posted as you iterate and evolve based on their feedback.

- *Book guests or speakers for interviews.* Many projects, including podcasts, books, and video channels, are great opportunities to speak to people you admire and turn their insights directly into the content. Make requests easy for them, and showcase how your audience appreciates the value they provide.

- *Partner with a good cause.* People you'd like to meet or get to know may volunteer with organizations you can also work with. Don't just participate, but become active and look for opportunities to collaborate with other more established individuals through shared working relationships. Find a cause, offer to help, and deliver.

BEGIN A PROJECT YOU CAN FINISH.

Each of these projects has an element of finality to them—similar to finishing a marathon.

One of the things about making this process fun is creating an obvious point where you can celebrate. Have celebratory moments throughout, but projects have a launch date, a release day, a kick-off party, etc.

This caveat leads to one of the biggest misconceptions about project creation—or perhaps one of the biggest pushbacks I receive from aspirational creators, entrepreneurs, and even start-up founders when looking for meaningful projects that necessitate collaboration.

"Why isn't a start-up on your list?"

I get criticism regularly for not including a start-up on my list of creation events. But the thing is, if every start-up founder is "killing it," or "crushing it," or "dominating," is anyone doing well?

Start-ups are certainly a way to show your work, but it wasn't something we observed that would fit as a project. The start-up itself doesn't build credibility. That happens well before the business gets anywhere.

Yes, successful people, we've observed on *Forbes'* 30 Under 30 list and beyond tend to start companies—lots of them. You might be lured into thinking that the path to demonstrate your purpose is just to start a company like these successful people. But the reality is often surprising to the uninitiated. Successful ventures come *after* projects rather than serve as the meaningful projects themselves. See Adam's story above.

Take Jaclyn DiGregorio. As a student, she completed a twenty-thousand-dollar Kickstarter for her business, CUSP 365, secured over seventy speaking gigs in six months, and was named one of the most promising entrepreneurs in Washington, DC, in 2018. You'd probably look at her and say she's demonstrating her passion through her start-up.

But step back and look under the surface. Her journey to early start-up success was almost a disaster when she invested thousands of dollars in an idea she had for a "portioning plate." Her fascination began with the idea, but no one was buying it. Her Kickstarter campaign almost completely flopped.

"I couldn't get anyone to care," she admits.

The problem, it turns out, was that Jaclyn's floundering business was selling a *what* without giving people an insight into her *why*. No one understood Jaclyn and why this business was so important to her and her potential clients. She hadn't taken Simon Sinek's advice to start with why.

But that changed with my course.

She explains, "I created a video course and wrote a book. Suddenly people were reading my story, and my insecurities were on display for everyone to see. People believed in me because I'd created something other people could judge for themselves."

Nearly every successful person—the emerging creator class—has used their project to provide the depth, expertise, and credibility to build their successful start-up venture. They weren't using their start-ups to build their credibility. They used the credibility they'd built through creation to start their business. It might seem like an issue of semantics to some, but in reality, the difference is quite significant.

Many of us will undertake something meaningful to find success— something that shows who you are and what you're passionate about *before* you can ever jump into a start-up and find business success. These projects enable the collaboration opportunities required to develop the relationships you're seeking.

Yes, you can demonstrate your passion in other ways. For art or design, you can work on a website, a mobile app, or another simple product. For a product or a problem you want to solve, you can invent something. Or if you're passionate about music, you can put on a concert. The opportunities for creating are limitless.

We observe four main "mediums" behind these nine meaningful, collaborative projects:

1. a video or video series
2. an event or conference

3. music available for free streaming
4. a significant written work

These four approaches are the most common because they tie directly to the person who created them—you.

You can put out a video series on YouTube, list an album on Sound-Cloud, or publish a book through CreateSpace without needing anything other than the tools to create it and the confidence to upload and share it. These options don't require corporations, production partners, or patents, and they are all quite simple to do on your own or with little help.

"I'm thinking about starting a blog," a friend told me. "It's my New Year's resolution. I'll write something weekly."

"Do not start a blog," I countered.

"But you said I shouldn't start a company yet. You said to continue exploring and investigating, so I'm going to do that and publish it on a blog."

"Do not start a blog," I said again in the same tone.

"I don't understand."

The New York Times recently revamped a section of its newspaper and put out a call for contributors. The media brand hoped to bring a "fresh perspective from young people," so they put out a call far and wide to attract submissions from tens of thousands of people looking for a place to share their voice.

The application was mostly standard fare, asking the applicant for information about their schooling, hobbies, writing experience, and opinions. But one section stood out to me—a link to your blog.

It wasn't the fact that they'd asked for a link; it was what was in the small print underneath: "Active blogs only, with a post in the past thirty days."

I chuckled for a minute. Harsh, no?

The digital world is littered with dead blogs, where the most recent post is years old. I recently realized that when I'd transitioned my blog from one platform to another, I'd never shut down the old one and the last post on the prior site was from May 2014.

Yes, the reader could go in and see that I'd written some interesting things if they wanted to, but something jumped out first. I'd stopped writing. My blog was dead. What does that say to other people about me?

This is similar to our fitness routines. When was the last time you went to the gym? If you have a membership and you haven't been to the gym in six months (guilty!), one can only and rightfully assume you've quit your goal to get in shape.

Plenty of people stick with their goals. They run marathons and train every day. There's fraternity among marathon runners. Even if you haven't trained in months and haven't completed a marathon in a year or a decade, anyone who runs a marathon can claim they've trained for something difficult and finished. No one judges that you haven't done it since then—just a hat tip that you put your body through the grueling training required to run twenty-six miles.

A blog is a gym. An article series, podcast season, video course, or book is a marathon.

**DON'T START A BLOG,
CREATE AN ARTICLE SERIES**

So, do not start a blog.

Okay, perhaps you're an anomaly and will prove me wrong by sticking to your plan to blog weekly, monthly, or daily. But chances are you won't. Even if you blog frequently, many individual posts rarely offer the depth required to prove you are an expert in something.

So, what's the difference between starting a blog and writing an article series? Put a number in front of it. Write a two-hundred-page book. Host a four-part speaker series. Publish a ten-part article series. Launch a twelve-episode podcast season.

Finish something meaningful that proves you have the forethought to organize this meaty and meaningful thing and offers your consumer a way to judge your depth for themselves. Creation events offer the ability to go fast and deep—and a way to finish something that stands on its own whether or not you ever do another one.

IT'S NOT (PRIMARILY) ABOUT MONEY.

You want money. Money comes in the form of a job or an internship you'd like to hire you, an investor in your start-up, a scholarship or grant for schooling, or an advance from a producer or publisher for your film, album, or movie. Mentors are the Problem Solvers who can help you solve those problems.

Just come out and ask for what you want. Right?

Not so fast.

Mentorship is a *free* transfer of assets. One of the quickest ways to stop a free transfer is to make the other person feel like their generosity is being taken advantage of. This makes sense. Forty percent of Americans viewed money as the most challenging topic to discuss with others, more than talking about death, politics, and religion. Directly asking for a job, an investment, or an introduction to someone about a job or investment can make someone feel skittish.

The three most common types of Super Mentorship in the research were: (a) academic (while the mentee is a student) (b) workplace (while the mentee was working at a company or organization), and (c) peer or near-peer (where the mentor and mentee are at fairly similar points in life/career). Why? My theory is that these times and scenarios are points when we have our guard down on being taken advantage of; we aren't outsiders or strangers. *We are at the same school or company or stage.*

My relationship with Steve Blank developed because I was a volunteer for a nonprofit in the start-up education world. Steve joined, and we collaborated on a project for that nonprofit. Based on our collaborations, he was instrumental in connections to investors for my start-up company a year later. But had I come out and said, "Could you introduce me to _____," it would have likely put him in a challenging spot. Or it would have put him in a clear spot—a simple no.

Projects make the process of developing a relationship for collaboration more natural. We run a much lower risk of feeling taken advantage of. Mentors are often pleased to speak at a group or organization, are happy to be interviewed on a podcast or for a book, and are happy to contribute their feedback on your research or product.

"Having a project to collaborate on plays to a knowledge-sharer's vanity, and that's 100 percent okay," Adam Saven told me. "I mean who doesn't want to be quoted in a book, sit in as a podcast guest, or feature in a documentary? Your ask could provide a way for the Super Mentor to raise *their* profile."

Money may be tangentially involved (eventually, you'd like to charge for your product, get hired in a field, or sell your music), but at the project stage, it's easier. That's one of the reasons why "my start-up" or "my business" are not on the list of common projects.

When studying uber-successful people and their mentors, most of them seemed to have a strong sense of what they wanted—jobs, access, opportunities, collaboration, etc. But they recognized the importance of patience.

A simple rule of thumb is this: Does a prospective mentor *typically* charge money for what you ask them to do? If they don't, great. You've got an easy way to make a small ask for them that's valuable for you. If they say they charge for speaking, coaching, or teaching, find a way to shrink the ask down smaller. You'll do a call with them when they are driving, you'll send them questions over email, or you'll ask for feedback on one feature or aspect.

Make people feel good about you and your project by making it about more than just money. Make it valuable and easy for them.

COLLABORATION IS ENJOYABLE.

As you look to build a network of mentors, it's best to view them as additive. Sheryl Sandberg was starting the *Women in Economics and Government* at Harvard, and she invited faculty members like Larry Summers to participate. But if he or any of the other faculty members said no, she was still starting it. Rahul Rana was writing a book, and if he couldn't land Josh Wolfe for an interview, he was still writing it.

Honestly, that's why these projects are meaningful and collaborative. Pick a project you're excited about. Pick a project you will enjoy working on. Pick a project that makes it easy for others to collaborate with you. Then the worst-case scenario is you still have a project you finished. Think about college. It's not a credential until you get your degree. You have to finish and get the degree.

Run the marathon. Invite others to run for a mile on the trip. Post your time. Then decide if you ever want to do another one.

For Lin-Manuel Miranda, creating came from a new musical project first performed for the president and then completing his musical on a topic he was passionate about and knew would teach others.

For you, creating might be a YouTube series like comedian Hasan Minhaj. It might be releasing a mixed tape for free like Chance the Rapper. It might be organizing an event like Elliott Bisnow. Or like Marie Kondo, it might mean writing a manuscript. Whichever way you choose to create your credibility, what's important is not the act of creating your account or getting something out there but the drive behind it.

Make your project meaningful for everyone collaborating.

SOMETHING YOU CARE ABOUT.

SOMETHING YOU CAN COMPLETE.

MORE THAN MAKING MONEY.

Make sure it's something you're excited about. Then, we begin finding ways to get them involved.

6

THINK SMALLER

The biggest risk to this process is giving up too early.

Part of that comes from the way we often retell success stories. We focus on the successful attempts, not the unsuccessful ones. I can almost guarantee you'll have unsuccessful attempts. We all do.

Michael Jordan has nine game-winning shots in his NBA career. But he's been trusted to hit a potential game-winning shot twenty-six other times and missed. You could look at this and conclude that he missed three-quarters of the time. Or you could recognize that he has hit the *most* game-winning shots of anyone in NBA history.

You've got to shoot your shot—no other way around it. But even more than that, you'll learn how to get the best opportunities for the lowest costs. There is no magical email template, no golden subject line, no perfect social media direct message, or perfect cold call. You will need to make a lot of high-quality attempts, and over time, strong evidence says some of your attempts will pay off (a few in major ways).

Making the right ask is much more effective when you've completed these aspects (chapters 4 and 5):

- You design mentoring to create opportunities (a.k.a. engaging Problem Solvers with your problems).
- You have a meaningful project to collaborate on.

In chapters 7 and 8, we'll help you be more tactical in creating the list of *new* people to engage with. You will need a set of targets combined with the consistency and patience to move your way through them. Your most transformative relationships are not built on perfectly created requests but on micro-requests that will build over time across multiple people.

This is where things begin to get fun. You'll learn to leverage the power of the micro-request.

BEGIN WHERE YOU ARE.

You've already got mentors. You just might not call them that yet.

Most of us already have people in our lives that have the potential to be very helpful in solving our problems. We either didn't realize they could help us or didn't know how to ask for their help.

It's time to take an inventory of your existing relationships. Start with a series of "who" questions, and investigate your access:

- Who do I know who has completed this project already?
- Who do I already know who has worked on something similar?
- Who do I know working in that industry or company or field?
- Who do I know who has already made this choice?
- Who have I heard speak, talk, or teach at an event or conference?
- Who do I listen to or watch when I need to learn something important?
- Who do I know who is closely connected to someone I'd like to meet?

———————

As you move from seeking general advice from Inspirational Mentors to tactical opportunities from Problem Solver Mentors, these questions become much easier to answer. In short: *Do I know anyone who has solved this problem already?*

Your initial list of connections might be small and uninspiring, or you might include someone you engaged with previously without developing any opportunities. Many of those relationships may need to be (smartly) rekindled through small acts of generosity.

Remember that you already have mentors; you will simply need to activate them through different requests, asks, and engagements to create opportunities.

LEVERAGE THE PSYCHOLOGY OF GENEROSITY.

Adam Grant, a Wharton professor and author, has studied the impact of generosity in various organizational settings—from salespeople and doctors to executives. He's discovered three predispositions to generosity:

- Givers
- Takers
- Matchers

Grant finds that Givers represent about a quarter of the population, and they are naturally generous and willing to help. Takers are the opposite and are more likely to view the downside of assisting others, so they're not as likely to help. Takers represent about another quarter of the population. Matchers are nearly half of people, and they believe in fairness. They believe in quid pro quo and do favors for people who have done favors for them, or they have a strong belief they'd be willing to do a favor in the future.

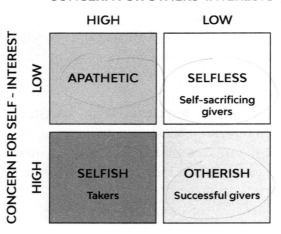

CONCERN FOR OTHERS' INTERESTS

	HIGH	LOW
CONCERN FOR SELF-INTEREST LOW	APATHETIC	SELFLESS Self-sacrificing givers
HIGH	SELFISH Takers	OTHERISH Successful givers

Adapted from Adam Grant's
"Give and Take" chart (p.158)

Mentor Fallacy: Most people are too busy, don't want to help, and aren't generous with their time.

Super Mentor Reality: Only 22 percent of people are takers according to Adam Grant and are unlikely to be willing to collaborate or work with someone purely to help the other person; 22 percent are givers who try to give without a second thought, and 56 percent are Matchers who try to achieve balance but are willing to give and be generous with their time.

It's essential to recognize what this active approach to mentorship means for you. You will be asking for favors.

***

Arlan Hamilton is an outsider who found her way inside the competitive industries of music, publishing, and venture capital throughout her career. Today, Hamilton is the founder and managing partner of Backstage Capital, an early stage fund focused on investing in high-growth businesses run by women, people of color, and LGBTQ. Hamilton recognized how generosity was her currency.

As a twenty-one-year-old, Hamilton was a fan of a Norwegian pop-punk group and wanted to see them perform live. But they weren't touring, so she reached out to them, asking if she could set up their tour herself rather than wait. The band took her up on the opportunity based on her success with an unknown Norwegian band. Hamilton would break into the music industry, managing touring for arena-stage musicians including Jason Derulo, Toni Braxton, and Kirk Franklin as a production coordinator and tour manager.

Breaking into venture capital would require those same skills, and she began looking to raise funds to invest in start-up founders from diverse backgrounds. She discovered they'd been long underserved for a reason. They often didn't have the funds to get into the conferences, clubs, schools, and companies where these connections were being made. Homeless and without access to those very same places, Hamilton began to share opportunities and the unique deal flow she had access to, offering value first to the people she'd eventually court as investors in her funds.

As Backstage has grown, Arlan isn't afraid to create the circles she wants to be in, create value for others first, and tap those she's helped when she needs it. Her limited partners include Mark Cuban, Netscape, A16Z founder Marc Andreessen, Slack founder Stewart Butterfield, and dozens of others.

One Meeting Away: Arlan Hamilton

Right Person. Mark Cuban, owner of NBA team Dallas Mavericks and investor on *Shark Tank*

Right Ask. When Hamilton first met Cuban, she was professional and shared the network of nontraditional founders she'd built and didn't make an initial ask.

Right Start. Then when she'd later revealed she was raising a fund to invest directly (as she was having trouble matching these founders to investors), he wrote her a check.

Right Time. Cuban gave Hamilton's Backstage Capital one million dollars to invest as she saw fit because he wanted to diversify his investments. Less than 10 percent of all venture capital deals go to women, people of color, and LGBTQ founders.

***

Generosity is the currency of influence today.

It's important to recognize the implications of this and how to leverage the public social circles you've created to help you in these efforts.

In some cases, you'll send a cold email or a direct message to someone to ask for a fifteen-minute conversation, and if you're lucky, that person is a Giver. If the person can help you out, and your ask is targeted enough, they'll likely be willing to offer their time somehow. The positive part of this is that you're likely to run into a giver about one in four times during your outreach. On the other hand, you'll reach out to a Taker about one in four times. You're unlikely to draw a positive outcome in those requests no matter what you do.

The important thing to note is that about half of the people you'll run across in your outreach are Matchers. Remember, Matchers are people who believe in fairness and are likely to do favors for others they know are generous or have previously done them a favor. You will face the challenge that Matchers won't know much about you due to a single, cold outreach. They are likely to presume you're just asking for a favor and are not generous. The challenge is that 50 percent of your outreach are Matchers, and unless you can prove otherwise, they're unlikely to offer their help.

But this is where how you use social media and engage your new circles can change this dynamic.

Remember, Matchers operate in a world of fairness. Grant recommends a technique called five-minute favors—positive activities where you are generous to others *first*. This creates a scenario where you're more likely to elicit a positive response from your cold outreach. It often creates opportunities for an initial engagement.

- Review their book
- Review their podcast episode or a video or theirs
- Review their products/apps
- Share or donate to their cause
- Share their articles/content

The activities are simple and should take you less than five minutes. You operate with generosity first, creating a much better chance of positive first engagements. You simply use social media to be positive and celebratory, operating with generosity. This is one of the most powerful ways to cultivate relationships long before building a direct one.

"I just congratulated a connection on LinkedIn," shared Terri Nakamura. "He'd just been appointed to another board of directors. A few days later, I asked if he could possibly help me line up an internship and he said yes. He initiated five email introductions, of which three resulted in personal follow-ups and subsequent phone conversations."

Research by professors James Fowler and Nicholas Christakis finds we become less engaged when content on our social feed becomes more negative. Be engaged, be generous, and create real, authentic positivity, which increases opportunities with others.

AIM FOR MORE IMMEDIATE GRATIFICATION.

"The winning team will do the most *outreach*—cold emails, LinkedIn connections, direct messages, etc.," I said to my class of thirty undergraduate students at Georgetown.

In this course, I found that a team dynamic that competes on the actions we control rather than outcomes we don't control is key in building the right behaviors. So we create a little competition and reward inputs rather than outcomes. Which team would do the most outreach? Recently, I began to add some sizzle to layer on the fun: "If anyone gets a reply, a like on social media, or sets up a meeting with someone who has fifty thousand or more followers or friends on social media, it's worth a bonus."

And the results bore that out, with the group receiving three to four more responses, replies, and engagement than when I asked them to target a minimum number of responses or replies.

James Clear, the author of *Atomic Habits*, describes this as making the process satisfying. Humans are poor at delayed gratification activities. As Clear writes, "What is immediately rewarded is repeated. What is immediately punished is avoided."

His advice: Feel immediately successful—even if only in a small way.

This is why I encourage you to engage with many mentors and in the context of projects. You'll be immediately successful and receive immediate gratification by scheduling a call you can use in your research, as an interview for your podcast, as a quote for your blog, or as a story in your book.

The benefit is much more direct.

If you'd like to make the habits repeated and sticky, you best involve others. We get immediate gratification from positive feedback and rewards. Create a group, a partner, or hire a coach. Design activities where you control the action rather than the outcome. Try to treat the outcome as the cherry on top.

MAKE REQUESTS THAT ARE EASY TO SAY YES TO.

People often ask for the *wrong* things at the beginning stages of the relationship.

- Can I pick your brain?
- Will you be my mentor?
- I'm trying to figure out my life. Can you help?

These questions are complex and potentially chaotic for the recipient. The questions require work to contemplate and effort to deconstruct. They can feel like a long-term commitment. They aren't things we can easily say yes to, so the easy—and all too common—response is no.

While there is no single magic template you can use, you should consider five important aspects when making a request that is easy to say yes to:

- Make it specific.
- Make it simple.
- Make it schedulable.
- Explain the opportunity.
- Acknowledge their capacity.

Even before you begin, make sure you rekindle the relationship. Here is a sample initial "micro-request" template to connect or reconnect with someone you already know, even casually, through email and social media.

SAMPLE EMAIL RECONNECTION MESSAGE

Hi [Name],

We originally connected through [Event/Meeting/Conference] [Person Who Connected You][Your School alum/student][Industry/Sector veteran/newbie][fellow entrepreneur/company alum]. [Reference the five-minute favor or another connection in these parentheses—e.g., "I recently [read your book/recent article] [listened to your podcast/a talk you gave at X][learned about your cause][started following you on Twitter/Instagram/YouTube] and was impressed enough to share it with my network."] I am working on a [project type] that I am hoping to release in the next year. The working title is [title] and it's a [twenty-word summary]. I thought your insights could be really valuable.

Would you be available to do a short twenty-minute phone interview in the next couple of weeks? I'm early in the process and would appreciate your thoughts.
[Your Name]

SAMPLE SOCIAL MEDIA CONNECTION REQUEST

Hi [Name]. Wanted to reconnect. We originally connected through [Your School alum/student][Industry/Sector veteran/ newbie][fellow entrepreneur/company alum]. Now I'm working on a [project type] about [twenty-word summary]. Based on [a relative achievement, a recent article they wrote, their experience in an industry], I think your insight can be really beneficial to the project. Thanks! [Your Name]

You can use this as a starting point and customize it for your project.

HOW TO MAKE IT SPECIFIC.

One of the easiest ways to create a more effective ask is to be specific on the outcome of the ask. As you'll see in the examples, you are requesting a short, twenty-minute phone interview or a chat.

> **Mentor Fallacy:** It's better to be general in our requests for help, support, or feedback and let our mentors guide us.
>
> **Super Mentor Reality:** The more specific our goals, the higher our performance and productivity levels. Make more specific inquiries, and you'll get more productive and helpful results.

The easiest way to make it specific is to ask yourself: "What do I most want out of this time?"

Researcher Howard J. Klein studied 162 undergraduate students to see how goal specificity affected their performance levels. He found that the more specific the goal, the higher the productivity levels.

How to make it simple. Do they have all the information they need to answer with a yes or no?

University of Toronto Psychology Professor Gary Latham found that the secret of goal achievement is exclusion. How do you remove things that aren't directly relevant to the goal itself? We like to feel a sense of accomplishment, and the more requests are aligned with that objective, the more we feel accomplished and willing to engage again.

Complex and ambiguous tasks are challenging because we attempt to address them as a whole. Smaller units are less ambiguous and can be interpreted more conveniently. By breaking your needs down into strategic units, we can build toward solving the more complex tasks.

HOW TO MAKE IT SCHEDULABLE.

These are not transactional relationships, and you should consider how to incorporate an interaction. Would this involve a call? Will you meet in person? Will you both be at an event to interact? Will you have a way to exchange digital, real-time communications via text messages or a similar channel? Even if your goal is a series of interactions over time, you want to begin with a first interaction. Add a specific amount of time you're looking for. Remember, the amount of time does not equate to the value of the interaction.

HOW TO MAKE THIS AN OPPORTUNITY.

Why should they make time for this? This is where scoping some of the details can highlight that your project is important—and finite. People can get excited about helping an aspiring writer, designer, researcher, or change maker. Communicate what you are doing and how they'll participate. How will they see the fruits of their work pay off? It's important to note that this isn't "what's in it for you" but more about "how will I know my time was well spent."

HOW TO ACKNOWLEDGE THEIR CAPACITY.

You're asking for a favor. Acknowledge that you appreciate them, their prior work, and the unique contribution they can make to you and your project. This could be one of the more important and under-appreciated parts of building these relationships. You want to share what specifically inspired you to reach out and that you believe their time will be important to your meaningful project. Any effort you make in advance to show your generosity—five minutes favors—can go a long way.

This first engagement is an important one. First impressions matter. But also, it's important to note that you don't need to overweight the first message itself as this message won't be the last one you send regardless of their response or lack thereof. At this point, it's better to hear nothing than no, and the first engagements and message position you for success.

You bear the responsibility. An inability to ask small, simple questions signals that you don't have the knowledge and would need to be taught or coached or may require a heavy investment. Consider asking yourself the question first. Does it require extensive thinking, planning, scheduling, or consideration? Can you make the ask itself more transactional? Can you create smaller steps to the larger question?

The simpler the initial requests—a well-scoped micro-request being ideal early in the relationship—the easier it is to come to a quick and hopefully positive resolution.

LOOK FOR THE SMALLEST INTERACTIONS TO START (AND BE PREPARED TO GO SMALLER)

"Is there any way I can just intern for you?" asked Blake Robbins on his phone call with venture capitalist Jonathon Triest of Ludlow Ventures.

"We're not looking for an intern," Triest replied, hoping to end the conversation with Blake. "We don't want to babysit anyone. We don't have time to teach anyone what's going on here."

That's a pretty definitive and clear answer to Blake's question.

After reading that conversation, you would probably be shocked to learn that Blake is currently a Partner at Ludlow Ventures.

In the start-up and venture world that looks for big visions, big exits, and big personalities, Blake found the power of asking *smaller*.

Blake Robbins is a *Forbes* 30 under 30 winner and is one of the leading proponents of the Creator Economy, a growing ecosystem that venture firm SignalFire defines as "the class of businesses centered around independent content creators, curators, and community builders including social media influencers, bloggers, and videographers, plus the software and finance tools designed to help them with growth and monetization." Blake has made early and successful bets in e-Sports, e-Commerce, and streaming.

Let's start with the good in Blake's story. He did lots of outreach, found his way to a connection, and made the ask. That's good; he took his shot.

Now to the not-so-good. His ask was too complex, too ambitious, and too much work for the person he was just meeting for the first time.

But here's the silver lining. He had a plan to make a smaller, micro-request.

"My junior year of college, I decided I wanted to be an investor," Blake shared. "But I don't think anyone was building start-ups or investing from Michigan State, so I would probably work at some oil company."

Blake quickly realized if he wanted to break into venture capital, he needed to start by identifying his aspirational peers, and he needed to find his "cousins." He started to build a list of venture capitalists he thought had similar backgrounds to his—people who hadn't gone the "MBA-to-investment-banking-to-venture-capital" route or were not successful start-up founders prior to investing. To his surprise, after a few weekends of digging, he'd developed a list of 200 people that met the criteria.

"I was much more shameless at that time," he admitted. "I felt like I had nothing to lose—zero downside to me sending this email. Worst-case scenario is they archive it; best-case scenario I can meet some really interesting people or I can get a job. The risk-reward of that was the simplest equation ever. I'm like, 'Hell yeah. I'm just gonna keep doing that.' And so that spiraled once I saw it worked."

Once he identified his list and reached out, he had to find his way into one of the most competitive industries. "Maybe ten or so of the two hundred responded. And thankfully, some of them were open with their time." Part of his success was in the fact that he'd been very specific in his targeting. They were all people who might "see themselves" in his hopeful and nontraditional path into venture investing.

He used a little social proof from Ryan Hoover, the founder of Ludlow investment Product Hunt, to get a call with one of the only venture firms in his backyard. Ludlow Ventures had its office in Detroit, Michigan, less than an hour from where Blake was studying. Boldness had gotten him this far, so on the call, he quickly made his ask.

"Is there any way I can just intern for you?"

"We're not looking for an intern," came the reply.

He was ready with his response. "I understand. Is there any way I can just have an email address?"

There was a pause on the other end of the phone.

"You don't have to pay me," he continued, "just give me an email address. I will just leverage that to set up meetings with interesting start-up founders. I will just send you my notes from those meetings. You never have to see me in your offices."

"I guess," Jonathan replied, considering the unorthodox request. "I don't see any downsides..."

With that simpler ask, Blake went to work. "Having this email address was enough to get my foot in many doors. And I reached out to every interesting founder. I again reached out to all the investors who ignored me from those initial cold emails, saying, 'Hey, I just ended up in venture. I'd love to learn from you now and start sending you deals. What areas interest you?' and now almost all of them responded. I was just building on my network and showing the access I could get for Ludlow."

The then-senior in college eventually got a job offer and a seat at the table at Ludlow because he brought an unusual network with him—one he built on the back of a simpler request of an email address.

Right Person. Jonathon Triest, Partner at Ludlow Ventures.

Right Ask. Is there any way I can intern for you? First, failure. Is there any way I can just have an email address and try to schedule some cool meetings for you? Second, success.

Right Start. Once he had the email address, Blake knew he would need to produce, and he took hundreds of meetings, created detailed notes, and provided regular updates.

Right Time. Ludlow was a newer and smaller firm, which meant smaller management fees for its operations. Being located in Michigan—far from many of the more common technology hubs in San Francisco, New York, Los Angeles, Seattle, and Austin—they needed to find creative ways to generate deal flow from high-potential start-ups. Blake offered to provide deal flow without any cost or overhead.

Blake leveraged one of the most important and underappreciated skills in Super Mentorship—the power of micro-requests.

Micro-requests are a superpower for the aspiring protégé. A micro-request is a piece of carefully scoped work, help, or support that can be completed quickly and without impacting the ability to complete other work or efforts. These are the "what's the downside" requests: small, tangible, and simple asks that require very little thinking and work from the mentor. But they enable a mentee or protégé to demonstrate their value and competence to the mentor.

Blake, however, nearly got trapped by his initial macro-request. "Can I intern for you?" is complicated and potentially chaotic. It involves negotiating a salary, finding office space, and deciding how to train and support someone. It feels a lot like, "Will you be my mentor?" or, "Can I pick your brain?" or, "I'm trying to figure out my life. Can you help?" He was asking Jonathan to do work when Jonathan had already signaled he was overly busy. But Blake's micro-request of,

"Can I just have an email address and send you notes from interesting meetings?" was simple. Of course, Jonathan could have said no, but this yes or no decision was simple.

Our effort to simplify our micro-requests to create "easy wins" is critical. Yes, it's an email address, it's a micro-project, and it's a question. But the power of a micro-request is transformative in establishing the first move.

ENGAGE IN INTENTIONAL AND FREQUENT ACTIONS WITH NUMEROUS PEOPLE.

"That one tweet changed my life."

Hyperbole like this is easy to dismiss. Stories about a single action that was transformative seem more a product of good fortune than a repeatable strategy or approach.

The author of the breakout book *The Almanack of Naval Ravikant*, Eric Jorgensen, built that life-changing tweet on a mountain of prior work, activities, time, and thought. Simple, small actions *can* lead to life-changing opportunities and outcomes.

He probably should have said, "I have ten thousand tweets that didn't change my life and one that did."

Jorgensen has been working on projects throughout his early career spending his day job working at a high-growth start-up. His extra time has been spent on a series of writing projects including Evergreen Business, a site he runs that curates some of the most impactful business ideas, frameworks, and wisdom from across the internet. As part of that work, he spends countless hours reading, watching, and listening to some of the most prominent thinkers in business.

One of those people was Naval Ravikant, the founder of start-up platform AngelList and one of the leading minds in the start-up economy. Ravikant's content is routinely shared and re-shared hundreds and thousands of times on social media, but for Jorgenson, he felt it risked being lost to the impermanence of the platforms.

He thought the content needed to be organized, curated, and given a permanent home.

"I had this simple idea and tweeted it," Eric said. "Naval retweeted it, and five thousand people were like 'Yes, so this; we want this book.' For me, it was a half-joke and half-real idea. And all of a sudden, it became very real. I'd never met Naval, and suddenly he's providing me all the material that would serve as the basis for the book."

The project became real instantly, but it grew into a collaboration well beyond what Jorgenson had initially thought.

"I wasn't clear it had to be a book—maybe a website or a blog. But the more work we did, the clearer the book was the ideal format. I'm thrilled that it is."

The book became a launching pad for Eric to collaborate with noted author and podcaster Tim Ferriss and dozens of others on a course that helps people learn some of the book's core insights.

But it began with a small ask into the universe to see if anyone—Naval included—was interested in the idea. If he had said he wasn't interested, or if no one had replied, he was out nothing. This micro-request certainly wasn't random, but it also wasn't a fleshed-out project at the earliest point. Funny enough, dozens or hundreds of previous tweets might have been equally as "thoughtful" as this one, but a combination of things led it to create the opportunity that has changed Eric's life.

One Meeting Away: Eric Jorgenson

Right Person. Naval Ravikant, founder and CEO of AngelList.

Right Ask. Have you thought about writing a book?

Right Start. That night, Naval engaged directly with Eric for the first time and offered access to all his materials but wanted Eric to be the main driver of the project.

Right Time. Naval had been doing more and more in-depth interviews, podcasts, and discussions. His content was being shared and syndicated broadly throughout the start-up ecosystem. When Eric tagged Naval in a tweet about writing a book, or helping to write it, the tweet went viral with more than five thousand people engaging with the tweet, including Naval, who retweeted it to his followers.

––––––––––––––––––––

Said another way, a single, life-changing tweet results from many non-life-changing activities.

Purposeful activities may only be simple actions. But consistent, simple actions give us the shot at a tweet, email, meeting, connection, or conversation that changes everything.

- Consistent, simple purposeful actions that compound over time
- You need to start making small requests

PART II

THE LAW OF
RIGHT PEOPLE

Find the people who have the power to transform your trajectory.
Learn how to connect with the people who have the opportunities
you're seeking.

7

BUILD A MAP TO THE PEOPLE WHO CAN HELP YOU

Imagine living in a close-knit neighborhood—the kind where everyone knows everyone, where you have block parties, kids play in the park and the pool, and you'll pop over the fence to say hello to someone out planting flowers, washing their car, or mowing the lawn. Now imagine you need to borrow a ladder to hang the ceiling fan you've just purchased. You walk to the neighbor with the biggest house in your neighborhood and knock once on their door. No one answers. You go home, put the fan in your car, and return it to the store where you purchased it. You conclude the fan isn't meant to be hung.

As ridiculous as this sounds, this happens to people searching for a mentor. They reach out to a single person, a single time, hear nothing and give up. Or worse, they never even buy the fan, assuming no one in the neighborhood would lend them their ladder.

"It's so disheartening to watch learners give up after just one attempt at making a connection," Adam Saven shared. "Especially when so many wonderful people around us are willing to lend a hand."

Turns out lots of ladder-owning neighbors would be more than happy to give you theirs.

The world is much more closely knit than we often imagine. It's remarkably easy today to figure out who in the neighborhood has a ladder, a bread maker, a bounce house, or even a propane blow torch. You need to map the helpers and the help.

When you realize you live in a world with plenty of people who can and want to help, you'll begin to see your neighborhood much differently. Your first neighbor may not be home, but knock on a few more doors, and someone will answer. While they may not have the ladder or the bread maker you need, they can point you to someone who might. Eventually, in a neighborhood like this, you'll find your way to the person who has what you need.

There is not one single person who will create opportunities for you. There's a web of help available to you, and your job is to begin mapping out that help.

IDENTIFY YOUR OWN HORIZONS

A guiding principle of Super Mentors is *many* people can deliver transformative opportunities to you. Our goal is to increase the odds of finding one who will provide a transformative opportunity dramatically.

But it's also important to recognize that most of us don't have a ready-made list of people in our heads or our lives. That's normal. Ask yourself who you admire in a particular industry, field, or arena, and most of us can reasonably easily identify a handful. For Zain Sandhu, his list was easy to come up with: Taylor Swift, Chance the Rapper, Kanye West, Lil Tay, and Frank Ocean. He didn't necessarily want to create music or know what he wanted in the industry, but he knew the musicians and artists he admired.

When we begin with big, well-known names, we tend to think it's almost ridiculous. I want you to be ridiculous. When I say aim higher, I truly mean it. Part of this act of aiming much higher makes our choices less difficult and makes this all feel more fun. When we aim higher on people we admire, we are less apt to censor ourselves. It sounds a bit ridiculous to rattle off names like Taylor Swift, Chance the Rapper, Kanye West, or any number of people we admire far off on the horizon, but they offer a real picture of who we believe *could* offer us these transformative opportunities. These are the people you'd love to be, be like, or be associated with on your horizons. Horizons are in the distance but visible. It's real, but it's far enough away that it's still blurry and uncertain.

Who are the people on your horizon?

- You admire Ava DuVernay, and you think you would love to be able to direct films like *Selma* and a *Wrinkle in Time.*
- You care about the climate and have seen Greta Thunberg's impact, and think you would want to contribute.
- You root for the Philadelphia 76ers and admire their general manager Daryl Morey, and think you would love to work in player scouting and analytics.
- You love Twitter and its founder Jack Dorsey and think you would love to start your start-up.
- You read *The Invisible Life of Addie LaRue* and nearly every other novel from Victoria Schwab and think you would love to write fantasy novels.

We humanized the horizon.

Even if you're unsure if these are your purpose or passion, or mission, they are people on your horizon who might help you find our way there. Most of us can easily identify the people behind what we admire, respect, and enjoy.

You're looking for specific people who could provide you with an opportunity to alter your trajectory fundamentally.

Specificity is key in this phase of your process. Most of the time, you'll know your initial list already because we are *already* connected and engaging with them in small ways. Maybe you're following them on social media. Perhaps you're reading articles about them in class or at work. Maybe you've seen them speak or shared their TEDx

Talk. You might be reading their books, watching their movies, or listening to their podcasts.

You most likely know your horizon, and if you don't, you can fairly quickly get to it.

Reverse Engineering Your Project

Picking a collaborative and meaningful project can be difficult. If you're unsure which project is the best fit for you, try to reverse engineer your project. Here's how:

Step 1. → Identify the people on your horizon.

Step 2. → Learn about their early career before they achieved breakout success.

Step 3. → Look for projects they tackled. Did they discuss or call out an article series or a book they wrote? Did they organize a concert, a conference, or an event? Have they taught a course or given a speech? Did they develop a product? Did they release a podcast, series of videos, or a YouTube channel? Did they publish some research or findings?

Step 4. → Examine the project in greater detail and learn the development process.

Step 5. → Repeat until you find a project that inspires or excites you. Then begin identifying any peer or near-peer mentors who have also worked on a similar project and might be able to talk to you about their process.

FIND YOUR ASPIRATIONAL PEERS

Chris is an entrepreneur, best-selling author and a vocal advocate for prison reform. He is also a convicted felon.

When he was seventeen, Chris was convicted of murder and sentenced to natural life in prison. He was a shy kid, but after violent threats to his family from his mother's ex-boyfriend and the attempted murder of his brother, Chris began carrying a gun. One night, the man who had threatened his family confronted him. Chris pulled the trigger and killed the man. He was convicted and assumed

132 · SUPER MENTORS

his life as a free man was over. While in prison, he created his master plan to become a better man by earning his high school diploma, taking college classes, and even starting a prison book club. He not only worked to improve himself but also his fellow inmates. A judge released him when he was thirty-three, and he got a second chance. He didn't take this chance lightly.

How could he quickly transition from an ex-con sleeping on a friend's couch after his release to a serial entrepreneur and best-selling author appearing on the *Today Show* and the *Daily Show with Trevor Noah*?

"I had to get back on my feet, so I started a business—multiple businesses," he told me. "Before I knew it, we were employing hundreds of people. My story of redemption was powerful. People began to tell me I should write a book to tell my story."

But Chris didn't know anyone who'd written a book. Breaking into the publishing industry is far from easy, and as an African American man, he was fighting an uphill battle. According to *The New York Times*, less than 10 percent of authors in major publishing houses are authors of color. Many first-time authors are already celebrities or individuals with massive followings. Chris had neither of those.

He needed help, but first, he had to understand the game.

"I read a lot," he said. "So, I knew what kinds of books I liked and what I wanted my book to do. It was going to be a memoir that could teach people something. Once I knew what I wanted out of this, the entire process was so much easier."

The next step was to figure out how to get help.

Chris didn't start with a large list of people. Most of us don't have a large list of people we admire in our heads, but we usually have a few we can quickly identify. Chris's initial list included Trevor Noah, Barack Obama, and Ta-Nehisi Coates, well-known names that would be a challenge to access. But this list identified the neighborhood he wanted to play in.

"I decided I first needed to find my 'cousin' books," Chris said. "I literally hired a guy—paid him two hundred dollars—and gave him a list of authors' books on similar topics and themes. Told him to find every person who had left a review of the book, every podcast that had interviewed them, and anyone who was a fan. I had to figure out what I was starting from."

Chris had figured out the power of aspirational peers—in other words, people who are not your peers *yet*, but people you aspire to be a peer to in the next three to five years. These people are his "cousins."

That list of Chris's aspirational peers became his target for mentorship.

One of those "cousins" was fellow Baltimore best-selling author Wes Moore, who went on to write the foreword of Chris's book *The Master Plan*. He didn't stop there. "Once I had the list, it was simply a matter of mapping the path to get there. I'd go to New York and meet with anyone I could. Who can get me to Alicia Keys? How can I find someone to plug me in with Van Jones and so on?"

One Meeting Away: Chris Wilson

Right Person. Wes Moore was a Baltimore native and the author of *The Other Wes Moore*, a *New York Times* best-selling 2010 memoir named by Oprah Winfrey to her Oprah's Book Club.

Right Ask. How can a first-time author get a seven-figure book deal?

Right Start. Chris engaged Wes in every aspect of the book development and writing process.

Right Time. Chris and Wes met through a prominent philanthropist looking to convene local leaders to discuss Baltimore's future. Chris shared his story and the discriminatory impact felt by generations of individuals being released from the prison system in that meeting. Wes would go on to write the foreword of *The Master Plan*.

The strategy paid off handsomely. Chris signed a seven-figure advance for his book and got featured on the *Today Show and* the *Daily*

Show—incredible results for anyone, let alone a first-time author with a criminal record.

"I knew I couldn't wait around for people to come to me to buy the book or sign me. I had to figure out how to get there and who could get me there," Chris explained. "But none of it mattered if I didn't know what I wanted out of it."

It's important to note that the most successful, the most well-known, or the most famous people won't be your Super Mentors. You're looking for the people who can be most helpful to you in context. While Wes Moore is well-known in some circles, most people wouldn't know him by his name alone. However, he was *accessible* to Chris and critically helpful *in the context* of what Chris needed.

It all started by finding his aspirational peers—his *cousins*.

MAPMAKING ON YOUR KNOWLEDGE GRAPH

Your knowledge gap between your aspirational peers and their peers is often much bigger than you realize. That's not surprising. Our minds can only hold a limited number of people. Anthropologist Robin Dunbar determined that the greatest number of connections anyone can maintain at one time is 150. That's why the process of mapmaking itself is remarkably valuable. You can begin to understand exactly how to make the most of your 150.

You are going to be creating your *knowledge graph*. The knowledge graph is a collection of people you find have interesting and relevant knowledge that you think could potentially provide you with some unique opportunities. You don't have to know the people or the opportunities directly, but assume that interesting people have access to interesting opportunities.

The exercise is valuable, but admittedly, it can be tedious. I'd urge you to spend time on this exercise first, and then if you need help, it's a great project you can outsource. As you read, Chris Wilson paid someone two hundred dollars to do a version of this exercise.

You don't need to know much to begin. Start by trying to identify two things:

1. Who are your aspirational peers? Who do you admire?
2. What sectors/industries/arenas are they playing in? What intersections do they operate in?

––––––––––

Let's make this a real demonstration—and remember this process is designed to be fun. Your mapmaking homework is to spend time online exploring, specifically on Google, YouTube, TED, and your favorite podcasting platforms.

Let's use an example in the political arena. Matthew Henry was a student of mine at Georgetown, and he had ambitions to potentially work in politics or run for political office one day. He had no established network, as he'd grown up in Australia.

"Run for office one day" is a broad aim, of course. Still, he was most curious about aspects of bipartisan politics and perhaps how technology could lead to more bipartisan opportunities.

STEP 1: IDENTIFY SOME "KEYWORDS" OR "KEY PEOPLE"
Start broad to guide us to make our map:
1. Who are your aspirational peers? Who do you admire?
   Progressive leaning candidates; Third-Party Candidates; Politicians and political operatives who work "across the aisle." Examples included Jesse Jackson, Madeline Albright, Patrick Kennedy (Congressman, Massachusetts), Major Richard N. Ojeda (Democrat in West Virginia), Ezra Klein (Vox political commentary).
2. What sectors/industries/arenas are they playing in? What intersections do they operate in?
   Politics; Technology; Bipartisan; Third-Party Candidates

––––––––––

His answers are broad and not fully formed. That's okay. We are focused on people—it turns out mentors *are* people—so our research won't be focused on "facts" or "topics" but on people. We'll want to focus our energy on the places and sources where we can learn about people and their expertise.

This is how we'll begin to access the knowledge graph.

STEP 2: RESEARCH THE KNOWLEDGE GRAPH

Imagine you were in a large auditorium with a thousand intelligent people. All of them could be interesting to talk to. Right now, they are just milling around, and so are you. You don't have time to talk to them, nor do you want to. There's knowledge in the room, but the graph is how we organize the knowledge we seek. It's like beginning to put some circles on the floor and having people stand in them based on their expertise. Then we'd draw smaller circles and Venn diagrams. I call this process your "knowledge graph." We simply need to search the knowledge graph to find who to speak to within our circles.

Your goal is to find people talking about the subjects you're interested in. We're going to explore the knowledge graph across these four digital communities. These digital communities give us access to knowledge directly from people—talking, speaking, presenting, teaching, and being interviewed:

1. Podcasts (Apple and/or Spotify)
2. TEDx Talks
3. YouTube
4. Google

PODCASTS (APPLE AND/OR SPOTIFY)

Start by searching for key people you've already identified. We begin with the initial names on our list and want to see their connections. Have they appeared on podcasts, and would we like to connect with the hosts or the other guests? Does the individual themselves have a podcast, and would any of the guests be of value to us?

For Matthew, that meant he started with Ezra Klein, one of his favorite political commentators at Vox. Ezra has a podcast, and Matthew searched through Ezra's guest list. An exciting author popped up that Matthew had never heard of—Lee Drutman. Matthew listened to the first couple of minutes and wrote his name down on his list. This phase aims to look for people Ezra is connected to or engages with. Go the other way. Look at the podcasts that Ezra has been on and see if those hosts are intriguing or exciting to you.

Once you've gone through the names of your aspirational peers, begin to look for the keywords you've identified to see if you could begin to identify people.

Matthew also searched for: "third-party candidates" and "two-party system."

TEDX TALKS

TED is a collection of speakers—people who have interesting or insightful ideas they've shared on the TED or TEDx stage. This rich resource in the knowledge graph uses a powerful algorithm that helps you see "what is similar" to a talk you like.

Matthew added keywords again to his search, including: "two-party political systems."

Find relevant talks, read part of all of the transcripts, and see what is similar.

YOUTUBE

You can find a lot of information and material on YouTube, so you'll need to curate your searches primarily around speeches, talks, and interviews. You can search for people directly as well as keywords.

Matthew searched for phrases including: "two-party political system."

GOOGLE

Google is even broader than YouTube but has a rich data set in the knowledge graph. Rather than searching keywords alone, you'll want to add words to limit your search. You can search for people directly as well as keywords.

- "Books"
- "Speeches"
- "Research" (scholar.google.com)
  Matthew used his keywords and added the limiters:
- Books → "two-party political system" + books
- Speeches → "two-party political system" + speech
- Research (scholar.google.com) → "two-party political system" + research

STEP 3: IDENTIFY RELEVANT PEOPLE AND STORIES AND ADD THEM TO A RUNNING LIST

At this stage, if you've started this work, you'll quickly see you've got a lot of names *already* to work with. This is just based on one keyword/phrase and a first layer of digging. You'll quickly build a huge list if you do this long enough. While you're doing it, you're learning more and more about the world that interests you.

A sample of what Matthew found:

- Podcast research
  - Ezra Klein
  - Lee Drutman
- TED research
  - Pia Mancini → www.ted.com/talks/pia_mancini_how_to_upgrade_democracy_for_the_internet_era
  - [TED recommends more like...] Beth Noveck, the former deputy CTO at the White House → www.ted.com/talks/beth_noveck_demand_a_more_open_source_government

- – [TED recommends more like...] Coder and activist Jennifer Pahlka → www.ted.com/talks/jennifer_pahlka_coding_a_better_government
- YouTube
  - – Vernon Bogdanor
  - – Sean Wilentz
  - – Yanis Varoufakis
- Google
  - – Books:
    - James L. Sundquist
    - Joseph Romance and Theodore J. Romance, Joseph Pomper, Gerald Lowi
  - – Scholar:
    - William H. Riker

TED TALKS:
Pia Mancini,
Beth Noveck

YOUTUBE:
Vernon Bogdanor,
Sean Wilentz

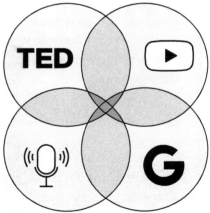

PODCASTS:
Lee Drutman,
Ezra Klein

GOOGLE:
James L. Sundquist,
William H. Riker

He very quickly identified the eleven interesting people above—a subset of the more extensive list he'd built. Most importantly, all of these people are engaging in the context of Matthew's interests. Many connect back to his aspirational peers.

STEP 4: FIND OUT HOW TO CONTACT THEM

As you'll see, I recommend an easy first step. Connect with and follow everyone from your mapmaking on social media. This is your "clubhouse" where you can curate that room of people talking to just those you're interested in listening to. Eventually, you'll want to reach out to them. Here's an important insight. Most people can easily find contact information, particularly if they have a public presence on the knowledge graph.

What's the secret? Just type in their name and add "Email" at the end. You can find other tools and resources. I've used a free tool called Hunter.io, but the easiest way is to Google their name plus email.

Matthew found the author Lee Drutman (whom Ezra Klein interviewed) to be fascinating, so he simply Googled "Lee Drutman" + "email."

Then you just hunt around the links until you find his email. While you're at it, connect on social media and LinkedIn.

STEP 5: RINSE AND REPEAT IN YOUR WARM NETWORKS

Ultimately, your goal is to connect with those in your knowledge graph eventually. So why not leverage whatever connection you may have to these potential knowledge sharers.

Take your keywords and key people and run them through this process at your alma mater. Have any fellow alumni been on podcasts, written books, or connected with your key people? Have any of these "cousins" spoken at your institution? You may even discover a professor you could add to your clubhouse. Remember, you're not looking for your Yoda or Glinda when making a knowledge graph. You are looking for people who share your interests and will connect with you over the right ask.

"Sharing something in common can help you get a response," Adam Saven shared, "but it's still on the mentees to make the right ask. You can't expect someone to kick down every door for you because you share the same alma mater or even took the same class with the same professor."

Adam finds that school affinity is a robust and long-lasting connection point not enough people take advantage of. "I'd encourage learners to seek out these communities when building their knowledge graph," Saven said. "These knowledge sharers have raised their hand to help. And if you give them a specific, small ask around a project, and you'll see powerful engagement levels."

ANTICIPATE THE REFERRAL AND MAKE IT FOR YOURSELF

Imagine if Chris Wilson had gotten meetings right off the bat with a Trevor Noah, a Barack Obama, or a Ta-Nehisi Coates. The discussions went great, and at the end, Trevor told Chris, "You know, you should meet _____."

Who would Taylor Swift introduce Zain Sandhu to? Who would Ezra Klein introduce Matthew Henry to? Who would Lin-Manuel Miranda introduce you to?

Who are those people?

This will almost feel meta, so the concept of aspirational peers can serve as a simple frame to identify who we aspire to be in the next three to five years. If things were to go your way, who would you like to be peers with? For Chris, that was a small set of diverse, well-read authors telling their own stories—Trevor Noah, Barack Obama, or Ta-Nehisi Coates.

This group isn't large, but it's tangible and specific. I identified four thought-leading professors who were also famous authors: Adam Grant, Brené Brown, Angela Duckworth, and Scott Galloway. The specificity of the list is critical, as it helps beyond abstract self-discovery.

Then the work begins. Create your map.

Who have they helped, supported, championed, collaborated with, hired, partnered with, or celebrated?

Look at who has previously interviewed them or spoken with them at conferences, podcasts, or events. Find out who has collaborated with whom, provided endorsements, or said nice things on social media. Identify genuine connections rather than superficial acquaintances. This is the process of mapping your knowledge graph.

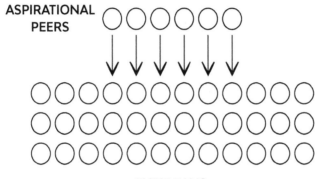

The key isn't to evaluate the list as you're building it; it's just to make it. Remember, a guiding principle is *many* people can deliver transformative opportunities to you.

Look through the list and begin to develop exciting individuals that you'd like to know. Find out who they are as well, what motivates them, and discover surprising pathways toward them.

Don't be surprised if the list has a range of people from very seasoned and experienced to peers or near-peers. As you identify candidates to engage, look for fit over fame. Can some individuals on the list open doors to your immediate? Mentoring experts point out that early in our careers, during schooling and the first five years of our career, people with three to eight years more experience than us can be a good fit. They are experienced but not so experienced they aren't relatable.

"Think about it like Waze," Adam Saven told me. "Those just ahead of you on the road can provide a good deal of insight on what they just passed. Is there an accident ahead? An obstruction on the road? Maybe even a speed trap to avoid? Someone on the road would want to learn that from someone who drove the road an hour ago as opposed to a week, a month, or a year ago."

Either way, know that the people on your list aren't likely to find you, so you'll have to work your way to them intentionally.

When you examine yourself and explore these internal and external components of self-awareness, one of the first steps is the awareness of your stage of mentorship. In the last part of the book (part IV), we examine the eight standard periods when mentor relationships tend to form and flourish: while in school, in our first job or opportunity, the second career, during early jobs/career, entrepreneur, career expansion, CEO to younger CEO, personal.

It's critical to understand the context of mentorship. Chris was beginning a second career (i.e., author) and needed to find mentors relevant to that specific challenge. Zain Sandhu was able to gain support from his professor (me) during his while-in-school phase but was ultimately looking for his first job or opportunity. As a result, he engaged with an entirely new set of people to navigate that stage of his life.

ITERATE AS YOU GO

As what we want or need becomes more apparent, it's tempting to feel daunted about how to get just that.

Raising funding for a new venture is one of the more challenging endeavors, with less than 2–3 percent of companies seeking capital, coupled with the fact that 70–80 percent of start-ups funded have at least someone on the team who has raised money previously. Leveraging mentorship as an access tool has become critical—not simply seeking mentors for advice or guidance but creating experiences with individuals designed to unlock fundraising opportunities.

Amy Nelson, the founder of The Riveter, a coworking start-up, has raised nearly twenty million dollars and has plans to open more than one hundred locations by the end of 2022. Her start-up represented a significant career pivot and transition, having spent a decade as a lawyer. The work to raise her company's first seven hundred thousand dollars was much more challenging than she'd anticipated, as she shared on a panel at the Seattle Female Founders Conference.

Her first couple of investors came organically by attending a series of start-up events. A woman had followed up with Amy after asking a panelist's question and by tapping unusual connections already in her network, including a woman in her daughter's co-op preschool class. But Amy quickly realized that approach would take too long or be too unfocused to get the capital she needed to secure her investors.

Her approach was redesigned around aspects of peer mentors—dozens of people who'd make warm introductions to these communities she was not a part of. But to do so, it required Amy to reframe her approach. She took stock of the funding landscape, identifying every investor in the region who had invested in companies in her space and people she already knew who had made start-up investments. "For the people I wanted to invest," Amy told a Y Combinator investor panel in 2018, "I found connections to them. I was super methodical about it, spreadsheet, going on LinkedIn. I want to connect to person X. Who can introduce me?" It wasn't simply the access to money but the people who could get her in front of those decision-makers.

Her success began to compound when other founders began to make warm introductions. She'd learned the importance of making it easy for them since she'd already mapped out the specific connections and targeted the ideal person to make them fit. Those connections—many of which came from these fellow female founders—would eventually lead Nelson to Hope Cochran, a Madrona Ventures partner who would lead a five-million-dollar round into the company.

Right Person. Hope Cochran (and a network of dozens of female founders in the Pacific Northwest).

Right Ask. Can I help you make your innovation space more attractive to women?

Right Start. Amy would follow-up, share updates, and keep building out the network she'd eventually need.

Right Time. Madrona had recently leased a second floor in their building to build out an innovation space for their portfolio companies. Nelson offered her insights about creating areas that attract and retain women beyond typical benefits in coworking spaces.

———

While our existing networks may be limited or seem to lack the reach we need, it's essential to design an approach that involves our work and feedback from those who may have recently been in our shoes.

Once you recognize where you are and what you need, finding guidance and support from your "cousins" gets easier.

8

OPERATE WITH A MODERN RELATIONSHIP MINDSET

Many of us have heard the quote: "You are the average of the five people you spend the most time with." Or a similar quote says, "Show me your friends, and I'll show you your future."

But it turns out researchers find that's not entirely true. We are influenced and affected by *all* the people we surround ourselves with. David Burkus, the author of *Friend of a Friend*, said, "You're not the average of the *five* people you surround yourself with. It's way bigger than that. You're the average of all the people who surround you. So take a look around and make sure you're in the right surroundings."

Mentoring is a relationship, not a transaction. You want to build a relationship that allows regular and routine engagement. But we also want you to have lots of mentors. In the old mentoring world, you could hold deep, intense meetings with dozens of people every week. When would you have time to get your work done?

The relationship mindset is critical for modern mentorship:

- Establish relationships with multiple mentors
- Create a mixture of relevant synchronous (live meetings/engagements) and asynchronous (updates and social media engagement) touchpoints
- Develop opportunities through a process

This is why it's essential to surround yourself with your aspirational peers and the extended networks you've studied. You should also create circles you'd like to be in. Modern mentors are so much more dynamic than ever before. They will still require a relationship mindset, but your engagement mirrors how most of us leverage social media and digital platforms to keep in touch with our friends and family. It's a relationship for the modern era.

Even if you've casually used social media in the past or view it as something more fun than valuable, create the proper circles and begin to participate in them.

It's remarkable to watch how you change when in these conversations, whether you are an active participant or simply an observer and consumer. Once you begin to get comfortable and familiar and realize you belong, you'll see opportunities to engage.

CREATE A CLUBHOUSE TO PLAY IN

You've done much of the hard work already by identifying your aspirational peers and beginning to map an extended network and web of their connections. If you've done this correctly, started with a half-dozen individuals you admire, and mapped out the people they endorse, they've worked with, recommend, and they celebrate, you're quickly able to create a reasonably large web around you. Networks have become visible today through the power of social media.

You'll simply need to add a layer of intentionality to your use of the platforms.

Anabelle Nuelle was an extraordinarily bright and engaging student of mine, but it was evident from our first discussions that she didn't have that compass or the map for where she was heading. She was an Arabic major beginning her final semester in college. While she enjoyed Arabic, she realized it would most likely take another decade of schooling to work in the field. Her answers were mainly opaque as we discussed what she hoped to do next.

"Forget what you've done in college for a minute," I told her. "Who do you admire? Anyone in the world, but focus on people who are maybe three-to-six years ahead of you. Who comes to your mind?"

She took a deep breath and reflected. I let the moment hang in the air.

Then, suddenly, she smiled, and I saw a moment of true joy flash in her eyes as she revealed her guilty pleasure. She was a foodie, and she loved spending her free time watching the Food Network, engaging with food Instagrammers, and cooking. She rattled off half a dozen names I'd never heard of, but these were her people, her aspirational peers, and cousins.

"Let's find a way for you to meet them," I replied.

And she did. For the next few months, she built her map of aspirational peers. She connected with them on social platforms and engaged with those she'd already connected with. Anabelle did cold outreach to find connection points and engaged with people she hoped to know. It was as if she finally permitted herself to be who she wanted to become.

Less than six weeks later, she returned to my office. "I got a job," she exclaimed. "In *food* marketing!"

She relayed the story of an informal conversation—a practice or informational interview—a conversation that, truthfully, couldn't have started much worse. As they began their scheduled phone call, the interviewer was late and admitted to not having read Anabelle's résumé.

"I guess, just tell me what you're into," the woman asked.

Anabelle explained the work she'd been doing to immerse herself in and understand the booming food social media economy, rattling off conversations and insights she'd gleaned along the way. She'd been engaging in this sector and began to build up an accidental competency and perspective in many ways.

The woman stopped her mid-sentence.

"Wait, this is incredible," she responded. "I'm working on a client pitch for a food company *right now*. Let me ask you a few questions..."

One Meeting Away: Anabelle Nuelle

Right Person. Georgetown alumnus at BBDO, a top marketing and advertising agency in Chicago, Illinois, focused on the consumer sector.

Right Ask. Are you currently working on any campaigns in the digital food marketing space?

Right Start. Anabelle followed up, helped with the pitch, and continued engagement. That conversation led to a job collaborating with the alumnus on a specific client opportunity.

Right Time. Anabelle was an Arabic major who wanted to make a transition beyond her major and took any opportunity to speak to people—regardless of whether it was tied to a specific job opportunity. Then, having spent nearly three months speaking with leading digital influencers focused on food, Anabelle was able to turn an "informational" interview into an opportunity to educate the alumnus on her findings.

Anabelle revealed that this "non-job" interview turned into a client strategy session and, days later, a job offer. All she had to do was build the self-awareness to create her circle of aspirational peers, and she found someone who went on to become her mentor in her first post-college role.

It begins by putting yourself in the right surroundings.

THE MODERN RELATIONSHIP PROCESS

Modern mentorship is built around collaboration—the power of "let's"—a simple framework for enabling small, shared projects that build on one another. Beyond just collaboration, *how* these parties collaborate is the most instructive.

There's commonly a build to the modern mentor relationship—something I call Stair-Step Mentoring:

STAGE 1: Micro Request for Advice/Guidance
STAGE 2: Micro Opportunity
STAGE 3: Opportunity & Access Acceleration

In chapter 9, we'll discuss the importance of feedback loops in advancing in the steps, but at the core is a series of micro-requests that build over time. These steps are not necessarily single steps but stages through which you'll engage with your potential Super Mentor. Think of each step as increasing levels of relationship trust or relationship capital.

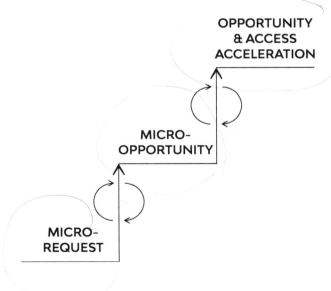

OPPORTUNITY
& ACCESS
ACCELERATION

MICRO-
OPPORTUNITY

MICRO-
REQUEST

HERE'S HOW STAIR-STEP MENTORING WORKS.

STAGE 1: Make an initial micro-request. Usually, this request is for advice/guidance to show you can take feedback and apply it. The goals are simple: (a) prove you can take and apply the guidance, feedback, and coaching; and (b) make the relationship into a "two-way street"; i.e., the mentor does their part, and you do yours.

This stage involves developing tight, specific micro-requests or asks. Early engagement may just be initial micro-requests, continued meetings, phone calls, questions, answers, etc.

Reflecting on my own Super Mentoring experience with Steve Blank discussed in chapter 1, my micro-request was coming by his ranch. For Blake Robbins (see chapter 6), his micro-request was a call with the partners at Ludlow, and when the initial request wasn't met, he continued through the help of a portfolio company founder Ryan Hoover. Later in the chapter, you'll learn about Mark Zuckerberg's micro-request to *The Washington Post* CEO Don Graham that rekindled their relationship after a failed investment bid.

STAGE 2: Identify and develop a micro-opportunity. Micro-opportunities go beyond a simple ask or request but are designed with some interactive effects. They share careful scoping of the work and collaboration, and they enable an opportunity that can be completed quickly and without impacting the ability to complete other work or efforts. Micro-opportunities are usually intended to be finite in some form.

The micro-opportunity stage is a chance to earn and build trust. For the mentee, this period can prove to the mentor that they are worthy of investment and will build shared value. These types of engagements are usually collaborative in nature, requiring some small action from both parties but still limited in scope. Common examples of micro-opportunities include (a) an interview, quote, material, or specific information in the context of your project (b) an introduction to someone in the mentor's network (c) a small project collaboration, review, feedback, or demonstration with the Super Mentor or (d) a more material project—usually initiated or organized by the mentee—where the mentor could provide more project guidance/coaching.

Steve Blank and I connected and discussed my post-start-up plans, which prompted him to suggest that I should consider teaching. This would likely be described as a macro-opportunity, a larger opportunity for consideration. But the micro-opportunity was our collaboration on a teaching program through the organization where we both were board members. He also facilitated two micro-opportunity introductions, connecting me with two of his peers to get their sense of my competence and fit for future projects. Blake Robbins's, "Just give me an email address," enabled him to create a micro-opportunity for him and the Ludlow team—less involved and complex than an internship while offering him an opportunity to showcase his talents. Zuckerberg's micro-opportunity involved ongoing informal discussions, collaboration on *The Washington Post*'s digital activities, or engagement in a series of advertising experiments.

STAGE 3: Begin looking for ways to accelerate opportunities and network access. This stage is where the protégé begins to experience the external benefits of the Super Mentor, as the relationship transitions from finite into indefinite and from directive (you should) to collaborative (we could). Often, a series of external feedback validates the Super Mentor's decision to increase access and opportunities.

Elements of pride and ego become more powerful as the Super Mentor recognizes that the protégé's actions and outcomes elevate their mentors. Feedback from others in their network creates cycles of more access. At this point in the relationship, mentees are at risk of leaping beyond their Super Mentor, a risk that can create backlash if not properly managed. These are relationships, not transactions.

In my relationship with Steve, he began to vouch for me to investors, and our experiences unlocked opportunities at universities and corporations that started to request me. At this stage, our relationship began to transition from active mentorship into passive support and collaboration. Similarly, Blake Robbins found himself being offered full-time positions at both Google and Ludlow. Those opportunities came after he'd shown his value over a near-two-year window to the partners at Ludlow. Zuckerberg and Graham came full circle three years after a failed investment, and Graham was invited to join Facebook's board of directors and make an investment in the rapidly growing network, an investment that would be worth forty-one million dollars in their 2012 IPO and more than $264 million by the end of 2020).

The mentee's mastery of micro-requests enables the Stair-Step Mentoring approach to work.

The power of feedback loops and follow-up we discuss more in chapter 9 is one of the most critical—and least leveraged—tools in unlocking the full potential of the opportunities.

INVITE THEM INTO YOUR COMMUNITY

We want to be a part of something—whether it's a club, a group, a school, a company, or a team. Your projects can offer you that framework to create connection and engagement.

Begin by getting to know a prospective mentor. Engage through social media, their newsletters, and updates, and learn about them through their public persona. Then leverage the five-minute favor framework (from chapter 5) to create digital engagement leveraging generosity. Finally, reach out to connect (often using platforms like LinkedIn and email). View your engagement through the lens of a project, and invite them to participate.

Don't be afraid to follow up, and don't wait too long. A well-timed follow-up a few days after your initial outreach shows you are serious about your invitation. The best salespeople will tell you that staying top of mind is crucial to getting a response. And even if that response is "no," at least you won't be holding your breath. Your follow-up doesn't have to be a new update either, but staying patiently persistent is one of the simplest things you can do to create an opportunity for connection.

GIVE YOURSELF PERMISSION TO JOIN THE CONVERSATION

The process of identifying the people who will most impact us is often as simple as looking beyond our existing circles into the circles we want to be part of.

"Out there on tour, I always noticed a difference between the front of the tour bus and the back of the bussers," John Jaxon Huffman told me. Today, Huffman is the founder and CEO of Creator Capital, operating at the center of the music industry. He founded his first music industry software start-up in 1996 and has worked with leading record labels, brands such as Coca-Cola, Coors, and General Motors, and thousands of artists.

But as a senior in high school, Huffman was a "back of the busser." He had broad ambitions in the music industry and got his first break as a backup dancer for Vanilla Ice. When the song "Ice Ice Baby" became the breakout song of the year, he found himself at the center of the music universe, but at the back of the bus.

Though the opportunity to dance for a top artist was an opportunity in the music industry, it wouldn't get him where he was headed.

Huffman began to position himself around the people he wanted to be: "I took everything seriously. I was eating well. I was sleeping well. I was staying in great places. This is a big deal to me. So pay close attention." He began to sit in the front of the bus... just listening.

"I would notice on these tour buses that an executive would get on," John shared, "and [I] would hear their conversations about what they were talking about. Paperwork would be left up front, and I would just try to read it to learn anything I could. I remember reading one contract from Ford Motor Company. They were offering us free Ford Mustangs if we put one in our videos. I was just a sponge."

Huffman knew the people he *already* knew wouldn't change his trajectory. As he listened, the executives getting on and off of the tour bus began to notice him. One day, Charles Coplin—the Emmy-winning President of Big Monkey Entertainment, who had produced the halftime show for the NFL Super Bowl, the NHL's Winter Classic, and been a producer for Disney—asked the twenty-year-old what he was doing on the tour.

"I told him I wanted to be the CEO of a major record label," Huffman admitted.

Coplin smiled and told Huffman he should come to New York, start working in his mailroom, and in thirty years, he could be the CEO.

"I pushed back," recalled Huffman. "I didn't just say, 'Let's go work in the mailroom.' I pushed back. I told him my thoughts about the future of the internet on music. And we kept talking."

Coplin joined the tour bus again, and Huffman would seek him out with new ideas and thoughts, especially about early digital technologies, like email and the internet.

"Charles gave me more, and that more was life-changing for me," shared Huffman. "He told me, 'You keep talking to us about the internet. You keep telling me I need email. And you have caught my attention. So why don't you start a company like that? We need these kinds of things at the company. We know you well. We'll become your customer.' And that was it."

One Meeting Away: John Huffman

Right Person. Charles Coplin was an innovator in branding opportunities across sport and entertainment.

Right Ask. How do you see the internet changing opportunities for your artists like Vanilla Ice in music and entertainment?

Right Start. John continued the relationship, engaging with his first potential client to turn them into an actual paying customer.

Right Time. In the mid-1990s, the internet was in its infancy but had captured cultural relevancy as younger consumers embraced online platforms and communities. One of the first intersections of music and the internet had garnered much attention as Severe Tire Damage, a rock band made up of engineers from Xerox, Digital Equipment, and Apple, first put its music on the internet. Most people didn't yet have email addresses unless they worked in the technology industry or were students or in academia.

We can learn a few things from Huffman's experience. Pay attention and be aware of what's already around you. We are often closer to the future we want than we realize, and today, with the power of the internet, we are a few strategic moves away from nearly anyone.

Ask questions, celebrate others, push back on things you disagree with, and participate in the conversations.

TAKE STOCK OF YOUR RELATIONSHIPS
AND FIGURE OUT THE NEXT STEP

Don Graham, CEO of *The Washington Post* Company, had a unique insight into why Facebook was not just another social networking platform—his children.

Graham first heard about this new social network sweeping college campuses through his daughter. Despite more dominant platforms like MySpace and Friendster, his daughter and her entire class were spending more and more time on Facebook. After hearing more about Zuckerberg's ambitions from her, Graham's daughter connected her classmate Mark to her father in 2005.

"We talked a little bit about Facebook as a business. The future tech titan did not then know the difference between revenues and profits." Graham wrote on Facebook in 2018.

Believing in Zuckerberg's vision and seeing firsthand the impact of Facebook through his children, Graham offered to invest six million dollars in Facebook. Zuckerberg accepted the offer, only to renege when Accel Partners offered to invest at a higher valuation, thanks in no small part to the advice from Napster founder and new Facebook President Sean Parker. It was shocking, but Graham, rather than feeling snubbed, was impressed by how Zuckerberg handled the situation.

He recognized the potential in both Facebook and Zuckerberg. At the time of the failed investment, Facebook was only nine months old. "The youngest of my four children was two years older than Mark; through my kids and their friends, I had an extensive experience of shy, awkward twenty-year-olds. Mark was, by a mile, the shyest, most awkward twenty-year-old I had ever met." He recognized that Zuckerberg would need coaching to turn into an executive.

How does a failed investment turn into a mentoring relationship? Small steps.

Most likely the first point in the relationship was structured more in terms of an investment decision or engagement than mentorship. That transaction failed or was not completed, and the relationship essentially reset.

Flush with Accel's capital and viral growth, Zuckerberg began to focus more and more on his own skills as an emerging executive and company leader. By 2007, Graham received an email from Zuckerberg that shared, "I'm a CEO now and would like to shadow you and see what you do."

It was a simple request, and one Graham was happy to entertain. This was Zuckerberg's micro-request. Graham had learned from Zuckerberg's insights already and had begun to examine how to weave more online initiatives into his businesses, *The Washington Post* and Kaplan.

One Meeting Away: Mark Zuckerberg

Right Person. Don Graham, the CEO of *The Washington Post.*

Right Ask. Could I shadow you and see what you do?

Right Start. Graham had a relationship with Zuckerberg, even though it had taken an unfavorable turn. But Zuckerberg had been cordial and not let the relationship turn negative, enabling a rekindling and eventually the offer for Graham to join the Facebook board of directors.

Right Time. Graham was one of the best-known media CEOs, having taken ownership of *The Washington Post* from Katherine

Graham and grown and expanding their footprint into other business lines. *The Washington Post* was an old media company that had maintained relevance in the new media landscape. As Zuckerberg's business was growing, he needed to learn how to be a CEO and be a CEO in a media business.

Graham brought Zuckerberg to his executive meetings, let him attend an investor conference, walked him through the newsroom, and the two chatted throughout the day. The relationship over the subsequent year enabled collaboration between the two regarding leadership or management insights and partnership opportunities. This established a foundation whereby the end of 2008, Zuckerberg invited Graham to join the board.

Graham joined Facebook's board and bought a significant number of shares, which he swore not to sell as long as he was on the board. Since the early days of Facebook, *The Washington Post* has consistently supported the firm by advertising its products on the platform. The relationship has been a mutual one, despite their age difference. "Don will have ideas and questions that he'll want to bounce off Mark, and similarly, Mark takes counsel from Don," one source close to the Graham family told the *Wall Street Journal*. "They have a very close relationship that focuses on business issues and dilemmas."

***

There's inherent complexity and chaos in sparking and building any relationship. Whether it's a failed relationship that's rebuilt or an initial rejection of the relationship, building a relationship is challenging. In understanding the approach to Stair-Step Mentoring and the ability to scope simpler and more apparent micro-requests and develop micro-opportunities, you can avoid adding to the complexity yourself.

Protégés learn agility to control what they can handle and the flexibility to navigate through what is out of their control. These relationships are rarely straight-line relationships but relationships cultivated through repetition and work.

YOUR PLAN

REALITY

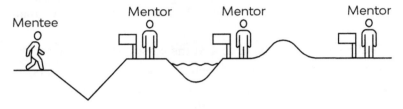

PART III

THE LAW OF RIGHT START

Begin mentor relationships small. Take steps to make it super. Learn how to grow relationships that lead to transformative career and life opportunities over time.

9

WIN THROUGH FAST FEEDBACK LOOPS

Three things appear to matter in cultivating Super Mentor relationships.

FOLLOW UP, DO IT FAST, AND CONTINUE FOLLOWING UP.

Yet, why do people hesitate to follow up?

My guess is much of it comes down to a mismatch of expectations. You've met someone interesting, someone you know could help you, and someone who has already provided you some value just through a conversation. You can see the potential.

So we begin to build up our expectations and project our expectations on them. As a day becomes a week after that first interaction, we tell ourselves that our follow-up needs to be even more mind-blowing and polished. A week becomes a month, and we're now worried we've lost your opportunity, and if we follow up now, they will scold us for the delay.

Adam Saven has seen this countless times. "Even if you approach a first call or meeting with the micro-request and follow the Super Mentor framework to the letter, you will still fight the urge to start viewing the mentor as your 'Hero's Journey Guide'—your Yoda or your Dumbledore."

Saven says this causes us to forget the basics of relationship building and feedback loops. "I can't tell you how many times I've seen learners forget to express gratitude. We saw it so much at PeopleGrove that we built functionality into our product to remind learners when our system doesn't see any words of thanks in a message!"

Four transformative words can change your relationship with anyone:

"THANK YOU. I'VE ALREADY..."

This is the art of micro follow-ups. Acknowledge the person and their time, and offer evidence their time is already impacting you.

I've already... been thinking about what you said... been building a list... been writing more notes... been brainstorming titles... been looking at dates... been adding things to my calendar...

Much like micro-requests, there's power in micro follow-ups. Think of them as another time for the person to identify an opportunity for you. You become top of mind in the *context* of your discussion. Perhaps just as important, you *remain* top of mind for future opportunities that come to your Super Mentors.

When you begin to think about each loop as an opportunity to engage and stay top of mind, you'll see it less as *the chance* to stand out but as a chance to engage.

EXPRESSING GRATITUDE THROUGH SIMPLE ACTS

It turns out many of us simply *overthink* following up with others.

University of Texas researcher Amit Kumar wanted to understand why people didn't express gratitude to others more frequently. He knew that when you ask someone how receiving appreciation from someone else made *them* feel, they'd report powerful and positive feelings. So you'd expect if we know how gratitude makes us feel, we'd be likely to do it more often.

But we don't.

Why then don't we express gratitude more to others? Kumar found a significant disconnect between what we believe people would feel from a simple act of gratitude. People who received gratitude were much more surprised, felt much less awkward, and felt much more positive about it. We just overthink it.

Providing simple feedback to our mentors—thank yous, summaries of what we learned, activities we plan to take, and early results—are materially more impactful than we'd think. It turns out that recipients of gratitude and feedback expect nothing, so nearly any feedback is positively received.

If you're concerned about your feedback being insufficient or awkward, try to think how you'd feel if someone expressed gratitude through a simple action.

FEEDBACK LOOPS MAKE YOU "TOP OF MIND"

The best opportunities won't operate on your timeline or timetable. Instead, you're playing for a critical moment:

"... AND YOU POPPED INTO MY MIND..."

Simple expressions of gratitude are memorable. When we are memorable, we remain top of mind for future opportunities.

Matthew Busel was a student of mine, and after graduation, he was trying to navigate a nontraditional career path. He was interested in the intersection of augmented reality and sports, but those companies don't necessarily interview recent graduates on campus for entry-level jobs. Undeterred, Busel leveraged that fact for an informal discussion and interview with Serge Kassardjian, the then-global head of Google's Media Apps business. It was brief, and Matthew followed up after the meeting with some of the research he'd done on the companies working on interesting augmented reality projects in the sports arena. Many people would look at those brief interactions through the lens of "nothing came of it." But Matthew stayed top of mind. He shared some of the articles he'd written and engaged on social media.

Then, in late 2017, Serge decided to cofound a new venture—NextRev Commerce—looking at virtual reality applications in commerce. Matthew popped into his mind, and after meeting again, Matthew sent him a short deck with his thinking. He sent it quickly after the meeting so he stayed top of mind. More than a year in the making, that opportunity would land Matthew a job as the first employee of NextRev and its first product manager.

One Meeting Away: Matthew Busel

Right Person. Serge Kassardjian, cofounder of virtual reality start-up NextRev Commerce.

Right Ask. How does Google think about augmented reality and virtual reality for the sports industry?

Right Start. While Matthew had no obvious opportunity at Google, he shared some of the articles he'd written and engaged on social media after their meeting.

Right Time. Google was exploring AR/VR but had not made a push into commerce, which led Kassardjian to leave and start a new venture focused on using virtual reality in commerce. Not many people had extensive experience in AR/VR, making Busel a perfect candidate to join the team.

———————

Had Busel used his time with Serge to discuss career ambitions or to pick his brain, or had Busel failed to provide feedback loops on his progression to Serge, it would have been unlikely Busel would be top of mind and "in context" for Serge's opportunity.

If you're struck by the work Busel put in to create a deck in just a short amount of time, remember you have identified a project at this point in the Super Mentors framework and are immersed in this work. Throwing four or five slides together with your ideas should be a breeze.

You aim to be "top of mind" to people who have the opportunities you want—even if the opportunity happens months or years later. Sheryl Sandberg's transformative opportunity with Larry Summers at the World Bank happened years after their first experiences working on a new student club and Sandberg's thesis. Wes Moore would write the foreword to Chris Wilson's book *The Master Plan* years after meeting at a Baltimore leadership summit.

But an important piece in earning these opportunities comes from placing yourself regularly and contextually in the view of your Super Mentors. This is why feedback loops are critical to creating moments when you'll "pop into their mind."

BUILD LOOPS, NOT JUST FEEDBACK

How do we grow?

Some people might say trial and error, practice, or experience. All of those are correct, but underlying each one is the idea of feedback. To improve, we must know what *needs* to be improved. Think of it like a swimmer trying to improve her speed. Hopefully, she jumps in the pool week after week for a swim, and the practice helps her improve. Or maybe it won't. But if instead of just swimming week after week, someone gives her feedback—lap times or splits to beat or more granular data about the firing of her muscles or blood-oxygen ratio—she can see the cause and effect of any changes she'd made.

• importance of getting feedback

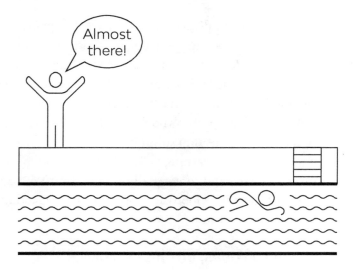

Feedback loops are one of the most powerful tools for growth, changing behavior, or improving performance.

Thomas Goetz, the executive editor at *WIRED* and the author of *The Decision Tree*, describes feedback loops as a way to "provide people with information about their actions in real time, or something close to it, and then allow them to change those actions and push them toward better behaviors."

Mentors operate similarly. Providing positive feedback unlocks their ability to provide you with more opportunities. For me, Steve Blank would become an advocate for an investor, helping us to secure funding for our new venture. But that opportunity came after a series of smaller engagements that netted positive feedback—from me directly or from others.

Remember, feedback does *not* only need to be positive.

A 2010 study by researchers at the University of Toronto and the University of California at San Francisco investigated the cause of failed mentoring relationships. The top two results were poor communication and a lack of commitment.

The study also found that reciprocity was the most cited reason for a *successful* mentorship experience. Both the mentor and the mentee should provide feedback so the relationship can develop to most effectively address each party's needs. However, these loops are mostly driven by you as the mentee.

We want these bigger opportunities, but they are often built on a series of smaller ones that net positive feedback.

TIGHTER FIRST MEETINGS MAKE
FOR TIGHTER FEEDBACK OPPORTUNITIES

The irony is that while some value does occur in our relationships from the first interactions, most opportunities and access come after that. Yet people aren't great at the follow-up necessary to unlock them.

One summer, I decided to track how people followed up on mentoring meetings. For ninety days, I agreed to meet with anyone who wanted to connect about start-ups, careers, or other challenges and opportunities they were seeking. As a professor, I'm probably more accessible than others, and given my experiences in start-ups, quite a few ambitious people are looking for support.

Over those ninety days, eighty-one people would schedule time with me. I spoke with someone and advised them about careers, life, and start-ups every day. They were fun and energizing. After every call, I'd offer them a small bit of homework—something that would take them a couple of hours max—and encourage them to schedule another call when they wanted to discuss what they'd learned. For most of them, I sent a recap email and a link to grab some more time on my calendar.

Any guesses as to how many followed up within six months of our meetings?

Zero.

That's right... none.

The only one of the eighty-one who would *ever* come back to discuss the call—a college senior referred by a former classmate—didn't follow up with me until an entire *year* after our call. Now you can probably see why I felt it was critical to write this book!

But what did I learn from this? Certainly, some of the lack of follow-up stemmed from these first meetings themselves. I hadn't scoped the conversations, so they weren't micro-requests—a specific, simple ask that was tied to a collaborative project opportunity. Instead, they were more open, free-wheeling, and "Can I pick your brain?" or "I'm trying to figure out my life. Can you help?" conversations. The outcome of these open, unstructured conversations reveals why the well-thought-out micro-request makes a huge difference in the start of a relationship.

Second, I also realized I hadn't made the homework fun and enjoyable. I'd told aspiring entrepreneurs to interview ten potential customers. Now, in my classes, I encourage my students to share the most unique experience, funniest experience, or most interesting conversation about their start-up. When anyone shares that they got kicked out of somewhere for doing interviews, the entire class gives them a standing ovation. The fun thing—as it turns out—really does matter.

Third, and most relevant to this part of the book, when I spoke to these individuals, I realized many believed the feedback they needed to provide me should be much greater than I was anticipating. If we spoke about career ideas, they thought they should wait until they landed a new job. If we spoke about a start-up idea, maybe they'd wait until they had a prototype or were raising money.

One of the most common responses of people who failed to follow up with me during my eighty-one meetings was over-scoping. For aspiring entrepreneurs who met with me to discuss their start-ups or new business ideas, my most common recommendation was to speak to five to ten customers and tell me what they'd found.

They'd build a threshold around feedback when they'd reached that specific number—five to ten—rather than feedback loops along the way. Micro feedback that does not create more work or actions for the mentor is more valuable than delaying beyond a particular threshold.

Think in feedback loops rather than feedback. Build on the power of small wins to show progress.

IT'S EASIER TO OVERDELIVER
THE FASTER YOU DELIVER

Melissa Proctor is the chief marketing officer of the NBA's Atlanta Hawks, one of the first female African Americans to hold the position in the NBA. Growing up as the daughter of an immigrant single mother, she learned the importance of working quickly, efficiently, and well.

Her rise to the upper echelons of the NBA began humbly as a ball girl, a role in which the Miami Heat had never had a woman hold before Melissa. But through a mixture of persistence and follow-up, she secured the job... only to realize later it was unpaid other than tips from the opposing team's equipment manager.

Melissa would parlay that experience into her first internship at Turner Broadcasting. As part of the program, Turner arranged informational interviews with executives, and Proctor was paired with Jennifer Dorian, the then-head of brand strategy for Turner. The interview proceeded as most informational interviews do, with Proctor asking her about her career path. But then she changed the tenor of the conversation.

"What keeps you up at night now? What challenges do you have?"

Dorian considered the question and shared some of the early work on a new project she was doing to help the network reach younger fans. Their fans were getting married for the first time, having their first child, and buying their first home.

"[Jennifer] was like, 'I don't know what to give them' as kits for these dramatic occasions in their lives."

Proctor went home and began drawing, sketching, and building out what she'd include in the kits. "It was fun, and it wasn't that big of a deal."

The next morning Proctor dropped off a folder with her ideas. "It blew her away. The fact that I took the time, effort, and initiative promptly to follow up, respond, and provide something made all the difference in the world."

What Proctor had leveraged was the fact it's much easier to over-deliver on your follow-up when you deliver quickly—in her case just twenty-four hours. It wasn't overcomplicated, and it wasn't intended to be polished. It was just "her thoughts."

One Meeting Away: Melissa Proctor

Right Person. Jennifer Dorian, head of the brand strategy at Turner Broadcasting and now the CEO of Public Broadcasting Atlanta.

Right Ask. What keeps you up at night? What are your points of pain? What challenges do you have?

Right Start. Proctor followed up quickly. She went home the night after her interview and created a series of sketches and promotional mock-ups for the kits that she sent to Dorian the next day

Right Time. Proctor leveraged her informational interview to learn about a current project Dorian was working on—dramatic occasion kits for TNT's younger fans.

Don't be afraid to caveat. "I wanted to get you something quickly," "these were just some notes and thoughts," "I wanted to see if this was the right direction," "I've already started to explore…" For Proctor, it was just something she played around with that night.

Researchers find when salespeople follow up within five minutes of a call or another engagement with a prospect, there is a nine-times higher likelihood of closing the sale. That's part of the delight that comes from near-shocking speed. "How did you do this so fast?" Would Dorian have been blown away if that project took Proctor a month or two? The follow-up bar, especially fast follow-up, is so low, meaning anything you do will be perceived even better.

The reality is like your initial requests. You don't need macro follow-up. Specific. Simple. Schedulable. Within twenty-four hours, are you able to follow up with a message that reads, "I've already _____"?

First follow-up, and then do it more quickly than anyone else.

Then do it again.

LEVERAGE THE POWER OF THE BACKCHANNEL

In 2008, at the start of the Great Recession, unemployment in the United States doubled to highs that hadn't been seen in a decade.

The very same year Charlie Hoehn graduated college.

Charlie started his career in one of the most challenging job markets.

"I applied to over one hundred jobs, and they didn't have any sort of one-click application," he shared. "I got ignored by all of them. It was very demoralizing."

His parents recommended that he consider graduate school—ride out this period and give it another try after things improved. But Charlie worried that would set him on a path and a career track he wasn't interested in.

He tried to refocus his perspective for inspiration and found a new set of voices on blogs and social media that resonated with him. People like *Tribes* author Seth Godin, *I Will Teach You To Be Rich* author Ramit Sethi, and life hacker and author of *The 4-Hour Workweek* Tim Ferriss offered a message outside the normal career track he'd been on.

In particular, Charlie found inspiration in Tim Ferriss. Tim was a *New York Times* best-selling author, popular blogger, and highly in-demand speaker. Tim was the pied piper of the "life hacker" movement that advocated for a way of life outside of the normal ways of doing things.

After one-hundred-plus jobs being rejected for Charlie, Tim's message of taking control of your life and career was powerful. He shifted his focus from graduate school or traditional jobs and set his sights on working for Tim.

"I had just gotten out of college, and I said to myself, 'I'm going to be his first full-time employee. I'm going to be his right-hand guy,'" Charlie said.

There was one big problem. Tim was notoriously careful with his time.

"I started buying into my frame of reference. And I viewed every single opportunity, every single piece of work I did, as moving me closer to my goal of working for Tim. It was the belief in changing my identity."

Charlie soon recognized he didn't have a straight line to Tim. But he'd leverage one of the most powerful tools at the foundation of Super Mentoring relationships to land a full-time offer from Tim.

FEEDBACK LOOPS.

"I realized if you want to work with somebody who's exceptionally high profile or a famous person, it's not a direct path," Charlie said. "I have to triangulate. And so I worked."

He built feedback loops with each person he worked with and leveraged those to provide evidence for his next mentors to backchannel their feedback forward.

Charlie recognized the need to triangulate to access someone like Tim Ferriss. He realized it might require him to find multiple people who could vouch for him to Tim.

We've discussed how developing Super Mentoring happens in stages: micro-requests, micro-opportunities, and eventually opportunity and network access acceleration. Successes at each stage create another opportunity or increased access. Small requests and opportunities—a meeting, an introduction, a project, a presentation, or a conversation—typically define the early stages of mentorship. Whether mentees recognize it, Super Mentors often see these initial engagements as trials.

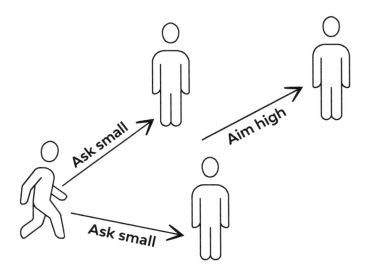

And if you want to unlock Super Mentorship, you mustn't fail these small, preliminary tests. Charlie became a master at creating feedback loops. He began studying the people he admitted and thinking of ways and opportunities for him to add value to the work they were doing.

He'd start with Ramit Sethi. Ramit had become a regular speaker on the conference circuit. "I know you speak, and you're really good on video," Charlie wrote. "But you don't have a demo reel. Based on stuff I found for you, I put one together or have you on YouTube."

This blew Ramit away. Charlie's message gave him a simple way to expand the relationship: "By the way, if you ever need somebody to partner up with or work with on an ongoing basis, I'm your guy."

Ramit solicited Charlie's ideas on other ways he could improve his speaking brand, and Charlie immediately shared his ideas.

Each engagement—each micro-request, micro-opportunity, and micro-project—is an opportunity to provide information and evidence *back* to the mentor. Super Mentors want to know their advice, requests, guidance, and coaching are being leveraged. Like Ramit, any potential mentor needs feedback to continue to provide further opportunities.

He explained, "Because I had those endorsements from people Tim trusted, he said, 'All right, let's do a trial run. Let's work together.' We started off with baby steps doing menial tasks. And as I kept performing, that ramped up, and he made me a full-time offer. I was his right-hand guy, and suddenly, I went from being a miserable college grad, working on my parent's ping pong table to sitting across from people who were changing the world."

INCORPORATE FEEDBACK LOOPS
INTO KEY DECISION-MAKING

Were it not for some timely guidance, Robert F. Smith might still be designing products for Kraft Foods or Goodyear Tire.

Instead, Smith became the world's wealthiest black man after founding Vista Equity Partners in 2000.

In 2019, the unassuming Smith shot to the front pages of newspapers and social media feeds. During his commencement address to the graduating class at Morehouse College, he pledged to pay off their student loans, immediately wiping an estimated ten to forty million dollars of debt from the graduates.

Twenty-five years earlier, Smith's graduation speaker changed his life.

Born in 1962, Smith grew up in a middle-class neighborhood in Denver. He was a child of parents with PhDs who stressed the value of hard work and education. After graduating from high school, Smith was admitted to Cornell University, where he studied Chemical Engineering. He then held several engineering-related roles at consumer-facing companies like Goodyear Tire and Kraft General Foods. He earned two patents for a coffee foam brewing process and a stainless-steel coffee filter at Kraft.

In 1992, Smith left Kraft for Columbia Business School. The early 1990s marked the rise of technology and the digital era, and Smith was interested in exploring innovation and entrepreneurship. He joined Columbia expecting to go into law, originally enrolling in a joint JD-MBA track, but later found it uninspiring.

Many of his classmates headed to Wall Street, but he still hadn't found his niche after more than a hundred interviews. It appeared Smith might return to consumer products.

Smith's graduation speaker was John Utendahl, a 1982 graduate of Columbia Business School and the founder of one the first black-run investment banks and the future vice-chairman of Deutsche Bank Americas.

Forbes reporter Nathan Vardi writes of that day: "Utendahl noticed the young African American man sitting among the other Columbia Business School graduates. Utendahl sought Smith out after the ceremony and invited him to lunch. Over tuna sandwiches, Utendahl convinced Smith to ditch his other plans and give investment banking a try, helping Smith land a job at Goldman Sachs."

While Utendahl felt strongly that a brilliant mind like Smith's could create transformational wealth in finance, Smith was initially unconvinced, having spoken to most of the Wall Street firms. Utendahl's help guided Smith to the mergers and acquisitions (M&A) side of finance and its leading player, Goldman Sachs. Smith changed his tune about finance and ultimately touted its value to his alma mater in a 2015 interview: "With the exception of warfare, [M&A] is how assets are transferred on this planet."

That guidance and coaching from Utendahl became the hallmark of their mentoring relationship for the next six years while Smith was elevated to Goldman's first M&A banker in the technology practice in Silicon Valley. Having worked closely with Apple, "Where we kicked out the board and invited Steve Jobs to rejoin the company," he became a trusted partner to tech's power players.

By 2000, Smith saw an opportunity beyond Goldman and founded Vista Equity Partners. He positioned Vista as one of the first private equity firms to focus on enterprise software. Through a series of deft transactions, he built the fund into a fourteen-billion-dollar firm with a portfolio of more than thirty companies employing over thirty thousand people.

Not being too strong-willed for coaching, but taking advice critically and thinking for yourself.

Right Person. John Utendahl, former vice-chairman of Deutsche Bank Americas.

Right Ask. What is the most inspiring emerging sector in the finance industry?

Right Start. Smith had largely made up his mind but recognized that Utendahl offered a different perspective and examined it to find a new way to frame an opportunity in finance.

Right Time. Financing of technology companies was in its infancy, and recognizing an opportunity for Smith to carve out his role in mergers and acquisitions in the technology sector at Goldman Sachs, Utendahl reframed the industry and reorientated Smith in a way one hundred job interviews couldn't.

Art Markman's examination *in Psychology Today* of the effects of a typical power dynamic in mentoring found that giving advice and seniority puts the mentors in power. Mentors often feel more powerful when mentees implement their guidance. One of the studies even indicated that knowledgeable people who want to boost their confidence often take the position of mentors to project their influence.

But as Utendahl showed, great mentorship comes from collaboration rather than directives. Smith could have simply brushed aside Utendahl, or Utendahl could have written off Smith as someone too strong-willed for coaching. Feedback fosters collaboration.

In many ways, Smith's commencement speech harkened back to the impact of one man's investment in him twenty-five years prior. But both men agree, firm advice didn't push Smith into finance; rather, a thoughtful series of conversations, connections, and persistence helped Smith find his path.

Feedback loops are critical tools in our most transformative decisions.

10.

EMBRACE THE UNANTICIPATED AND UNEXPECTED

An adage as old as time says something to the effect of:

LUCK IS WHEN PREPARATION MEETS OPPORTUNITY.

In the Super Mentor experience, what you'll see is that aspect of luck—unanticipated, unexpected moments that are transformative in some form or fashion.

Are you open to the unexpected? Are you ready for unexpected opportunities that may not be on your timetable or plans? Or are you at a point where you have a specific problem you need help with on a more urgent timeline?

A mentor may not be the best solution to your problem.

Mentors can deliver the unexpected and unanticipated—but exceptional—because their relationships are usually less in our control. We aren't paying them, we can't guarantee their interest, and we don't necessarily know what or if outcomes will even come. So while we anticipate something good happening, it's often better or different from something we didn't even see ourselves:

- How Jennifer Dorian opened a path for Melissa Proctor to become an executive in the NBA rather than a coach
- How Larry Summers would offer Sheryl Sandberg the opportunities to work at the World Bank and the Treasury
- How Naval Ravikant would encourage Eric Jorgenson to write the book rather than as the author himself
- How Steve Blank helped to design and unlock my path as a new type of professor at a school I likely wouldn't have gotten into as an undergraduate

---

In studying nearly three hundred recent graduates and current students who did not currently have a mentor, I saw a pattern as to how they were thinking about mentorship.

Now that I'm looking for a job, I need a mentor to help me.

And quite frankly, this thinking is a big reason why people are hesitant to embrace mentorship. They can't control the outcomes, the timelines, or the uncertainty.

College students are probably the most susceptible to this "need a job" trap. The four-year degree has become a predefined ladder with steps to be completed in order.

"Students arrive at their institution with this idea that the path is already laid out," Adam Saven told me. "If I major in this thing, take this class, get this internship, *then* find a mentor... I'll get a job." Of course, when students are ready to get a job, most still have no idea what they want to do.

"But that's okay," Adam continued. "The key is to inject social capital earlier in the process. Seventy percent of students enter college planning on networking with alumni, but only 27 percent of them do it. What if every school required students to have at least three conversations with alumni before they declare a major or their second year ends? By involving mentors earlier in this process, we begin to not only build social capital but open student horizons to the unexpected and shift their mindset."

Saven finished with a call to action for students. "Don't wait for your school to do this for you. Commit to having those three conversations without someone forcing you."

As you embrace modern mentorship, remember that *the mentee or* protégé *plays the most important role in these relationships.* And that's exciting. But it also means you'll need to be ready for the truths of this new reality.

Are you ready for the unanticipated and unexpected?

Recognizing what you can and can't control leads to exceptional outcomes.

BUILD THE MINDSET TO BE MENTORED

Let's start with an essential but perhaps nonobvious question:

Do you *want* to be mentored?

We know the data says that most of us believe mentorship is critical to career and life success. Yet most of us don't have a mentor. Maybe you don't need a mentor but a coach. Or maybe you've got a clear plan, and it's about execution at this stage. Or maybe you're not ready yet and need more self-discovery.

Early in my thirties, I found myself in some challenging and new scenarios running a start-up company backed by big-name investors. I didn't embrace mentors because I thought mentorship was when you were young and partially because I was looking for something more transactional—coaching.

Mentorship is a free transfer of assets, but it's important to know that it's more like playing a slot machine than going to the bank. The bank has high certainty. You give them your money and get it back with interest. Playing the slots is highly uncertain. You pull the lever repeatedly, and most times, nothing happens other than you losing your money. But every once in a while, if you play long enough… jackpot.

Here's a simple test to determine if you're in the right place for mentors.

How *urgent* is the problem you're facing?

- Have you just graduated and need a job or do you have a fine job, and you're looking to make the right transition? (Coach versus Mentor)
- Is your start-up running out of money in six months, or are you considering whether to grow your business, and the right approach is to inject more capital? (Coach versus Mentor)
- Have you finished your script, book, event agenda, or first podcast season, or are you developing the project and still open to it evolving? (Coach versus Mentor)

Is this a three-to-six-month problem (coaching) or a six-month and beyond problem (mentoring)? Mentorship is an activity like going to the gym, potentially lots of work with little immediate results. And the results you get might not be what you were hoping for.

Readiness matters in building successful mentoring relationships and building them into Super Mentors. And you can certainly engage both—coaching for selected urgent needs and mentoring for less urgent problems.

When you begin to look for the pattern in those who are open to mentoring by their Super Mentors, we describe some common patterns as the protégé mindset. These individuals all believe in their potential, are clear in running toward it, and are resilient when life throws challenges or incredible opportunities. In other words, they operate at the intersection of three key mindsets of successful people. This intersection of mindsets and skillsets makes them masters of unlocking the power of their relationships.

Three important aspects can help control what you can and embrace what you can't possibly anticipate or expect in your mentorship experiences:

- Engaging the Right People (**Not** a single person)
- Openness to the Right Opportunities (**Not** a single outcome or path to the outcome)
- Patience for the Right Time (**Not** giving up too early)

Magic lies in the uncertain and unexpected. But if you need the certainty of outcomes on your timelines, perhaps a mentor isn't the ideal construct for you.

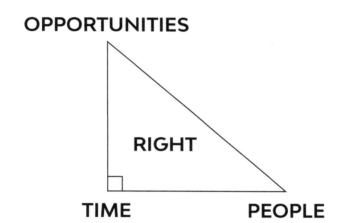

OPPORTUNITIES

RIGHT

TIME   PEOPLE

LOOK FOR A TYPE OF PERSON, NOT THE PERSON

Remember, you don't *need* a mentor or someone who formally calls themselves your mentor. You need to establish relationships with numerous high-potential individuals. Opportunities don't always travel on a straight path.

Christina Qi fits into that camp. She's a *Forbes* 30 under 30 winner, the founder of DataBento and Domeyard Fund, and one of my former students. In her 2016 blog post titled "No, I don't have a mentor, and I'm doing just fine," she writes. "Whether I was in college, in a lab, or preparing for my first internship, people encouraged me to regularly meet with a formal mentor. And while I found positive role models and lifelong friendships during each experience, I never found a mentor. Something must be wrong with me. Why can't I find a mentor? Am I not likable enough?"

But clearly, Christina has a circle of individuals who operate as mentors—formal title or not. She counts luminaries Robert C. Merton, the 1997 Nobel Memorial Prize in Economic Services, and Gregg Schoenberg, cofounder/showrunner for *The Financial Revolutionist* in her close circles.

She turned to people like Robert, Gregg, and others when she needed specific guidance, help, or opportunities instead of following the formal mentor programs that have become popular. When Christina received media opportunities, she could speak to Gregg, a showrunner, and Robert to understand challenges within the hedge fund and financial services sectors.

One Meeting Away: Christina Qi

Right Person. Robert C. Merton, Gregg Schoenberg, and others (informally).

Right Ask. Can we discuss this opportunity?

Right Start. She's built an informal board of advisors she leverages regularly and routinely to work through the opportunities.

Right Time. Christina receives speaking, writing, advising, and board opportunities regularly, especially as one of the few female hedge fund founders and managers.

Don't get hung up on the term because having the wrong mentor is worse than having no mentor. Feeling somehow incomplete without a mentor, as Christina recalls feeling, isn't useful.

In my case, I'm not sure if any of my Super Mentors would lescribe me as their mentee or protégé if you asked them. The label ; different from the actions. Everyone who's had formal or informal

Increasing my circle & having clear asks of people

Super Mentors was very active in their personal development and surrounded themselves with the right people.

ENGAGE THE RIGHT PEOPLE (NOT A SINGLE PERSON)

CREATE MANY OPPORTUNITIES

You'll see time and time again in Super Mentor stories that the person was not "dead set" on a single mentor or relationship. Or even if they were—in the case of Charlie Hoehn designing relationships to get him to Tim Ferriss—the route there was seldom a straight line.

There's not just one person who can help you but a category of people. Designing for delight is about surrounding yourself with those people—your aspirational peers or your "cousins" as Chris Wilson described them.

Jeff Morris Jr. wanted to be where the action was. Throughout his career, he ran into the toughest problems but was always humble, aware of his place and step in the greater journey. He grew up in the belly of tech, hailing from Atherton, California, in Silicon Valley's heart. He went to high school with Meg Whitman's (former CEO of HP) son, his high school football coach was the legendary Bill Campbell (Steve Job's friend and business coach), and his grandfather was Mervin Morris, the founder of the Mervyn's Department Store empire.

"Everyone I grew up with was in tech, and everyone I met who wasn't from here wanted to be in tech," Jeff shared with me. "I wasn't interested in it."

So he pursued his path in the entertainment world, attending UCLA and earning his MFA from USC's noted film school. Eventually, he landed a job at United Talent Agency and began a career in entertainment. He soon realized his heart was back home, creating great technological products, which meant he needed to find the *right* way to get back into the place he'd left.

Like many people, he was initially fixated on a small number of rocketship companies: Zynga (social gaming) and Foursquare (location-based check-ins). He tried to leverage his connections, tried cold applications, and tried to get an audience at events with any of the executives. Nothing worked.

"I wasn't going to settle, but I also realized it was a specific company. It was a specific *type* of company."

So he expanded his search and refocused his efforts.

A few months later, a cold email landed in my inbox with a first line: "If my pay-to-be-hired contract seems like a bargain, that is fine. I am a single twenty-six-year-old male, I live a very lean lifestyle, and I can afford to place a bet on the most intriguing start-up concept I have ever heard."

The message was from Jeff Morris Jr.

"Wait, is he serious? He's willing to *pay us* to work here," I asked Adam Coomes, the very first hire we made at Zaarly.

"Yup. That's what he said," Adam replied with a shrug. "What do you want to do?"

"I want to meet this guy."

Jeff Morris Jr. remains one of my favorite people I've ever hired and worked with early in his career, and his remarkable cover letter is something of lore. We hired JMJ, as we called him. He became a superstar from nearly the moment he joined, helping develop and execute our community-first strategy to build active, thriving communities of users to launch our business in the biggest markets in the country. Zaarly launched the first nationwide hyperlocal business *successfully* and raised nearly fifty million dollars in no small part because of those early successes.

Jeff's experiences were *not* what he'd anticipated but part of the delight of the openness to the types of people you hope to meet. Jeff's work would include experiences like his last-minute scramble to find a rabbi in Los Angeles to come to Ashton Kutcher's home and designing a viral marketing campaign that involved a "human display" window where an actor was live-streamed using the Zaarly product for seventy-two hours.

While the specific opportunities and outcomes may have been different than he'd anticipated, his openness led to the eventual results.

One Meeting Away: Jeff Morris Jr.

Right Person. Bo Fishback, Eric Koester, and Ian Hunter (founders of then-start-up Zaarly).

Right Ask. Can I pay you to work for your start-up for two months?

Right Start. Forty-eight hours after sending the email, Jeff was in Kansas City and was one of the hardest workers I'd seen, regularly asking for more opportunities and almost never wasting those he received.

Right Time. At the time of receiving Jeff Morris Jr.'s email, Zaarly was less than two months old and only had an office in Kansas City, Missouri, making Jeff's offer to join—We didn't let him pay us. We hired him—and move to Kansas City critical for attracting early talent into the company.

Jeff would leverage these experiences to be hired as the first Director of Product for Tinder, helping grow its mobile app to be the top-grossing product in the AppStore by 2019, and the Director of Product and Growth at Lambda School, the fastest growing coding school in the country. Today, Jeff is a full-time investor at Chapter One Ventures, the venture firm he founded.

BE OPEN TO THE RIGHT OPPORTUNITIES
(*NOT A SINGLE OUTCOME OR PATH TO THE OUTCOME*)

THE BEST OPPORTUNITIES MAY
NOT COME ON YOUR TIMETABLE

"Ernie and I were, 'Holy crap. He's willing to do this!'" Zak Penn said. With the help of *Ready Player One* author Ernest Cline, Penn was making a big ask.

They'd already landed their dream director in Steven Spielberg. They asked him to create a sequence in the movie that featured a film within a film that Spielberg revered—Stanley Kubrick's adaptation of Stephen King's horror classic *The Shining*. Kubrick and Spielberg were friends, and Spielberg even described Kubrick as a mentor. When Kubrick finished shooting the Overlook Hotel scenes at London's Elstree Studios, Spielberg took over the set to film the Well of Souls snake pit for Raiders of the Lost Ark.

In some senses, Spielberg was paying forward the relationship he built with Kubrick to this new generation of storytellers in Penn and Cline. Penn and Cline spent nearly a decade trying to make the record-breaking film with Spielberg.

"It was nostalgic for me because I first met Stanley Kubrick on the set that I depict in *Ready Player One*," Spielberg told *Entertainment Weekly*. "The main living area with the grand fireplace in the Overlook is where I first encountered Stanley in 1979 when I went to look at the sound stages. They were about to build the sets for *Raiders of the Lost Ark* in Elstree Studios. When I found out Stanley had completed a set and was planning his shots, I asked if I could meet him."

Kubrick created history in 1968 with the creation of scientific realism through innovative special effects in his Academy award-winning film, *2001: A Space Odyssey*, which had a profound effect on Spielberg, then a film student.

In the years that followed, the directors were often described as having very different styles and approaches, to the point that Spielberg even confessed he wasn't a fan of *The Shining* when he first saw it, but it grew on him with time. Yet, meeting Kubrick in the late 1970s was an important step for Spielberg, as Kubrick inspired him to level up his game.

As Spielberg first approached Kubrick, who was setting up shots for an upcoming set, Spielberg observed Kubrick was using a model of the set to test shots with a Nikon camera.

"I looked at that, and I said, 'You've got the whole set, and you're looking for shots on a small quarter-inch of the scale tabletop model?' And Stanley said, 'Yeah, what's wrong with that?'"

That terse beginning makes it more surprising that their relationship developed to the point that Kubrick would count Spielberg as a trusted confidant. Kubrick saw a charisma in Spielberg that ensured his confidence in Spielberg's willingness to learn and make brilliant movies. For Spielberg, Kubrick's natural cinematic genius encouraged him to learn more and try out newer techniques in filmmaking. He was overjoyed that he could reinvent himself through his cinema, an approach to the art that has given him a near-fifty-year career at the forefront of filmmaking.

Just how did the notoriously private Kubrick come to trust Spielberg? Time and persistence. Following the success of *The Shining*, Kubrick hoped to make a sci-fi epic based on a short story by Brian Aldiss titled "Supertoys Last All Summer Long." *A.I.* would be a movie set in a future where climate change and robots had taken over the world. The project was ambitious, and Kubrick realized no one could quite conceptualize it like Spielberg. "He and Spielberg spoke all the time," shared Kubrick's brother-in-law Jan Harlan. "I have six or seven years' worth of correspondence between them over *A.I.*, which I recently passed over to Spielberg along with over a thousand drawings."

The pair built a near-twenty-year relationship that continued beyond Kubrick's death in 1999. Spielberg decided to make *A.I. Artificial Intelligence* as a tribute to his friend and mentor. "Stanley had a vision of this project that was evolving over eighteen years. I am intent on bringing to the screen as much of that vision as possible along with elements of my own," said Spielberg.

It's fitting that their relationship came full circle, with Spielberg recreating the iconic Overlook Hotel scenes in *Ready Player One*. Like with most of their relationship, it simply took a little time and patience.

HAVE PATIENCE FOR THE RIGHT TIME (NOT GIVING UP TOO EARLY)

DEVELOP THE PROTÉGÉ MINDSET

Again, ask yourself: Do I *want* to be mentored?

Modern mentorship requires a different mindset—some might say a radical one—from what you've been told is mentorship. You're not engaging a single person. You're not set on a single path or out-come, and you're not on your own timetable. The protégé mindset requires you to:

- Engage the right people
- Be open to the right opportunities
- Have patience for the right time

And while these traits may not be natural, you can work on a core set of principles to the protégé mindset to build and create the mindset necessary for modern mentorship.

Exceptional mentees and protégés *make* Super Mentors rather than being *made by* their Super Mentors. Christina Qi is correct. She doesn't have a mentor, and she's doing just fine. She and Jeff Morris Jr. have a mindset to be mentored in that both are individuals who work to leverage those around them to accelerate their success.

But make no mistake: They were not "made by" anyone.

A GROWTH MINDSET

This protégé mindset is based on a clear belief we can get better with an understanding that effort is essential. People like Jeff and Christina put in extra time and effort—in some cases taking risks that others may steer from—which led them to higher achievement. Those risks are often motivated by the people they choose to surround themselves with.

Super Mentor Reality: Only approximately 60 percent of people have a growth mindset; others believe their character, intelligence, and creative ability are fixed.

Stanford psychologist Carol Dweck studies the importance of our mindset in achieving success. In her groundbreaking book *Mindset*, she asserts that our mindset can be divided into fixed and growth mindsets. A fixed mindset assumes that character, intelligence, and creative ability are static givens that cannot change in any meaningful way, and success is the affirmation of that inherent intelligence. As a result, people with fixed mindsets avoid challenges, give up easily, see effort as fruitless or ignore useful negative feedback, and feel threatened by the success of others. On the other hand, a growth mindset thrives on challenge and sees failure not as evidence of unintelligence but as a heartening springboard for growth and stretching existing abilities. People with a growth mindset desire to learn; therefore, they embrace challenges, persist in the face of setbacks, see effort as a path to mastery, learn from criticism, and see others' success as lessons and inspiration.

, So you need to put a lot of effort into your Spruce

GRITTY

Jeff's snap decision to move to Kansas City to work for a fledgling company wasn't in pursuit of a clear path but a clear curiosity to be satisfied. Zaarly wasn't the first company he applied to. He'd reached out to every company that caught his interest, including future success stories like Uber and Airbnb.

He was persistent. He read everything he could, met everyone who interested him, and took risks. He had grit. Even the first line of his cover letter made that clear.

Charlie would work on a summer-long project that marketing guru Seth Godin shared in his blog. He then cold-emailed Ramit Sethi and collaborated on a series of video-related projects. Charlie then leveraged that experience to get hired as a videographer by four-time *New York Times* best-selling author Tucker Max as he turned his book into a movie. At each point, Charlie started small, but he delivered quickly.

His actions were feedback to the mentors that their advice, guidance, or suggestions improved him. They saw these improvements in the work he delivered every time.

"Three people independently recommended me to Tim," Charlie admitted. "Only one I explicitly asked, 'Hey, would you be willing to make an introduction to him? I have some ideas for him.'"

One Meeting Away: Charlie Hoehn

Right Person. Ramit Sethi. Seth Godin. Tucker Max. Tim Ferriss.

Right Ask. Is this free work useful?

Right Start. Once he got his foot in the door, Charlie knew he had to do exceptional work in order to make himself recommendable for whatever came next.

Right Time. Charlie enjoyed video production, and 2008 and 2009 were the early days of video's explosion through YouTube and other social platforms. Charlie leveraged micro-projects—free work—to demonstrate value, and to create backchannel opportunities to grow into increasingly higher profile mentor relationships.

You might wonder why they were willing to vouch for that kid who was rejected from one hundred jobs. It's because he built feedback loops to show he would deliver on any test, challenge, or trial.

The term "grit" was coined by Angela Duckworth, a psychology researcher at the University of Pennsylvania. Grit is passion and perseverance for long-term and meaningful goals—the ability to persist in something you feel passionate about and endure challenges and obstacles that come your way. This type of passion is not short-term, and it is not about intense emotions or infatuation. Rather, it is about having a long-term focus, direction, and commitment to succeed in the set goals. This kind of passion and focus enables people to stay committed in their course to success even when the task is difficult or boring.

Duckworth and her team of researchers studied people in challenging environments—from basic training to competitive graduate schools—and found that grit was the primary predictor of success. While talent is certainly a contributor to success, Duckworth writes in her book *Grit* that "what drives success is not 'genius' but a unique combination of passion and long-term perseverance."

Similarly, researcher Linda Phillips-Jones writes in her paper "Skills for Successful Mentoring" that "grittiness can be achieved by mentees striving to learn quickly, showing initiative, following through, and managing the relationship." And that's exactly what Jeff did.

In studying these stories of Super Mentors, I observed among mentees the same passion and grit touted by Duckworth and Phillips-Jones in building Super Mentoring relationships—perseverance to long-term goals and objectives. Jeff didn't stop at the first no or the dozens of start-ups that didn't hire him because he didn't have the right skillset. The protégé mindset focuses on achieving the ends that motivated them to seek mentorship in the first place, even if it doesn't pay off immediately.

BEYOND FRAGILE

In Christina's blog post on mentorship, she writes, "Something must be wrong with me. Why can't I find a mentor? Am I not likable enough?"

These feelings of self-doubt can often be crippling. And what's interesting about the concept of mentorship is we often believe that others have exceptional mentors. While a third of people report having a mentor, I'd argue a much smaller set of mentors create transformational experiences—Super Mentors.

Mentoring relationships are very different among the highest achievers than those we see in the movies. High achievers don't *need* a relationship to be successful. Instead, they see these relationships as mutually beneficial ones that can help them accelerate aspects of their success. Plus, as we found in our research, many of the most successful Super Mentor relationships were not formalized with any titles and were forged at various points in our lives and careers. Christina might well follow the pathway of Oprah or Twitter CEO Jack Dorsey and develop a formal mentor relationship much later in her life or career.

Having a mentor will not guarantee you success; your ability to work through the common challenges to *cultivate* a Super Mentoring relationship routinely leads to transformative outcomes.

Anti-fragility is an important trait for working through those challenges and cultivating the protégé mindset.

In his book *Antifragile*, author Nassim Taleb defines anti-fragility as the aptitude to benefit from shocks, thrive and grow when exposed to volatility, randomness, disorder, stressors, and love adventure, risk, and uncertainty. Anti-fragility goes beyond resilience and robustness. Resilience is the capability to remain unchanged and unshaken in the presence of shocks, whereas anti-fragility is the knack to continue growing amid inhibitions. Anti-fragility is the mechanism behind anything that has managed to survive and evolve through time.

Both Jeff and Christina worked through their shocks. For Jeff, the role at Zaarly was not the end but the beginning of a decades-long journey to define and establish himself. After three years as a marketing and operations specialist, he was ready to progress into building products, but his experiences didn't translate to the roles he wanted. He'd be making a lateral move rather than a forward one. It was a struggle to reconcile. He was told that he needed to learn to code to get the jobs he wanted, so he swallowed his pride and enrolled in a coding boot camp. Back to the laboratory, he thought.

The coding boot camp didn't start for several months, so he decided to experiment and learn independently. He looked inward for product ideas he wanted to use and turned to the internet and peer mentors for guidance. Before the boot camp started, Jeff launched three successive products to become number one releases on Product Hunt (Slack Chats, Requests for Startups, Startup Adoption Agency). He became a finalist for Product Hunt's Maker of the Year in 2015.

"I never completed in the boot camp," he admits. "Tinder reached out to hire me for a lead product development role. And they never once asked about my coding skills."

The mentorship journey is characterized by obstacles that can easily throw mentees off the rails. Whether those obstacles are humbling guidance, not having a formal mentor, or the common shocks of an early career trajectory, resilience and persistence through shared struggles allow successful Super Mentor relationships to grow.

Buster Benson, author of *Why Are We Yelling?*, propounds that people can live an antifragile life by sticking to some simple rules: building in redundancy and layers, embracing randomness, avoiding single points of failure, being open-minded, and observing traditions and building on them.

That's where these elements build into designing for delight—redundancy of not depending on a single person, randomness in embracing wonderful and surprising opportunities, and persistence to recognize that multiple moments lead you where you're headed.

This same framework is the core of the protégé mindset in many senses, having the mindset to be mentored.

EMBRACE PERSISTENCE ABOVE ALL ELSE

University of Toronto medical Dr. Sharon Straus studied hundreds of mentoring relationships in academic hospital settings. Her 2010 research found that a lack of persistence by the mentee is a leading cause of failed mentorship. Her study revealed that mentees who lack persistence were poor communicators, barely acted on feedback, and lacked commitment.

That's right... it's not them; it's you.

> **Mentor Fallacy:** Mentoring relationships fail because of a poor fit between the mentor and mentee.
>
> **Super Mentor Reality:** Mentoring relationships are often reported to be a good fit but fail instead because the mentee is poor at follow-up and commitment.

You'll need to reach out more, follow-up more, provide more feedback, and realize that this relationship may not yield anything transformative despite all that work and effort. So you'll need to do it again.

You'll often see periods or phases of mentor-building in highly successful people, and we'll discuss these specific periods or phases more in the rest of part IV. While this advice seems obvious and simple, implementing it isn't easy.

Mentorship for mentorship's sake is hard to maintain from a momentum perspective, especially if you have early silence in your outreach. When in doubt, work backward: I'd like to speak to a dozen people over the next sixty days for this research, this book, this product, this event, cause. Persistence is often an easy word to throw around. It implies if you are *not* persistent, you're lazy or not hard working. I think of it in a more outcome-focused way.

People give up much too easily and quickly when building transformative relationships. I have been called a pusher in my courses, which is a polite way of saying I strongly encourage (read as force) them to engage and outreach much more than they'd do if left to their own devices. That's where you'll find the importance of a project in these efforts. Rather than just reaching out for a mentor… now you're reaching out because you want to interview someone critical of your course, book, podcast, product, cause, or research. It's contextual and creates a reason for continued effort and persistence.

You need the outreach, the follow-up, and these feedback loops for an outcome—hence why it's important to scope the opportunities you'd like and tie them more directly to the projects you're tackling.

One of my students shared that she'd reached out to two people who didn't reply to her, so she stopped thinking it wasn't working. A week later, she'd try again, and this outreach would directly lead to three email introductions and job interviews. The reframing happened when she reimagined why she was doing the outreach. It wasn't to find a mentor or to have conversations. It was to help her get an internship that fall.

Celebrate these mini-milestones—a reply, an introduction, a like on your social media five-minute favor, a meeting, or something else you didn't expect. Make these moments of delight truly delightful. BJ Fogg, Stanford professor and the author of *Tiny Habits*, advises people seeking to build any new habit to overly celebrate small wins. "I do a dance of joy and celebrate as if I've won the Super Bowl when I complete a new habit I want to build. My wife thought it was crazy when I'd do this after completing five push-ups, but that's what it took to create that habit."

Celebrate. That builds a habit that creates persistence.

While this isn't a perfect analogy, 80 percent of sales happen after the fourth follow-up. When in doubt, remember these activities are tied to outcomes.

***

For many of us, a freeing feeling comes with recognizing that we have much greater control over our own success. Super Mentors are additive to that success. but we are not dependent on them. When we begin to operate with the protégé mindset, others are drawn to us. They recognize that we already believe in our potential; we are running toward it, and we are resilient when life throws us challenges and obstacles.

No, you certainly don't *need* a mentor. But recognizing the mindset that leads to Super Mentoring relationships is the foundation they are built upon.

. There is a bit here - leveraging a propel to make a connection

PART IV

THE LAW OF RIGHT TIME

Mentorship has seasons, so engage the ideal mentor at the right time in your life. Learn how to identify stages and mentors that can support you through them.

11

THERE IS A "RIGHT" TIMING FOR A MENTOR

What follows in the subsequent chapters are a series of deeper dives into the core phases and stages of mentorship based on the research. Thank you if you've made it this far in the book. I hope that means you've enjoyed it. You'll be able to unlock much of the value from the book in its first ten chapters.

I decided to include these next nine chapters to help go deeper into mentorship with more specific stories, examples, and explanations of the impact and importance of timing in mentor relationships.

The book is built on an extensive study of the mentor relationships of high-profile individuals and validated by data provided by Adam Saven and the team at PeopleGrove. In this analysis, we extracted some patterns and lessons that provide a valuable way to begin to build targets based on your needs, stage in life, and the type of people you're targeting.

While these relationships certainly contain a right time component, I'd encourage you to view this as more of a framework than hard rules and approaches to follow.

FINDING A PATTERN IN MENTORSHIP

Most studies and research into mentorship have been focused on structured or assigned mentoring programs, such as academic mentor-match programs and workplace mentorship, or "natural" mentorship where relationships were built outside of a formal program. And while these insights are certainly useful, I was unable to find any research, studies, or reviews that analyzed the mentoring relationships of highly successful people.

As I explored different ways to conduct research, I considered whether to focus on a more quantitative approach by focusing on a survey or study of a pool of individuals such as the chief executive officers of the Fortune 500, tenured professors, or attending physicians. While that approach has some merit, I concluded that my aim of the research and the book was to offer a broad range of stories across industries and highlight those that may be well-known to the reader.

For the purposes of the research, we were able to develop an extensive analysis of 142 high-profile mentor-mentee pairs. We would describe this as qualitative research.

We began the process with a variety of keywords, websites, lists, and books that would describe two individuals as having a mentor-mentee or mentor-protégé relationship.

To scope our project into the list of 142 relationships, we made the following determinations:

1. We only included relationships where the mentee had a Wikipedia page on our list. This was a simple way to focus on relationships we felt were high profile from a reliable source.

2. We researched publicly available sources that detailed mentor relationships. With the help of several researchers, we dug into these origin stories in books, magazines, interviews, and other media.

   a. We excluded mentor-mentee familial relationships and relationships that a direct family introduction had facilitated. While those relationships might have been valuable, we wanted to focus on relationships that were not facilitated through family since not everyone has access to those relationships.

b. We excluded mentor-mentee relationships with insufficient sources to map the story of their mentorship, including how they first met or were introduced, opportunities created by the mentor for the mentee, and any key advice or guidance provided.

c. We excluded mentor-mentee relationships where we could only uncover evidence of "advice" in the relationship. If we were unable to find evidence of a specific opportunity, like an active, collaborative action step, we did not include them.

Based on this exclusion process, we could operate in high confidence these relationships met our definition as Super Mentors. We recognize that without full confirmation from each party, we may have over or under included some people.

We then looked for different patterns across these 142 pairs of mentor-mentee relationships classified as Super Mentoring relationships. Many of the pairs were hard to pin into a single category. For example, peers at work could be work mentors and peer mentors. So in some cases, we chose or left them uncategorized if we felt it was safer. Remember, we are using this as an unscientific descriptive study rather than looking for predictive patterns.

Among this pool, many more men were represented. Just twenty-four female mentors and twenty-three female mentees or protégés were present with ten mentor-mentee pairings having women-women relationships. This divide has several possible explanations. Perhaps successful women are less likely to disclose their mentors, are less likely to describe relationships as mentorships, or there is less female mentorship. These are interesting and important questions but fell outside this book's scope. However, given these findings, it's perhaps not a surprise that Sheryl Sandberg, who herself benefited from Super

Mentorship, has become such an outspoken advocate for the need for female mentorship.

From a macro perspective, the qualitative findings are consistent with and have been incorporated into the four laws of Super Mentors: right ask, right person, right start, and right time.

THE FOUR LAWS FOR THE "AVERAGE" PERSON

You might be thinking, I'm not Mark Zuckerberg, and I don't know anyone whose parents own a newspaper like *The Washington Post*. It can be difficult to learn about high-profile mentorships like Zuckerberg and Graham and then bring it down to your level.

That's where I got excited by understanding what Adam Saven had been building with PeopleGrove, a platform designed to use technology to facilitate many of the modern mentoring principles I'd first seen in my research.

Millions of students and alumni at the institutions they work with have leveraged the opportunities found in their college networks to advance in their career and get where they want to go. Adam and his team are constantly evaluating activity in their platforms and studying the outcomes of these learners.

So when I called Adam up to talk about the laws of Super Mentors, I could feel the excitement on the other end of the line. "This is just what we've been working on," he exclaimed. "We've seen so much change around mentoring in just the last two years that we launched a few projects to measure what's different."

To narrow the field, the data scientists at PeopleGrove looked at recent messages and connection requests from across their platforms, looking for patterns. They did not separate student requests from alumni requests, as both groups are learners.

Additionally, the company recently surveyed its users and received nearly three thousand responses. These surveys asked learners to describe the impact of social capital on their career journey.

These projects helped our team demonstrate that these Super Mentor patterns weren't just for the rich and famous but played out every day among those ambitious enough to put them to use.

THERE ARE SEASONS OF MENTORSHIP, BUT THEY ARE MORE FUNGIBLE AND FLEXIBLE THAN RULES

In studying these individuals and their mentoring relationships, we found a strong level of self-awareness and self-advocacy in the mentees. Perhaps, that can be credited, in part, to the ways we tend to retell history. Many times, our success narratives don't quite account for good fortune and timely opportunities. But it was clear that successful people have multiple mentors tied to key periods and phases of their lives.

While we were not analyzing every mentoring relationship exclusively, the relationships were more fleeting than lifelong relationships. Individuals such as Mark Zuckerberg and Warren Buffett disclosed multiple Super Mentor relationships.

And as a result, if you're fortunate, you'll likely have an opportunity for multiple Super Mentors that align with different seasons of your life and career based on your needs. This section of the book expands on that idea because it's critical to recognize both the period you're in and the types of Super Mentors best equipped to help you through that period.

MENTEE PHASES

We found that these Super Mentor relationships were common and clustered in the eight life phases or periods below.

1. **While In School.** This phase describes when the mentee is in school and coincides with the academic/professor mentoring type.
2. **First Job or Opportunity.** Mentoring relationships during this stage occur early in a person's career while they are trying to get that first "real job" or "first big break."

3. **Second Career.** The second career describes a life stage where mentoring relationships focus on a mentee who has succeeded in an area but is now looking to extend into a new arena.
4. **During Your Early Jobs/Career.** This phase occurs once a person has landed a job but needs help navigating the next steps.
5. **Entrepreneur.** Starting a company can be very difficult. Having experienced founders around is one of the key ways a person can make it through that time.

6. **Expansion of Career.** Generally, the mentee has been a high achiever in the past but needs a push to move to the next level.
7. **CEO to younger CEO.** These people have "made it," but one has been at it longer and can share what it's like to be at the top. It doesn't only have to be in business but is at the pinnacle of the career, so to speak.
8. **Personal.** This phase describes situations where a person needs guidance that focuses less on career and more on personal life, such as family, love, hobbies, etc.

For example, Steve Blank's mentorship came at a key phase in my life called *second career*, when the mentee or protégé is transitioning to a new role, industry, or career path. This transition in my late thirties from a technology start-up founder to a professor/academic was supported by Steve's Super Mentorship.

SUPER MENTOR CATEGORIES

We were able to put each of our 142 Super Mentors into a category listed below.

1. **Sees a younger version of themselves (a.k.a. "The Mirror Effect").** These relationships typically evolve from someone "following in the footsteps" of another person. Often, someone sees their mentor as someone they aspire to be or whose path they'd like to follow. Bob Dylan grew up listening to Woody Guthrie in high school and eventually befriended him as a young musician. The relationship aided Dylan's rise.

2. **Academic/Professor.** The relationship usually begins as a professor/administrator to student relationship but can evolve into a longer-term relationship. This is one of the most common early career mentors. Still, it's rare that these turn into Super Mentor relationships, often because students are unaware of how to cultivate that relationship transition. Examples include Dr. Benjamin Mays, former president of Morehouse College, developing a relationship with Dr. Martin Luther King Jr. that continued beyond King's college days; Jean Arthur and actress Meryl Streep; Frederick Terman and HP founders Bill Hewlett and David Packard; and Benjamin Graham and Berkshire Hathaway founder Warren Buffett.

3. **Work.** This mentorship develops through work, usually between someone senior at a company and a younger, high-achieving person. Perhaps, a CEO takes a fast-rising manager under his wing. For example, Larry Ellison mentored Marc Benioff Oracle, and when Marc went off to start Salesforce, he left with Larry's blessing, an investment, and Larry in a role on the board.

4. **Peer Mentor.** These relationships between two parties are equal in status, but one member has more specific knowledge about something. For example, Bill Gates and Warren Buffett are two of the richest and most financially successful men globally, but Bill describes Warren as someone who often asks for advice. Other examples include Intel founder/CEO Andy Grove and Steve Jobs, director/producer Todd Phillips, and actor/director Bradley Cooper.

5. **Investor.** This mentoring relationship centers around an investor or investment and is most common in the start-up ecosystem. Often, the relationship begins as an investment but takes on very different relationships from there. Examples include Dennis Crowley and Ben Horowitz, the Partovi Brothers investing in Drew Houston at Dropbox, Don Graham of *The Washington Post,* and Reid Hoffman of LinkedIn (and formerly of PayPal) investing in Mark Zuckerberg at Facebook.

6. **Shared Struggle.** The shared struggle mentor is drawn to a mentee because they share some type of struggle. For example, both Steve Jobs and Mark Zuckerberg were misunderstood outsiders, who had to battle to retain decision-making control of their companies but ultimately became dominant cultural forces.

7. **Luminary.** These relationships typically begin when the future mentee tries something in an industry, and an already successful person takes them under the wing. Examples include entertainers Carol Burnett and Vicki Lawrence, fashion icons Christian Dior and Yves St. Laurent, and aviation industry pioneers Sir Freddie Laker and Richard Branson.

8. **Collector.** Certain people surround themselves with younger up-and-comers who they can learn from and share wisdom with. Examples include SNL creator Lorne Michaels, Steve Jobs, NFL Hall of Fame coach Bill Walsh, and my mentor Steve Blank.

In my life, Steve Blank is best defined as a *Collector*, a type of Super Mentor characterized by a tendency to "collect" multiple protégés, as he did with Eric Ries, Derek Andersen, and me. The Collector has intense, bounded relationships with protégés, and once they conclude, both the Collector and protégé move on.

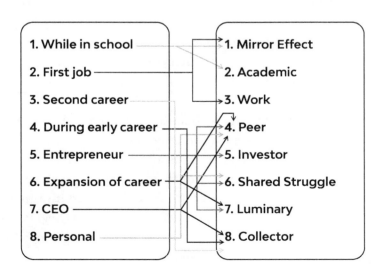

1. While in school   1. Mirror Effect

2. First job   2. Academic

3. Second career   3. Work

4. During early career   4. Peer

5. Entrepreneur   5. Investor

6. Expansion of career   6. Shared Struggle

7. CEO   7. Luminary

8. Personal   8. Collector

THE IMPORTANCE OF RIGHT TIMING

Meaningful relationships build on repetition. Sometimes that repetition is over a long period of time and other times it can be over a shorter, intense period. But in most cases, mentors and mentees will recognize it was "good timing" that they met.

In our research, we saw certain common 'seasons' to mentorship—common periods when mentorship appeared to be particularly impactful for many of the people we studied. These particular 'aligned' moments in the mentors' and mentees' lives seem to be more likely to result in a Super Mentoring relationship.

In many ways, these relationships were formed similar to how long-lasting friendships are built. In his book *The Like Switch*, former FBI agent Jack Schafer shares four critical components to developing a friendship: proximity, frequency, duration, and intensity. These components are often at the core of mentoring relationships that seem to form naturally.

Mentor Fallacy: Developing a relationship is primarily driven by fit or similarity.

Super Mentor Reality: The four key factors in developing long-term relationships are proximity, frequency, duration, and intensity. Similarities are often much less important than these aspects that create momentum behind the relationship.

When you're seeking help from mentors, you may meet someone who seems to be a perfect candidate for a mentor and yet you can't form a relationship. It may be one of those four elements is missing to form the relationship. It may not be an aligned time for both parties, which is why it's important to create many casual mentors for some to turn into Super Mentors.

But even short duration or frequency engagements can be transformative. It's a fallacy that time spent together is the best predictor of transformative opportunities.

Timing matters, both for you and any potential mentor. Sometimes a failed mentoring relationship is just a matter of wrong timing, and sometimes a Super Mentor happens to deliver the perfect opportunity at the perfect time.

It's also why modern mentoring isn't about putting all your eggs in a single basket.

While Steve's role as my Super Mentor remains one of the most transformative mentor experiences, our relationship has changed over time. Those six months were crucial to my growth and established a foundation for a long-term relationship, but I haven't needed that same level of support since. Most successful people will note multiple mentors and several Super Mentors during their journey. As I reflected on my own life, I've been fortunate to have a series of mentors, including Dan Chellman, Todd Glass, Steve Blank, and Scott Case.

Each of these mentors provided me with unique opportunities, and all of them came at key junctures and in key roles that I—the protégé—needed at that time. Dan was a Work Super Mentor during my life's first job or opportunity phase. Todd was a Luminary Super Mentor at the law firm I worked at; he was not my direct supervisor but was critical in helping me grow my network as a young lawyer during my early career phase. Steve was a Collector Super Mentor who aided me in transitioning into a second career in my late thirties, and Scott was a Peer Super Mentor in my entrepreneurial endeavors.

And as you examine the role mentors have and can play in your life, I've found this framework to be helpful, looking backward and forward.

Your lack of people and engagement with others - tried to go it alone.

12

THE MIRROR EFFECT

We've all heard the phrase "opposites attract." But can the same be said of mentoring relationships? Not so much.

"Meeting Maya Angelou on those pages was like meeting myself in full," Oprah Winfrey wrote in O *Magazine* in 2000 about her mentor. "For the first time, as a young black girl, my experience was validated."

As an ambitious black woman, Oprah was often forced to see a future for herself with few examples of others who looked like her. For many people, not having role models whose experiences they can relate to can be discouraging, and that discouragement can hold them back. For that reason, Maya Angelou played a critical role in giving Oprah a vision of her potential. But perhaps just as important was that Maya saw elements of herself in Oprah.

Our analysis of 142 high-profile mentor-mentee pairs identified nine best-exemplified scenarios where the mentor saw themselves in their eventual mentees, including Oprah Winfrey and Maya Angelou. Other examples included technology entrepreneurs Steve Jobs and Mark Zuckerberg, entertainers Ingmar Bergman and Woody Allen, and directors Stephen Spielberg and J.J. Abrams.

However, the actual similarity is less important than the initial perception of similarities. Super Mentor relationships possess stunning levels of mirroring, where a Super Mentor and their protégé display strong similarities across observable characteristics like upbringing, career path, gender, race, socioeconomic background, and schooling. There were, of course, outliers, but "seeing a younger version of themselves in the mirror" was a typical pattern.

Why?

In a mentoring relationship, the first stages are often characterized by minimal information—an email, a brief interaction in person, or a third-party introduction. Not unlike romantic relationships, there's often a sense of "love at first sight." The same holds in relationships where mentors and mentees report a "connection at first meeting," a sense they clicked right away.

A research group led by R. Matthew Montoya labeled that experience as "perceived similarity" and have found that when we first read about a stranger—without having met them—and find we have a great deal in common with them, it substantially increases our perceptions of them. Even dating site OkCupid has found the importance of emphasizing similarities of interests, such as television preferences, in initial matches. When we see a stranger who has similarities to us, we simply like them more. That is partly because we don't have anything else to base our perceptions on when we haven't gotten to know someone yet. Still, even more than that, those perceived feelings of similarity are driven by deeper psychological feelings.

Researchers Adam Hampton, Amanda Fisher Boyd, and Susan Sprecher had strangers fill out a questionnaire expressing their likes and interests. Then, they shared others' blind answers about their likes and interests and allowed them to choose a partner based purely on those answers. The team found that people were more likely to select partners to work with based on similarities and steer clear of those they perceived as having different interests and likes.

They theorized that when looking to engage with a stranger, we seek those we perceive to be similar, as they validate our interests, a feeling of greater certainty of being liked, an expectation of more fun and enjoyable experience, and a belief that those like us can offer us the greatest opportunities for growth and self-expansion.

Similarities play a big role in Adam and his team-building products. But they take it one step farther than just driving connections through shared majors. "Course of study, hobbies, and interests are all great things to connect over. I've gotten many meetings by sharing my love of reality television. But the greatest conversations happen when we share the same *passions,* like building things or storytelling or complex problem-solving. The mentor will do the same if I can bring how I use that passion in my day-to-day life. I learn far more and build a stronger connection that way."

Specifically, in the case of mentoring relationships, it's much less important that you have a lot in common but that you and they *think* you have a lot in common. While someone different from us may offer us more opportunities to expand our knowledge or experiences, studies, such as Hampton's, find that we perceive we would gain more from those similar to us.

I recently received an email from a stranger who referenced a specific start-up I'd worked on in the past and shared, "Looks like we are both interested in marketplaces, and I'd love to learn any insights you learned along the way."

While I had little about the person other than a short message, it's logical to assume I would decide that we must have something in common. And while the reality could be far from that, he masterfully captured the *opportunity* to develop a relationship by highlighting our shared similarities at the outset.

To be clear, I'm not suggesting we should only seek mentors who are similar to us—in fact, quite the opposite, as people with unique and different experiences and backgrounds often yield the most fruitful opportunities. But as we initially build a relationship with prospective mentors, strong evidence supports perceived similarities as being critical to unlocking the first stages of the relationship.

The question now arises. How can you tilt the mirror just right to drive a connection through perceived similarities?

***

Oprah was a victim of sexual abuse at the hands of her relatives from the early age of nine years old. Trauma early in life can lead to feelings of doubt, worthlessness, depression, and anxiety, yet experts have found that processing childhood trauma is often facilitated through developing a relationship with other victims.

Maya Angelou had a similarly challenging childhood. As she shares in *I Know Why the Caged Bird Sings,* Angelou, like Oprah, had a childhood marred by sexual assault. She was sexually abused by her mother's boyfriend, which trauma resulted in her loss of speech for several years. Following her grandmother's death, her guardian, Maya had to start her journey, a journey the world would look upon in wonderment.

One Meeting Away: Oprah Winfrey

Right Person. Maya Angelou

Right Ask. Should I share my traumas publicly?

Right Start. When they reconnected, their relationship formed as Oprah dug deeper into Angelou's process to share her childhood trauma. Oprah had achieved success, but reaching into the next levels of her connection came from Angelou's ability to guide her through Oprah's process of revealing her childhood sexual assault and trauma.

Right Time. The pair had connected years earlier, but during a chance encounter in Chicago their relationship was cemented and built.

When Oprah Winfrey first read Angelou's memoir in her twenties, her mind resonated with the words written there: "I was captivated from the very first page, when an awkward young girl in a lavender taffeta dress stands up in church in Arkansas and forgets the lines of a poem she's reciting: 'What are you looking at me for? I didn't come to stay... I just come to tell you, it's Easter Day.'" She wondered how a book could resonate so beautifully with moments from her life and believed her life as a young black woman was validated only by the words Angelou had written in the book. She felt an instant connection with the author, whom she hadn't yet met, but that admiration would shift to guidance after a series of brief encounters.

SEEING OURSELVES IN YOU

The Super Mentor you want, or will eventually need for what's next, is probably someone you don't know yet. That person may be several degrees outside of your circle and several years ahead of you.

Recognizing that you need to find a way to spark an initial connection to unfold the relationship, how can you identify and leverage your similarities?

To be frank, it's a powerful experience as a mentor to see ourselves in someone years younger than us. Part of the power of these relationships is that mentors hope to help mentees avoid missteps they may have made. Still, another part of it comes from mentors' ability to identify the opportunities they would have most benefited from.

Jessica Carson worked for me as a venture capital associate, helping our team identify and invest in promising companies. I saw her raw charisma, intellect, and ability to draw on her insights from studying neuroscience to create unique connections between the start-up founder's mind and psychological triggers. Those connection points led me to encourage the entrepreneurship center at Georgetown to bring her in as its first expert-in-residence focused on founder psychology.

On the one hand, I knew she'd be an exceptional resource because of what she'd done, but I was equally convinced this experience would accelerate her forward because of what my own experience being hired as a professor had done for me.

This is why Super Mentors are often able to offer guidance and opportunities to their mentees. They benefit from hindsight.

Traditionally, the fundamental idea behind mentorship is passing on wisdom and providing a support system for people who want to further themselves in education, career, or personal life. Typically, society associates wisdom and life experiences with age. Dr. Bill Thomas, an author, and eldercare specialist observes that, culturally, people tend to romanticize the notion that everyone gets smarter with age. As a result, most people seek mentorship from senior individuals. These relationships are formed less because of age or experience and more for relevant experiences that tie to the mentee's goals or ambitions.

"Seeking advice from those ahead of us has always been the tradition," Adam Saven told me. "And subsequently, as we gain more experience, we expect to serve as mentors for others." Saven also noted, however, that in his experience, the best mentorship outcomes occur when the mentor is three to five years older than the mentee. "It's often easier to see ourselves at the next ideal step than at the top of the stairs. We can model ourselves after those right before us, knowing that we're on our way toward our ideal."

Saven's team saw this clearly in the data. Using graduation year as a marker, the team looked at who mentees most frequently reached out to. The most common delta was five years, followed by four, and then three.

"This was interesting because using graduation year takes age completely out of the equation," Saven elaborated. "The national average age of a college student today is over twenty-six years old. Someone who graduated five years ahead of a mentee could theoretically be as young as twenty-five and as old as… well, unlimited. The experience matters, not the age."

Experience alone is rarely enough to create that deep connection; it must be the *right* experience or shared experience. To achieve desired goals and objectives, mentors must assimilate different approaches. Adam believes that for successful mentoring to occur, mentors must know their mentees' thought processes to understand their strengths, weaknesses, and actual needs. National Academies of Sciences propounds that discernment of another person's mental processes largely depends on the similarities between the people. For example, a mentor who shares a social background with a mentee is more likely to understand that mentee's thought process, perspectives and challenges.

As I found with Jessica Carson, her actions to highlight and develop our similarities allowed our relationship to develop to provide new opportunities.

***

Maya Angelou was a beloved Black author and entertainer. In that way, she was a natural fit for Oprah's mentor. Perhaps more importantly, however, Angelou and Oprah shared similar childhood trauma. Angelou told her friend, "I have the blessing of seeing our connection and the courage to admit what I see."

In the late 1970s, as a Baltimore reporter, Oprah got her chance in a brief, five-minute interview to meet Angelou. Years later, a chance encounter on a Chicago street sparked their Super Mentor relationship. Oprah had buried much of her shame of her childhood and saw how Angelou had reclaimed power over her story. In an interview from 2013, Oprah asked Angelou what she would say to a younger version of herself. Angelou's answer offered a glimpse into her guidance to her mentee when she replied, "I would encourage her to forgive. It's one of the greatest gifts you can give yourself, to forgive. Forgive everybody."

Forgiveness and self-healing connected Oprah with the world, as her vulnerabilities drove the intimacy with her fans and viewers. Angelou offered Oprah guidance and a picture of success that Oprah may not have seen on her own. Oprah credits their relationship with helping her reach the heights she has achieved. On one occasion, Oprah said, "She [Angelou] was there for me always, guiding me through some of the most important years of my life... The world knows her as a poet but at the heart of her, she was a teacher. 'When you learn, teach. When you get, give' is one of my best lessons from her."

And perhaps the most powerful wisdom was a simple three words from Angelou: "You are enough!"

***

Identity is a major component of mentorship. Identity also offers a roadmap and hope for the ambitious mentee when framed as a younger version of a mentor. For a Super Mentor, it's usually important to create a balanced relationship of motivation and support.

"Mentoring teenagers can be challenging," wrote YouthBuild mentor named Shania. "However, when you put yourself in their shoes and spend time with them without overstepping boundaries, mentoring outcomes are likely to be positive."

The YouthBuild organization finds that great mentors strive to be friends, not a parent or authority figures, to their protégés. In other words, the lesser the differences—social, experience, age— between the mentor and mentee, the better the understanding of mentee strength and needs and, hence, better mentoring outcomes. In some senses, these relationships lean on the similarities without the baggage of a long history that you'd find in a family or long-term friendship context.

Many mentors try to bridge mentor-mentee differences created by age by seeing the mentee as this young version of them and treating them as they'd like to have been treated. Despite the age difference, they avoid hierarchical relationships. In the pamphlet "The Wisdom of Age: A Handbook for Mentors," the authors observe that most mentors take this persona and approach. This allows the mentor to directly relate to the mentee's challenges and develop mentoring strategies that resonate with the mentee.

As we seek mentorship, it's important to recognize the importance of that identity in the connection and the opportunities that can result. The concept of mentorship can mean many things to different people. You would probably get ten distinct answers if you asked ten different business professionals what mentorship means to them. Mentors come in varying personas. While some see their protégés as younger versions of themselves, others see them as buddies in the same struggle, colleagues, investors, or customers.

***

Bob Dylan didn't meet his mentor until years after he'd been inspired to follow in his path. Bob Dylan was a great fan of Woody Guthrie and aspired to achieve success in his early life. The two later met, and Woody Guthrie realized he and Dylan had many similarities, like Maya Angelou and Oprah.

Dylan's love for poetry drew him to music at a young age. Woody Guthrie had the most significant influence among the musicians who inspired him. In 1961, Dylan dropped out of high school and moved to New York not only to pursue his dream of becoming a musician but also to meet his idol Woody Guthrie someday. Dylan read Guthrie's autobiography *Bound for Glory* and became obsessed with Guthrie's mythical portrayal of himself. Ellen Baker, Dylan's friend, told Rolling Stone, "He [Dylan] so absolutely became Woody Guthrie in the months I knew him well... 'We're going to go see Woody in New York,' he used to tell me all the time. He was painfully sincere in his feelings. He had an obsession about Woody Guthrie and going to see him." By the time Dylan met Guthrie, Guthrie had become seriously ill. Dylan frequently visited the legend and played his songs, and on one occasion, Guthrie gave him a card that read, "I ain't dead yet."

Guthrie passed away in 1967, marking an untimely end of Guthrie's brief relationship with a young Dylan.

Dylan wrote about his relationship with Guthrie in his memoir *Chronicles: Volume One*, "His [Guthrie's] repertoire was beyond category. Songs made my head spin, and made me want to gasp. For me, it was an epiphany. It was like I had been in the dark and someone had turned on the main switch of a lightning conductor."

One piece of advice from Guthrie that Dylan vowed to remember for the rest of his life was not to worry about writing songs but to focus on singing. Dylan attributed his musical success to his resemblance with Guthrie.

One Meeting Away: Bob Dylan

Right Person. Woody Guthrie

Right Ask. Am I a songwriter or a musician?

Right Start. Dylan had been learning from Guthrie long before the pair met. Those encounters helped Dylan cement his trajectory, mirroring his hero's path.

Right Time in many ways. Dylan was very early in his career and in need of a musical mentor to help him navigate his early trajectory. Even though their time was brief before Guthrie's death, his influence changed Dylan's musical trajectory.

This story encapsulates the Mirror Effect. Dylan fell in love with Guthrie's work at a young age and chose to follow in his footsteps. He later met his mentor, who immediately took him under his wing. Guthrie understood Dylan's strengths and weaknesses and advised him to focus his energies on singing instead of writing songs. Although their relationship was brief, their friendship-based mentorship changed the lives of both men.

***

This "younger version" Super Mentor persona taps into our identity—the power of familiarity without the burden of history—and involves a relationship that typically evolves from someone following in the footsteps of another person. When the mentor takes the mentee under their wing, they perceive the mentee as a younger version of themselves.

Most mentors assume this persona because of the traditional understanding of mentorship and the tendency of older people to be more willing to offer mentorship. The psychology behind this persona revolves around increasing mentor-mentee similarity for better outcomes. As an active mentee, recognize that while surrounding yourself with people of varied backgrounds and experiences is the most powerful way to develop new knowledge and opportunities, finding ways to create that initial perception of similarities is critical to unlock and expand the relationship into Super Mentorship.

13

IT'S ALL ACADEMIC

It's perhaps not a surprise that academic mentors were the largest category of Super Mentor relationships in our analysis of these high-profile mentor relationships, with more than 20 percent of Super Mentoring relationships developed with a professor or teacher.

Most of us first find ourselves on our own as adults in college with a very present need for guidance, coaching, and opportunities. The academic setting has served as the foundation for many mentoring relationships. And in this analysis of our 142 high-profile mentor-mentee pairs, we identified twenty-nine that originated from academic relationships including Sheryl Sandberg and Larry Summers, Warren Buffett and his mentor Benjamin Graham, Bill Hewlett, and David Packard and their mentor Professor Frederick Terman, and even astronaut Dr. Sally Ride and her professor-turned mentor Dr. Arthur Walker Jr.

In many ways, colleges and universities were built on a mentor-like relationship between students and their professors and instructors. The apprentice-like relationship between a professor and her students was the hallmark of academia. But as higher education has become more common, those bonds have become less common.

Today, less than half of college graduates say they had a mentor in college. In its study of more than 5,100 US college graduates, Strada-Gallup found that only 25 percent of respondents "strongly agree" and 18 percent "agree" that they had a mentor who encouraged them to pursue their goals and dreams.

Mentor Fallacy: Academic mentors are professors or teachers.

Super Mentor Reality: While about two-thirds of mentors in college are professors, mentors can be staff members, alums, or peer mentors.

Of those who did have a mentor, professors accounted for nearly two-thirds of mentors for college students (64 percent). These relationships often stay active well beyond graduation, with 71 percent of these graduates having spoken to their college mentor in the past year. Sadly, these numbers are worse for students of color. While 72 percent of white students cited a professor as a mentor in college, only 47 percent of racially underrepresented students pointed to a professor. Similarly, first-generation students are less likely than students with a college-educated parent to have had a professor as a mentor.

This social capital gap that emerges in college is a problem that Saven sees in their mentoring data. "The research on mentoring in college doesn't paint a very pretty picture," he told me. "Almost three out of four first-year students say they plan on networking and building relationships, but only one out four graduating students completed that goal. And for students of color and first-generation students, the numbers of those participating in social-capital-building activities are even lower."

This lack of mentorship represents a great missed opportunity. As academic priorities become higher, it's even more important for ambitious college and graduate students to develop and cultivate these relationships.

***

The important relationship between student and teacher is not new. Two pairs of teacher-student mentors formed the foundations of philosophy: Socrates and his mentee Plato and Plato and his mentee Aristotle.

While the surviving evidence of their relationships is not complete, it's clear that both relationships went far beyond the modern student-teacher model. Aristotle was born in 384 BC in Stagira, Chalkidice in Northern Greece, and lost his father at a young age. He was invited to join Plato's Academy in Athens at seventeen or eighteen. Under Plato's tutelage, Aristotle blossomed as a student of logic and philosophy, building on his ideas of the real world and what differentiated it from fantastical ideas. Aristotle remained in Plato's Academy for two decades. He ultimately became one of the most well-known philosophers of all time, and Plato's influence is evident in his work.

Plato primarily studied with and learned from Socrates but pushed beyond his mentor's ideas to form his own. He passed these ideas on to a young Aristotle at The Academy. Aristotle questioned aspects of his mentor's ideas about real life or life as we know it on Earth. Eventually, he left Plato to strike out on his own and spend the latter half of his life pushing back on some of Plato's insights.

Plato's imprint remained deep, bringing Aristotle back to Athens to found the Lyceum, his school. And following Alexander the Great's conquest of Athens, he became a mentor to the young emperor, Alexander.

The world of academia, however, has drastically changed since ancient Greece.

While professors represent a critical interface for the students, the average professor only spends 15 percent of their week doing activities with students, Colleen Flaherty writes in Inside Higher Ed. Nearly all of that time spent with students is actually in group settings *inside* the classroom teaching (14 out of the 15 percent). In comparison, less than 1 percent of a professor's time is spent on meetings, coaching, mentoring, and student-centric activities.

Is this a bad thing?

Not necessarily. As I mentioned earlier in this book, we saw throughout our study of Super Mentoring relationships that more time does not necessarily equate to more significant impact or outcomes.

For some of my Super Mentoring relationships with students—Rahul Rana and Anabelle—my one-on-one time with each was relatively small. Both Rahul and Anabelle individually spent less than an hour in one-on-one engagements with me. *How* we spent our time mattered. The same held for the academic Super Mentors of Sheryl Sandberg while at Harvard, entrepreneur Michael Dell as a student at the University of Texas, and Warren Buffett as a Columbia University graduate student.

Perhaps nowhere is the Protégé Effect on display than in the case of academic mentors.

***

Warren Buffett sought out his Super Mentor, Benjamin Graham.

He described his strategy to create a relationship with Graham as, "I made a pest of myself."

The then nineteen-year-old future investing whiz read Graham's book *The Intelligent Investor*, and it immediately made sense to him. He even described it as, "By far the best book about investing ever written."

But he nearly missed the opportunity to meet his future mentor. After Harvard rejected his graduate school admission, Buffett considered continuing his studies in Nebraska when he stumbled on a review of Graham's graduate seminar. Realizing Graham was teaching a class at Columbia, Buffett sent a hasty letter to Columbia, asking if they'd permit him to enroll despite missing the deadlines.

"They said yes, and that was the reason I ended up at Columbia," Buffett shared with Louisa Serene Schneider.

Apart from developing the idea of value investment, Graham is known for creative analysis and the usage of financial analysis in stock investments. Having lost a major portion of the money he'd earned in the stock market in the market crash of 1929 and the Great Depression, Graham learned a hard lesson on the importance of analyzing market securities. And he shared these real-world insights with students every week.

In the seminar, Buffett was enthralled as Graham shared real-world examples and experiences to teach. He described it as "like learning baseball from a fellow batting .400."

Buffett shared with his alma mater how he was taken by Graham's approach in and out of the classroom: "I wanted to go to work for him and he gave me an A+ in the course, but he turned me down on going to work. But I kept trying to 'propose' myself to him—and one way was to send him ideas about stocks. He'd eventually give me one or two little orders... but at least he was paying attention. He sent me at least two job opportunities. Apparently, he was talking me up to other people even though he didn't have any need."

Nearly five years after Graham met Buffett in his seminar, he invited Buffett to discuss an opportunity together "the next time Buffett happened to find himself in New York." As Buffett recounted, "I made sure to find myself in New York about twenty-four hours later."

Graham asked Buffett to work for him, providing Buffett with the opportunity to gather the capital he required to create Buffett Associates Ltd. in 1956. Working for Graham served as a foundation for Buffett's future as an investor. Graham was the chairman of a small insurance company named GEICO, and Buffett eventually joined him on the board before acquiring the entire company through his corporation, Berkshire Hathaway.

Buffett wrote of Graham's impact on his life in a tribute to Graham in *Financial Analysts Journal*

In 1976, "I knew Ben as my teacher, my employer, and my friend. In each relationship—just as with all his students, employees, and friends—there was an absolutely open-ended, no-scores-kept generosity of ideas, time, and spirit."

When Buffett began teaching, he modeled his teaching style on Graham's in later years.

Right Person. Benjamin Graham, author of the Intelligent Investor.

Right Ask. Is it okay if I send you some ideas for stocks to invest in?

Right Time. After being a consistent "pest" for five years, Graham provided a much bigger opportunity by introducing Buffett to a small insurance company named GEICO that would become one of Buffett's first and largest investment successes.

Right Time. Buffett first met Graham in his graduate school class and asked to work for Graham, who turned him down.

Buffett's pest-like approach to his academic mentor may seem extreme, but it's more common in many ways than people might imagine. First, Buffett identified a key trait in many academic Super Mentors: Graham was more than just a professor; he was a *practitioner* professor. In other words, he enjoyed teaching and mentoring others but had a network well beyond the academic halls. Second, Buffett continued his relationship beyond the classroom and engaged with his future boss and partner for over five years. Third, Buffett drove the relationship. Buffett recognized the value of his then-professor and invested in the relationship.

***

Graham's work as an author and practitioner attracted Buffett. Still, beyond his work in finance and investments, Graham's role as a teacher demonstrated a clear interest in impacting students. To be candid, the pay of most academics—particularly practitioner academics—isn't why they do it.

A role in the classroom offers an interesting opportunity to build a collection of impressive former students, something many professors relish.

Boston University professor Gerald Powers was called "one of the most formidable men on the PR scene" in no small part because of the network of students he's taught and mentored in his near-thirty-year career. *PR Week* wrote, "He's taught three thousand students throughout his career and has helped spawn such PR greats as Ray Kotcher, president of Ketchum in New York, Roger Bridgeman, founder of Bridgeman Communications in Boston, and Andy Lavin, founder of A. Lavin Communications in New York."

Powers shared, "'I have no friends in the classroom and none in the grade book, but I have a lot of friends outside. I'm fiercely loyal to my students but they are to me, too, which is very gratifying."

Beyond the guidance and coaching, that network of former students often makes professors so valuable as mentors.

One such mentor who groomed the first American woman in space—astronaut Sally Ride—was her Stanford professor Arthur Walker.

Ride said of their relationship, "He instilled confidence and made me believe I could accomplish what I set out to accomplish."

Walker was born in 1936 and grew up in a time of great racial unrest. Many tried to stand in his way. He excelled in science as a young boy, but his parents were justifiably concerned by the challenges of becoming a black scientist in 1950s America.

His mother made sure that the school system did not stifle her son. Walker's wife, Victoria Walker, said of her mother-in-law, "She paid a visit to the school and told them in no uncertain terms that her son would study whatever he wishes."

After excelling in school, he began his career in science as a member of the US Air Force. He later earned the opportunity to work at the Space Physics Laboratory of the Aerospace Corporation as one of the only men of color in the lab. From there, Walker spent twenty-seven years as a professor of Applied Physics at Stanford University. And his first graduate student would become a major part of his legacy.

Ride attended Stanford University in the late 1970s, where she earned a master's degree and PhD in Physics. During this time, she came under the mentorship of Walker. He supervised her research and was critical in helping her navigate the relationships she'd eventually need within NASA. He doubted that the space program would welcome a woman, but Walker, who'd battled obstacles of his own, insisted she pursue it.

Ride became a pioneer, taking three space flight missions with NASA—STS-7, STS-2, and STS-3—and helping in the mechanical evolution and development of the NASA space shuttle's Canadarm robot arm.

One Meeting Away: Sally Ride

Right Person. Stanford professor Arthur Walker worked at the Space Physics Laboratory of the Aerospace Corporation as one of the only men of color in the lab.

Right Ask. How do I become an astronaut?

Right Start. Ride recognized it took more than intellect to succeed in the space program, so she learned from Walker the soft skills necessary to thrive at NASA.

Right Time. Walker had experienced being a pioneer as a man of color in the space industry. He guided Ride during her PhD and navigated the key relationships that would lead her to command three space flights of NASA's space shuttle.

Walker passed away in 2001 after a battle with cancer. His impact reached far beyond Ride to include Condoleezza Rice, the sixty-sixth United States Secretary of State, who shared her own experiences with Walker in the *New York Times* as a fellow black faculty member at Stanford University writing:

"He was an inspiration for generations of young physicists and worked tirelessly to increase the number of underrepresented minorities undertaking graduate work in the sciences. His most lasting contribution to academic life at Stanford was his mentoring of graduate students, thirteen in total, a majority of them from sectors of society underrepresented in science, namely women and African Americans."

The impact of our professors can be genuinely transformative, as this period of our lives is one of the most wide-open we have ever experienced. The number of choices before us is vast and daunting. But recognizing who can transform you and how to develop that relationship is far more complex than sitting in the back of a classroom and doing well on a test or paper.

14

WORK ALLIANCE

When I was in high school, I told the student newspaper that one day I would be a CEO of a Fortune 500 company.

I truly felt like this was my destiny.

A few years later, however, I found myself unsteady and lost in my first job, which was supposed to be the first step of a career path that I'd mapped out in my head. I took the job at Morgan Stanley because that's what my peers were doing, and my career counselor had assured me this was the right step on the road to get me where I was supposed to be. Get a prestigious job with a fancy title, get a graduate degree, go into upper management at another prestigious place, and then get promoted until I was a CEO decades from now.

But this picture in my head didn't match my reality. The job, the boss, the role—none of them were the right fit for me. That ambitious, self-assured high school kid found himself in an unfamiliar place and mindset. The job made me anxious, depressed, and unsteady. My boss gave us daily tasks—dials per day—and he commented on a whiteboard outside the bullpen on each of us when he tallied up the day's dials.

I decided to tell my boss I was leaving after just seven months.

"You're unremarkable. Look around," he said without lifting his fingers from the keyboard. "The people in charge of places and companies like this didn't go to no-name schools. They have MBAs and

PhDs from the best schools on the planet, and they worked in places that will never hire you now. Your credibility is shot in this industry."

I sat in stunned silence, barely hearing what else my boss was saying to me. This wasn't at all how I'd imagined this conversation going.

He didn't wait for me to respond. "Honestly, it's a good thing you quit because if you hadn't, I would fire you on Monday anyway. Leave your badge and get out."

My hands were shaking as I slowly removed the badge from my pocket and placed it on his desk. I never made eye contact as I left, and I never saw him again.

This conversation would haunt me.

***

So much of our value is wrapped up in our work. We spend approximately fifty years working, and we often introduce ourselves by where we work or what we do.

Our analysis of 142 high-profile mentor-mentee pairs identified dozens of relationships that touched on shared work experiences, categorizing sixteen as the primary way the relationships began. Some were informal mentoring relationships between Warner Avis (CEO of Avis Rental Cars) and Shark Tank's Robert Herjavec or comedic actresses Carol Burnett and Vicki Lawrence on the set. Some were more structured mentorship on the job, such as between fashion icons Christian Dior and Yves St. Laurent or Yahoo! CEO Marissa Mayer and Google founders Larry Page and Sergey Brin, and CEO Eric Schmidt. Work is hard, and navigating cultures, hierarchies, and our trajectories are particularly complicated.

Workplace mentorship exists to help newer employees develop skills and gain knowledge in their areas of expertise. The following statistics show that the benefits of mentoring at the workplace can impact mentees, mentors, and the organization itself.

According to a Gallup study of mentees and mentors who engage in constructive mentorship programs, 90 percent report positive relationships with colleagues, 89 percent report feeling valued, and 89 percent assert that mentorship allows them to contribute to the company's success. A similar report by Deloitte propounds that while training can increase output by 24 percent, mentorship can increase organizational productivity by over 88 percent. Wonder, a firm specializing in research, indicates that workplace mentorship can increase job retention of mentees and mentors by 72 percent and 69 percent, respectively. About 77 percent of organizations with active mentoring programs record a reduction in employee turnover.

It's not a shock that the Work Mentor persona is one of the most common Super Mentor personas. We spend a lot of time with our colleagues, which opens the door for mutually beneficial relationships among the mentee, mentor, and organization.

Starting any new job often requires learning from experienced coworkers. And even more so early in our work career, we're forced to learn how to work after more abstract experiences in college or graduate school.

In some professions, mentorship is built into career progression. For example, recently qualified doctors and lawyers go through structured or unstructured apprenticeship programs to master their art, forcing them to keep learning throughout their earlier career stages. But beyond the basic skills of doing the job, a set of skills, traits, and decisions enable high-potential employees to accelerate into management, into in-demand roles, or to other opportunities.

As the name suggests, work mentorship is a mentorship relationship that develops through work, usually when someone more senior at a company mentors a younger, high-achieving person. We often see top management executive officers or chief executive officers taking fast-rising managers under their wings. The primary objective of mentors who take this persona is to create an alliance between the mentee and the business. This alliance is based on probity, and its fundamental goal is to positively impact the organization while benefiting the mentee.

In this shared alliance companies minimize the risk of losing high-potential employees who feel stuck or stifled by empowering those high-potential employees to tackle increasingly complex and important work for their organizations.

This setting is ripe for Super Mentorship, but why is this still so rare for most employees and organizations?

***

"I know it's an accounting job," I shared with Dan Chellman, the man who'd become my boss and one of the Super Mentors in my life, "but I'm not an accounting major and..."

Dan stopped me. "I can teach you accounting, but I can't teach you the other things *you* have."

We spent the rest of the interview talking about everything from the student organizations I'd been involved in and my summer jobs in high school to, most shockingly to me, what I eventually wanted to do *after* this job.

It was a wildly different conversation than any I'd had with my last boss and in my last role. It was reassuring, and that was just what I needed.

Chellman wasn't an accountant either—at least, he didn't major in accounting in college or ever earn his Certified Public Accountant's license—yet, he was the Chief Accounting Officer for a fast-growing public biotechnology company that would be bought by Roche Diagnostics Corporation for $3.2 billion just four years after I'd left.

Dan was exactly what I needed after stumbling in my first job after college. He was a numbers guy, and as a numbers guy, he knew Ventana Medical Systems didn't have a big budget to hire people for the finance and accounting function. He needed to find people with ambition and teach them the skills on the job.

But he also realized how powerful building trust was in creating the relationship. LinkedIn founder Reid Hoffman writes in his book

The Alliance: Managing Talent in the Networked Age, "Psychologist Arthur Aron of SUNY Stony Brook discovered that asking participants in an experiment to share their deepest feelings and beliefs for a single hour could generate the same sense of trust and intimacy that typically takes weeks, months, or years to form."

Dan recognized that successful Super Mentors build alliances with their work mentees, even if the truth isn't always perfectly aligned with the company's goals.

***

Reid Hoffman was well aware that employees and employers are sometimes at odds. That fact is a big reason why formal mentorship programs often fail inside organizations. Mike, my boss at Morgan Stanley, wasn't particularly interested in my long-term objectives. I filled a role to him, and my job was to do the tasks he needed done. My job was to call prospective clients... every day. He failed to realize that the task wasn't connected to my goals, so I struggled to do it.

Why should I be dialing one hundred numbers a day, hoping to get one decent conversation, getting yelled and cursed at, and being rejected constantly? I'd ask myself at the end of nearly every day.

I now recognized that the task was never connected to my long-term goals. What did making one hundred brutal calls per day teach me? How to get better at selling would be critical if I hoped to become an executive one day. But Mike wasn't concerned with how I was growing; he was interested in whether I was effective in the task, and clearly, the answer to that was no... or at least not yet.

Dan Chellman was different. He knew my goals were not to become a Chief Accounting Officer, but he was central in helping me recognize the importance of the skills I'd learn under his watch. He even went on to write my letter of recommendation for law school and kept me on as a part-time analyst for the first two years of my graduate studies.

As a result of his coaching and mentorship, my contributions were far beyond those of staff accountants. I led multiple software system integrations, presented to the board of directors on multiple occasions, and took the lead on drafting our public filings with the Securities and Exchange Commission. I worked much harder on work that wasn't necessarily any more glamorous than dialing one hundred numbers a day.

Harvard professor Teresa Amabile is a coauthor of *The Progress Principle*. She highlights the most critical aspect of work motivation—progress. She writes, "Of all the things that can boost inner work life, the most important is making progress in meaningful work."

And for work mentors, this excerpt contains an important insight into their role in unlocking employees' potential—helping them see progress toward their aims and goals. Amabile continues, "If you are a manager, the progress principle holds clear implications for where to focus your efforts. It suggests that you have more influence than you may realize over employees' well-being, motivation, and creative output. Knowing what serves to catalyze and nourish progress—and what does the opposite—turns out to be the key to effectively managing people and their work."

Hoffman found the same challenges when hiring and managing the necessary influx of ambitious talent at fast-growing LinkedIn. They could attract incredible people, but they quickly found their progress plateauing.

Even in a start-up environment, the relationship between the employer and his employees felt disconnected. Reid realized that his employees didn't necessarily want to be progressing merely within the company they were currently at; they wanted to progress toward their individual goals and objectives beyond their current employer. Hoffman writes in the *Alliance*, "As much as companies might yearn for a stable environment and employees might yearn for lifetime employment, the world has changed. But we also can't keep going the way we've been going. Trust in the business world (as measured by the proportion of employees who say they have a high level of trust in management and the organization they work for) is near an all-time low. A business without loyalty is a business without long-term thinking. A business without long-term thinking is a business that's unable to invest in the future. And a business that isn't investing in tomorrow's opportunities and technologies—well, that's a company already dying."

LinkedIn began to understand how to change that relationship—to be transparent and open that a disconnect existed between employees and their employers. Employees had to trust the company to share their objectives without fear of being fired or ostracized for planning to leave someday; simultaneously, managers had to feel comfortable investing in employees who might leave. The company began a new approach called the "Tour of Duty," which were multi-year "tours" that created a shared commitment to projects or activities that would benefit both the company and the employee. Employees were invested in projects and mentorship that would require a two-year or more "tour" to complete. The employer knew that investing in the employee would make them more valuable and recognized that they might leave afterward. This bold idea made some LinkedIn insiders extremely nervous.

"What do the results of a successful tour of duty look like for a company?" asked Hoffman in his book. "A successful mission objective delivers results for the company for either quantitative or qualitative goals, such as launching a new product line and generating a certain dollar amount in first-year revenues, or achieving thought leadership in a specific market category, as measured by the writings of industry analysts. At LinkedIn, for example, managers ask, 'How will the company be transformed by this employee?'"

Companies' formal mentorship programs often fail because employees are unwilling to share their individual, longer-term goals. There's a fear of retribution for having any views of ourselves beyond the company. I spoke to a senior executive about her younger employees, who shared, "I give them everything they ask for, yet they still leave."

In many ways, that's the hallmark of a successful Work Super Mentor. They see mentorship as an alliance.

And my relationship with Dan Chellman reflected the same approach. We trusted each other, and that allowed us to achieve together.

Super Mentors recognize that if they provide mentees everything they need, the mentees *will* leave, but in many senses, they (the mentors) will have driven great value from the mentees during their employment.

***

Larry Ellison and Marc Benioff's relationship is probably one of the best modern mentorship stories brewed at the workplace. At just twenty-six years old, Benioff, now CEO of Salesforce, was a thriving executive star at Oracle under CEO Larry Ellison's wing and soon became Oracle's youngest VP—thanks to his close relationship with Ellison. Benioff was one of Ellison's closest friends and most trusted lieutenant during his thirteen years at Oracle. Carlye Adler writes in *Fortune*, "They sailed to the Mediterranean on Ellison's yacht, visited Japan during cherry blossom season, spent Thanksgiving together, and even double-dated." Today, Benioff is one of the leading CEOs globally, heading one of the most prestigious tech companies worldwide. His net worth is estimated at $3.6 billion, making him among the richest people in the world.

Ellison's professional life had a rocky start. After high school, he enrolled at the University of Illinois, Champaign, where he was named science student of the year. His aunt/adopted mother died during his second year, prompting Ellison to drop out of college. The following fall, he enrolled at the University of Chicago but dropped out after only one semester and began to hop from one job to another until he settled at Amdahl Corporation. In 1977, Ellison and two of his Amdahl colleagues founded Software Development Labs and soon had a contract to build a database management system—which they called Oracle—for the CIA. The company had fewer than ten employees and revenue of less than one million dollars per year, but in 1981, IBM signed on to use Oracle, and the company's sales doubled every year for the next seven years. Ellison soon renamed the company after its best-selling product. For the past few decades, Oracle has multiplied to become one of the leading companies in Silicon Valley, with Larry Ellison's net worth valued at over eighty-eight billion dollars.

Marc Benioff had a different start. In 1982, Marc graduated from high school and attended the University of Southern California. He earned his Bachelor of Science in Business Administration in 1986. Before college, Marc was already a successful entrepreneur at age sixteen. The videogame company Epyx had published his Crypt of the Undead, Escape from Vulcan's Isle, the Nightmare, and King Arthur's Heir. Marc used the fifteen-hundred-dollar-a-month royalty to help him pay his way through college. At twenty-three, Marc joined Oracle, a firm that shaped his entrepreneurial journey.

Benioff left a strong impression immediately, winning Oracle's Rookie of the Year award in his first year. Three years later, Benioff became Oracle's youngest VP at twenty-six. He was already a star executive, making over three hundred thousand dollars a year by then.

Many inside and outside of Oracle saw similarities between the pair with their sales-first mentalities, charisma, deep passion for technology, and a willingness to be on a stage. As former Oracle president Ray Lane told *Fortune* reporter Daniel Roth, "Marc would get people believing in his vision and supporting whatever project he wanted to do... Marc's one of Larry's favorite children." The two were so close that rumors began to circulate about their relationship. "It's weird... People said I was related to Larry Ellison... that I was his nephew, or that Larry was my babysitter, or he mowed my parents' lawn," Benioff told *Fortune*. NetSuite's Zach Nelson said, "We heard that [Benioff] washed Larry's car as a child."

When Benioff first started building Salesforce in 1999, he was still working at Oracle. He says Ellison always supported his outside endeavor, permitting him to split work at Salesforce in the morning and Oracle in the afternoons. Ellison even let Benioff take a six-month sabbatical before starting Salesforce. Then, after ninety days of running Salesforce, Ellison suggested Benioff take another leave of absence from Oracle, offering to have him back if Salesforce didn't work out.

"He was my mentor for more than a decade as well as a close friend," Benioff says about Ellison in his book, *Behind the Cloud*.

One Meeting Away: Marc Benioff, founder and chairman of Salesforce

Right Person. Larry Ellison, CEO of Oracle

Right Ask. I want to build software to support salespeople, and I don't think we can use Oracle to do it.

Right Start. Benioff split his time between his new venture, Salesforce, and Oracle but always made sure to overdeliver on his promises to Ellison.

Right Time. Ellison has been known as a collector and cultivator of talent, having produced countless executives and founders of companies. Many individuals would have worked on a side project like Salesforce outside of the eyes of their boss. Still, Ellison created a culture of trust and was supportive of the work, even serving as the first investor in the start-up and serving on its board in the early days.

Ellison even invested the first two million dollars in Salesforce, introduced Benioff to top venture firms to fund the new company, and joined its board of directors. He simply asked Benioff not to take more than three people from Oracle to Salesforce when he left the company.

Their relationship wasn't always positive, though. Oracle eventually launched a competitor service to Salesforce. The move prompted Benioff to force Ellison to resign from the board. Despite their fallout, Benioff still likes to call Ellison his mentor. In 2013, he even said, "Oracle has been there with us when we have had problems. I also just wanted to thank Larry as well. [Oracle is] always there for us whenever we need them. They are a true partner. They've always been a true partner."

In a TechCrunch Disrupt interview, Benioff admitted, "He's my mentor. He was our first investor and first board member. There is no one I've learned more from than Larry Ellison."

***

Modern workspaces have forced a new approach—an alliance—to create the foundation of trust necessary to drive better outcomes from high-potential employees. Employees *want* mentorship. It's one of the single most cited benefits that people desire from their employer. But the truth is that mentorship beyond advice on how to do our job better requires a different level of trust and a longer-focused perspective on the relationship. Employees are more likely to be productive and stay at the company if the employer promises them development and delivers it.

Finding a boss or mentor at your workplace requires tact as a mentee, as the alliance framework is still far from the norm. Even Reid Hoffman admitted, "Few of the managers we spoke with for this book worried that the tour of duty framework might give employees 'permission' to leave. But permission is not yours to give or withhold, and believing you have that power is simply a self-deception that leads to a dishonest relationship with your employees. Employees don't need your permission to switch companies, and if you try to assert that right, they'll simply make their move behind your back."

However, if you find a Super Mentor within your workplace, remember this person can bridge the gap between employers and employees by providing opportunities for all parties to benefit. By receiving the tools to be a high performer in your current situation, you become equipped for the next, bigger step while the company reaps the benefits of your hard work.

15

PEERS AND NEAR-PEERS

I am at a point where I should be giving guidance not receiving guidance.

I'm too old for a mentor.

These are perhaps the most common—and most fundamentally incorrect—responses I hear in response to the research of Super Mentors. Many people simply believe you age out of being mentored or you can't be both a mentor and be mentored.

The truth is mentors may be more important the more advanced you are in your career. The power of a mentor doesn't disappear when you hit twenty-four or thirty or forty-five or eighty.

Quite the opposite: Mentors become *more* critical to reach the next stage.

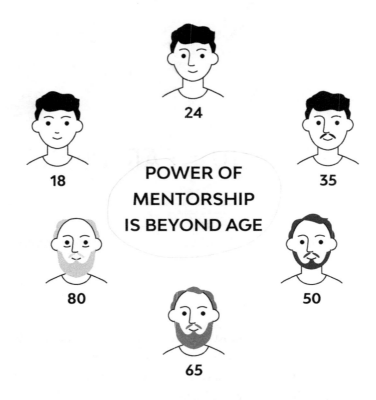

POWER OF MENTORSHIP IS BEYOND AGE

24

18

35

80

50

65

We regularly observed this type of mentorship in second career or expansion opportunities, and it's compelling as ambitious people plateau or find themselves at crossroads moments. Twenty-one of our high-profile mentor relationships were categorized as peer or near-peer mentorship, including billionaires Bill Gates and Warren Buffett, directors Stanley Kubrick and Steven Spielberg, celebrity entrepreneurs Jillian Michaels and Suze Orman, entertainers Bradley Cooper and Todd Phillips, and music icons Ray Charles and Quincy Jones all point to the transformative nature of these peer mentoring relationships.

Why?

As you'll see, the more we know, the harder it becomes for us to learn. And that can be detrimental to our growth.

Enter our peers.

Peers are not necessarily defined only by age. While being a similar age can designate you as a peer, sharing an equal number of years of experience in a particular activity, industry, or skill can also make you a peer. For example, if you are in your midcareer and take up computer programming, your peer may be someone who is also an entry-level software developer despite the potential for a many-decades age gap. Peers are usually approximately three to five years ahead or behind you in terms of age or experience with the challenge you're facing.

"Some of the more exciting mentorships we've seen in our work happen between two alumni of an institution," Adam Saven told me. "It's reflective of the simple fact that a career path is anything but linear. We're seeing older alumni reaching out to their younger peers as they start a new career journey."

The knowledge and growth that can come from our peers and near-peers changes how we learn and how rapidly we can accelerate our understanding. Learning directly from people we trust and respect offers a safe place to be curious. Everyone, from Oprah and Buffett to Cooper, has found their breakthroughs due to peer mentorship.

Once you move beyond the limiting belief you've outgrown the need for a mentor, peer mentorship becomes a remarkable superpower.

* * *

Bradley Cooper shattered many of the early perceptions of the handsome film star. Cooper has been nominated for various awards, including eight Academy Awards and a Tony Award, and has won two Grammy Awards and a BAFTA Award.

Following his breakout role in *The Hangover*, he became one of Hollywood's leading men, starring in blockbusters, including *American Sniper*, *Limitless*, *The Place Beyond the Pines*, *Silver Linings Playbook*, and both sequels of *The Hangover*.

But as Cooper shared with NPR's Rachel Martin, it wasn't until 2014 that he stopped and reflected on where he was headed: "And then I hit thirty-nine and I stopped and I said, 'What do I really want to do?'"

Cooper decided he needed to take more risks and make films that would push him.

He wanted more control. He wanted to direct.

And to do so, he enlisted help from his mentor. The man who helped catapult Cooper to leading man status was *The Hangover* director Todd Phillips. Phillips met Cooper at Cooper's audition for *Starsky & Hutch*. While Cooper didn't get that job, the pair realized they both were real film fanatics and attended the *There Will Be Blood* premiere together. When it came time to cast *The Hangover*, Phillips immediately thought of Cooper, but the studio had other ideas. Phillip's told Cooper, "Yeah, budgetary problems; they're going to need a name."

Cooper didn't have a name... yet. But Phillips eventually got his way and hired Cooper for the role that would change his life and cement the pair's relationship.

Having created and directed comedies like *Due Date*, *Road Trip*, and *Old School*, Phillips was already well-known in Hollywood. He was impressed by Cooper's curiosity about filmmaking during the filming and off set. Following the breakout success of *The Hangover* and Cooper's increased fame, the two remained friends, and in 2014, Cooper got the chance to learn from the best director he knew.

With Cooper looking to take on the edgier and more serious material, he needed a partner and a mentor if he wanted to convince studios he could make the transition from in front of the camera to behind it. The two formed a new production company in 2014.

"Todd is one of the smartest, coolest guys I know," Cooper told Justin Kroll of Variety. "He also happens to be one of the best filmmakers in the business and I am honored and excited to be his partner."

Cooper leveraged that relationship to dedicate the next four years to his most ambitious project—directing and starring in a new take on *A Star Is Born*, featuring Lady Gaga. The film tells the story of a broken musician who falls in love with an aspiring musician and helps make her a star, revealing his struggles. The film was ambitious, not only because it had already been made famous by the 1976 version starring Barbra Streisand and Kris Kristofferson but also as it was a high-profile directorial debut.

Some people suggested the project was too ambitious for a first film and encouraged him to consider directing a pilot or a commercial. Still, Cooper felt otherwise, in no small part because of his partnership with Phillips. Phillips had begun taking risks of his own by directing more serious fare. His 2020 film *The Joker* surpassed one billion dollars in box office receipts, and Cooper earned a producer credit on the film.

One Meeting Away: Bradley Cooper

Right Person. Todd Phillips, director of *Hangover* Trilogy, The *Joker*, *Due Date*, *Road Trip*, and *Old School*

Right Ask. Would you like to attend the *There Will Be Blood* premiere?

Right Ask. Phillips kept looking for an opportunity to work with Cooper. Once they began work on *The Hangover*, Phillips saw that Cooper was interested in much more than just acting and spent extensive time observing the craft of filmmaking from his future partner.

Right Time. The relationship between Cooper and Phillips started with a decision to see a film together. That connection would eventually lead Phillips to push to cast Cooper in his breakout role in *The Hangover*, where he got a firsthand look at Cooper's passion for filmmaking. The pair would eventually partner in a production studio, where Cooper would make his name as a director with *A Star Is Born*.

Cooper had a shining directorial debut.

A Star Is Born released in 2018 to commercial and critical acclaim and earned eight Academy Award nominations. Plus, first-time director Cooper was nominated for Best Director by the Golden Globes, Critics' Choice Awards, and Directors Guild of America. And while Cooper is undeniably talented in and of himself, he achieved such success with the help of his friend and mentor, Phillips.

***

Karla Lassonde is a cognitive psychologist at Minnesota State University and studies the link between humility and learning. She writes, "It is almost impossible to sit across from a kid searching the night sky for popular constellations and stars and not get into it."

Children don't expect themselves to know everything. They are incredibly open and humble with what they know or wish to know. Therefore, learning is relatively easy for them.

As we become adults, we become more self-conscious about what we are expected to know. It's prevalent for adults to overestimate their knowledge of everything from historical facts and trivia to home repairs and driving directions, getting progressively worse the older we get.

Professor of Philosophy and Religion James S. Spiegel found that to change our knowledge, we must be open-minded and aware that our beliefs can be incorrect. However, we are more prone to defend our current beliefs than admit they may be wrong as adults. We are less open to new information—what researchers Stanovich and West call "myside bias."

Essentially, the problem is that the more we know, the less we are willing to learn for many of us. In our view of mentorship, the more we know, the less we think we could benefit from mentorship.

Lassonde developed the Humility of Learning framework, which correlates to the style of peer or near-peer mentoring outlined in this chapter and what we observed in practice in these peer and near-peer relationships.

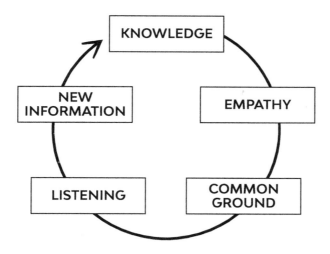

In short, the more we know and the more experience we have, the greater the need for a safe learning environment.

Imagine if Bradley Cooper dropped into a USC film class for pointers or called up Spielberg for some ideas. There's an internal pressure to have all the answers when we *believe* others are watching. Our peers and near-peers offer the learning environment we most need.

Two central theses of Lassonde's Humility of Learning framework are empathy and common ground—how we understand another's perspective and link our experienced-based general knowledge with others, respectively. Looking at these two elements helps clarify why Bradley Cooper was able to become an award-level director with his debut film.

Learning from Phillips allowed Cooper to admit his current knowledge may be insufficient for the task, thus allowing him to acquire new knowledge much more rapidly and effectively. That learning process was exponentially more straightforward because it was done with someone (a) who understands him and whom he understands and (b) who shares a common ground—their set of experience-based general knowledge—with one another. Yes, Cooper was talented, but directing a feature film at the very highest levels takes decades to master. By embracing peer mentoring with Phillips, he was able to accelerate his learning in dramatic ways.

It's not just that Phillips was a great director who could teach or coach Cooper. Peer mentoring sets up a learning environment that makes learning and growth so much more effective. These are the central tenets in peer or near-peer mentoring. And in many ways, when you are more experienced, peer or near-peer mentoring is perhaps the most effective way to learn.

***

Jillian Michaels became a household name with NBC's *The Biggest Loser.*

She is a personal trainer, businesswoman, author, and television personality who has worked with and trained several celebrities to help them meet their fitness goals. Achieving incredible professional success gave her plenty of opportunities, but she also struggles with where to focus next.

However, a true powerhouse such as Jillian did not see a need to be mentored in the traditional sense of the word. She had plenty of ideas that she wanted to implement, so much so that it created a fog around her that was hard for her to operate through.

Enter personal finance expert and Jillian's mentor Suze Orman. Orman invested deeply in owning her platform and digital presence, something Jillian had struggled to execute at best.

Orman reflected that a person like Jillian didn't need much mentorship. She just needed a "sounding board for her already great ideas." She needed guidance and firmness to help make tough choices to focus, cut where necessary, and invest in the future.

"Her problem was too many great ideas all going in different directions," she said. In other words, what Orman was actually providing was a safe place for Michaels to learn.

"Suze has already traversed so many of the paths I've yet to walk as a businesswoman, and hearing from her experience has saved me invaluable time, money, and resources," says Michaels.

Jillian has a tough exterior. At times, she was portrayed as meaner and more demanding than she was, which bothered her. Jillian needed to define herself and not let others define her to unlock her highest potential. The same applies to everyone else who might be afraid to be criticized or perceived differently. Once we have enough clarity on what we want, and whether our motives are apt to the standards we have set for ourselves, it does not matter how others interpret it. How we are perceived from the outside only takes us far enough.

One Meeting Away: Jillian Michaels

Right Person. Suze Orman

Right Ask. How do I transition to building my brand and platform?

Right Start. Michaels leaned on insights from Orman as she navigated COVID lock-downs, which changed how she delivered fitness education and coaching.

Right Time. Michaels was a well-known television star for her work in NBC's *The Biggest Loser* series. Still, as she looked to establish a platform and digital presence, she turned to Orman, who'd navigated a similar transition from a television financial advisor into a digital brand—something few had done as successfully as Orman.

Today, guided by Orman, Jillian Michaels has transitioned to owning her digital presence, embracing a new medium and way to connect with her fans. But beyond consultants and experts, often peers and near-peers can provide us a place to be open with what we don't know and wisdom to help us figure out what we do.

***

Who is the right peer or near-peer for mentorship? It's perhaps easier to decide when your peers are Todd Phillips, Bill Gates, or Suze Orman.

Researcher Jordan Grimmer studied the decision-making process of more than 500 people to understand how we select whose advice to trust. What he found was people tend to choose their sources of advice based on the seriousness of and investment required for the request. People prefer peer advice for simple requests, like where to have dinner or dating advice. On the other hand, for initiatives requiring significant resources and time, like choosing a college major or selecting stock shares to buy, more people prefer to seek advice from experienced mentors. The smaller the investment, the more we tend to trust friends over experts, but the more we feel we should know, the more we look to trusted experts.

A real sense of humility comes from seeking guidance from people our age or perhaps even from those younger than us. I remember feeling slightly uncomfortable when students in my executive-level courses were older or more experienced than me. Remember, the most important thing we can do to cultivate successful peer mentorship is to create a safe environment for learning, and at the core of safe learning are empathy and common ground.

Even our use of language in peer mentoring relationships can affect the outcomes. We tend to interpret advising as an act of power. As a result, people may resent advice from a peer or near-peer. Remember, approaching a peer who has achieved more than you in one aspect of life can feel a bit humiliating, but you'll be surprised that this same peer likely views the aspects of your life where you've achieved more in the same manner.

My former business partner Scott Case was the founding CTO of Priceline.com, a breakout dot com success story that eventually grew into a seventy-billion-dollar travel giant. Given our age difference of just a few years, I spent our first coffee meeting intimidated by what he'd achieved and accomplished. While I entered the conversation expecting to be the only one learning, Scott was equally fascinated by my experiences with my last mobile app company. That shared environment for us to collaborate and learn led to a friendship that would become a business venture.

Our relationship demonstrates a difference between peer mentoring and other Super Mentorship types—more often an *exchange* of guidance, coaching, and opportunities.

Author Ben Casnocha notes that simply packaging our advice as peer advice comes across as less condescending and can change the dynamic. Sharing your struggles with living up to any advice—"it's something I've struggled with, too"—can help reduce the stacked power dynamic. Casnocha suggests using less authoritative phrases like, "I'm trying, too" and "I would…" For example, "I know reading frequently works because I am also trying to read more often, working." Or, "If my performance in class dropped, I would try to read more frequently to get the concept."

Peer mentoring most often fails when either party appears to be projecting power.

***

Imagine sitting in a room and listening to the conversation between a seventeen-year-old Ray Charles and a fourteen-year-old Quincy Jones in the din of a dimly lit bar. What would the two talk about? Did anyone happen to see this moment that changed music history?

Charles won seventeen Grammy Awards, including eight posthumously, and was honored with the Grammy Lifetime Achievement Award in 1987. *Rolling Stone* ranked him number ten on their list of the 100 Greatest Artists of All Time and number two on their list of the one hundred greatest singers. Not to be outdone, Jones was one of the most successful producers, songwriters, composers, and film and television producers in history, with a record eighty Grammy Award nominations and twenty-eight wins.

And on that one night in 1948 at the Black Elks Club, Jones, the young trumpeter, introduced himself to the piano-playing phenom and began a friendship that lasted their entire lives.

Jones wondered if he was too young or not talented enough to make it as a musician but found inspiration in Charles.

"Ray had his own apartment and two suits," Jones shared with NPR. "It was amazing. But I guess what impressed me the most with Ray was that he was so independent, and his sightlessness did not hinder him at all. It's one of the treasured, cherished friendships that I really have because as kids we used to talk about everything."

Charles had been completely blind since he was seven. He taught Jones how to read braille and introduced him to his musical influences, including Nat Cole, Charles Brown, and Charlie Parker. But perhaps more than anything, the two found in each other someone equally driven.

"It's so hard to describe Quincy because you know, we're so close," Charles discussed in an interview with Harvard's School of Public Health. "He was just an energetic young kid and he really loved music. He wanted to learn how to write, and of course, I knew how to write, and that drew us together because I could help him out and show him some things about how to compose. I would work at night from 1:00 to 5:00 in the morning, get home at 6:00 a.m., and Quincy would wake me up at 9:00 a.m. and say, 'Hey man, show me how to write…' I said, 'Man, do you know what time it is?' He said, 'I don't care man.'"

Genius often requires someone to believe in who we can become, and Charles and Jones were fortunate to have found that in one another.

"We used to dream about the future," admitted Jones, "like wouldn't it be great to work with a symphony orchestra? One day we're going to do that. One day we're going to have three girlfriends each, you know? One day we're doing movies together. We're going to do all of that stuff, and we did it. That's what's amazing. We did, you know, "In the Heat of the Night" together. And we did "We Are the World," all of those things, everything, the girls. So we did. It's amazing to dream and have your dreams executed like that, you know."

Ray Charles died June 10, 2004, just two months before the release of his final album *Genius Loves Company*. The posthumous album sold over five million copies and earned eight Grammys. That same year, Jamie Foxx starred as Ray in the Academy Award-winning feature film, portraying Charles's life and career. The film memorialized Charles's greatness while shining a light on the power of his relationship with Jones, a relationship where each person was made better—and made great—by the influence of the other.

One Meeting Away: Quincy Jones

Right Person. Ray Charles

Right Ask. Can you teach me to write music?

Right Ask. Jones saw a friend and a partner in Charles, and the pair became inseparable.

Right Time. Charles was a protégé in the music industry, and Jones was young and ambitious. Both leveraged their passion and experiences as young African American men to navigate the industry.

"That's what mentoring is all about," shared Jones. "There's one person who sees that glimmer in the eye and sees the question marks in your eye… and just two or three words could make a difference in your life."

***

While mentorship is perceived to be most impactful early in our lives, peer mentorship represents a counterintuitive setting that many of the most successful people in this book harnessed for their breakthroughs. At the core of peer mentoring is establishing a safe environment for our growth and learning—as captured in the Humility of Learning framework—and, most often, the shared exchange between peers and near-peers. Part of the reason it's so transformative is because of the level of self-awareness and humility it requires, but I suppose if Ray Charles and Bradley Cooper are believers, the rest of us can learn a thing or two as well.

16

INVESTED

Babson College reported that more than twenty-seven million Americans started or ran new businesses in 2017, and estimates say more than 525 million people globally are entrepreneurs.

Entrepreneurship is attractive to more and more people because of owners' autonomy and agency in their ventures. But the flip side of this autonomy and agency is that the uncertainty and ambiguity that come from doing something new or challenging often require entrepreneurs to consult with others to learn.

As a fellow entrepreneur once shared with me, "Starting your first company doesn't come with an employee handbook and a welcome video."

Enter the Investor Super Mentor.

We've already seen the impact *The Washington Post* CEO Don Graham had on Mark Zuckerberg. Their relationship began as a potential investment and then turned into a mentoring relationship, only to circle back to an investor mentor.

Drew Houston and Arash Ferdowsi credit the success of Dropbox to the impact of Investor mentoring from fellow entrepreneurs the Partovi brothers. Foursquare founder/CEO Dennis Crowley counts entrepreneur-turned-investor Ben Horowitz as his Investor mentor. Michael Dell leveraged venture investor-turned-operator Lee Walker in the early days of Dell Computer to move his personal computer manufacturing operation from his dorm room to a professional venture.

Investor Super Mentor relationships go beyond simple capital investments and involve coaching, guidance on strategic matters, and access to various resources. Many of the savviest entrepreneurs we studied in our research were incredibly strategic in building relationships with investors that they were able to offer more than just access to capital. Aligned Investor mentorship focuses on creating shared financial outcomes between investors and the founders.

But, as we will see, money, power, and failure can also quickly change the relationship dynamics.

***

Starting any new business is challenging, and managing our psychology as entrepreneurs riding near-daily highs and lows is a job in and of itself. As a serial entrepreneur and investor, starting a new company is a lonely and isolating job. In particular, when you employ people who buy into your vision and follow you into a risk-filled experience, the pressure is immense. Lakshmi Balachandra writes in her essay "Investor Mentor: Evaluating the Entrepreneur as Protégé," investors who tend to focus on personal capabilities and qualities of entrepreneurs (the "I invest in people" type of investor who is often seen as "angel" investors in the earliest stages of a new venture) view themselves as mentors to start-up entrepreneur protégés.

Saad Khan, a founding partner at Uprising Ventures, invested in start-up companies, including Pandora, Change.org, Upworthy, Lending Club, Lyft, and Good Eggs, and in an initial start-up of mine. Saad shared a simple philosophy over coffee that guided his nearly two-decades-long career as an investor.

"Do no harm," he said. "My job is to do no harm to the business itself as an investor and do whatever I can to the founder and team trying to build it. We believe in them, and we know changing the world is hard. I'm laser-focused on the people because none of this would even be remotely possible without them."

In our regular check-ins, the conversations were always about the person first and the business second—a familiar mentoring-like engagement. That mantra aligns well with most entrepreneurs' needs when starting a risky and uncertain venture.

Researchers Chuck Eesley and Yanbo Wang examined the impact of mentorship on emerging entrepreneurs in their paper "The Effects of Mentoring in Entrepreneurial Career Choice." They note four major obstacles faced by novice entrepreneurs when starting any new venture:

- stigma or fear of failure
- self-efficacy or concerns about their entrepreneurial abilities
- general lack of information about entrepreneurial careers
- lack of social connection to strategic resources necessary to succeed

---

Despite a growing practice of teaching entrepreneurship principles in colleges, universities, and trade organizations, the nuances of building businesses often require levels of guidance and coaching far beyond what's available in textbooks or lectures. Further, the right mentors may provide access to those strategic resources—from funding and talent to customers and distribution.

Perhaps no aspect of Investor Super Mentors is greater than their role in helping entrepreneurs manage the fear and self-doubt that comes from running their venture.

***

Dennis Crowley became a cult hero in the start-up world. He already developed the Dodgeball app that created a game-like feel to a night out on the town and sold it to Google in 2005. By 2009, with the explosion of the iPhone and improved location tracking, Crowley launched Foursquare.

Foursquare debuted at South by Southwest (SXSW) and was an instant success. It enabled users to "check in" to venues and share their locations with others. It used gamification to reward its most active users by including the ability to earn perks and discounts if you were the "mayor" of specific venues, bars, clubs, or stores. By cultivating a strong sense of fear of missing out (FOMO), Foursquare was a breakout winner of 2009 and was called "the next Twitter" by Mashable and TechCrunch. By 2010, Crowley raised more than thirty million dollars in funding and turned down a reported one-hundred-forty-million-dollar acquisition offer. Times were good for Crowley and Foursquare.

Sitting at the center of what looked to be the next great technology company, Crowley was able to pick his partners to fund the company. Perhaps, it's not surprising he chose an investing partner who was very proactive in supporting founders and backing them as the visionary leader of their start-ups.

"We had our pick of the litter," Crowley told *Forbes*. They chose upstart fund Andreessen Horowitz to lead their 2010 round to bring in fresh capital. Netscape founder Marc Andreessen and Opsware cofounder and executive Ben Horowitz founded the fund, and both had deep industry experience.

"Ben and Marc, they've gone through this many times, and they see it as their duty to educate us," Crowley said.

By 2013, however, the company began to stall. Users fled the app; targets were missed, and the company began to have serious discussions about the direction of its product. This stagnation took its toll on Crowley.

In a 2021 interview with *The Profile* founder Polina Pompliano, Crowley shared that in December of 2013, while he was reading Nick Bilton's book *Hatching Twitter*, he began to consider whether his board might fire him like Twitter's had fired Ev Williams, the founder, and former CEO. Crowley doubted he was the right person to run Foursquare.

His internal fears and doubts were exacerbated when a meeting notice from his board members Ben Horowitz and Albert Wenger arrived, scheduled ominously for Friday, December 13th. He feared the worst.

That Friday, he met with his board members, who asked him about his plans for the holidays. He stopped them.

"Gentlemen, if you have something to say to me, just say it. Just break the news," Crowley blurted out.

Horowitz and Wenger looked confused. What "news" was he talking about?

"You guys aren't here to fire me right now?" Crowley continued.

"What's wrong with you?" Horowitz responded. "We just wanted to check in before the holidays."

While he wasn't being fired, the situation elevated Crowley's feelings of uncertainty. He was unsure if he was the right person to lead the struggling start-up as it was transitioning from a consumer-focused product to a business-focused data company.

"Sometimes, it's hard to have those hard conversations," Crowley shared with Pompliano. "So you need a moment like this one that *forces* the hard conversation to happen."

One Meeting Away: Dennis Crowley, cofounder and CEO of Foursquare

Right Person. Ben Horowitz, founder of venture capital firm Andreessen Horowitz

Right Ask. Am I the right person to continue to lead this start-up through the next stage?

Right Start. Crowley was able to lean on Horowitz, who had been in a similar experience in his own ventures. Those experiences had first drawn Crowley to take capital from Andreessen Horowitz. That experience and Horowitz's support helped Crowley build the company to its next stage.

Right Time. Horowitz had been in Crowley's shoes, building and growing a company from an idea to a large organization and had experienced the doubts and uncertainties.

Having an investor who is more than just a source of money is often crucial at seminal moments for founders and leaders of hypergrowth ventures. Horowitz has continually maintained that helping founders grow and remain as CEO is core to his investment philosophy. That strong principle enabled their relationship to remain strong while Crowley worked to transition from CEO to executive chairman. While it may be easy to assume that an Investor mentor is providing "free" advice, in many cases, the investment of time is in addition to funds or capital. In that way, we might describe a "value added" investor as an investor who gives you capital and is willing to invest time, expertise, and experience to guide the individuals receiving that investment.

Admittedly, there is an inherent tension, akin to that with Work mentors, that exists with Investor mentors. Crowley wouldn't have been the first founder to be replaced by his board. Investors are looking to maximize returns on their investments, while founders may be wary of being replaced by more experienced managers or executives. Steve Jobs was famously replaced as founder-CEO by a seasoned executive, only to eventually return to champion the next phase of Apple's growth.

Recognizing the tension, relying on shared, aligned principles, and understanding that the value of mentorship may outstrip the capital alone can facilitate successful Super Mentoring.

***

There's reason to believe that mentorship is pivotal, especially in high-growth start-ups like Foursquare or Facebook.

TechCrunch studied more than seven hundred tech companies and their founders and categorized 13 percent of the start-ups as top performers based on their growth, investors, and outcomes. They found that entrepreneurs led nearly all companies that were graded in the top performance tier with strong mentorship connections to founders of other successful companies.

They noted the example of two of the top-performing New York-based ventures—handmade and vintage marketplace Etsy and health technology company Flatiron Health—were each led by founders who other successful New York-based start-up founders had mentored. Caterina Fake from Flickr mentored Chad Dickerson of Etsy, while Brian O'Kelley of AppNexus mentored Nat Turner of Flatiron Health.

Their research hoped to find what the elite startups had in common (the researchers found that 13 percent of all startups analyze met their definition of elite). Perhaps the most surprising finding was that one-third of the founders of elite startups were mentored by other founders of peer elite startups, three times higher than those without mentoring this mentorship. And while investors' industry-specific knowledge and connections to partners and other investors certainly help their mentees succeed, sharing approaches to manage the mental aspect of founding a venture can't be understated.

Not all aspects of mentorship are created equally for a founder.

. For entrepreneurs, the type of support needed from mentors varies depending on the entrepreneur's experiences and prior history. A Kauffman Foundation study of nearly 550 entrepreneurs examined the biggest benefits of formal start-up mentorship programs. What entrepreneurs valued from their mentors varied, in some measure, based on their experience. Nearly 65 percent of university-aged mentees found that guidance was the single most important contribution from their mentors to the success of their ventures. In comparison, only 35 percent of non-university-aged founders found guidance valuable. Founders who were past university age were more than twice as likely to point to less formal networks as the most important support they received.

Michael Dell realized he needed both guidance and access to network resources to grow Dell Computers. His mentors helped him become the youngest CEO in history to head a Fortune 500 company.

As a college entrepreneur, Dell felt like he was in over his head and leveraged breakfasts with a leading technology innovator and University of Texas academic George Kozmetsky. At that point, Dell required guidance, and the guidance he received from Kozmetsky was hugely beneficial. Dell shared with his alma mater of his mentor, "George Kozmetsky's guidance in management issues, workforce motivation, and strategies needed [in order] to remain technologically competitive has been invaluable in helping Dell Computer Corporation grow to be a more than two-billion-dollar company."

But Dell soon needed more than just guidance, so he turned to venture capitalist Lee Walker. He initially asked Walker for his help in vetting a candidate for Dell Computer's first president. Walker had dinner with Michael Dell and the prospective president for Dell's two-year-old company, who just happened to be a Brooklyn native. Unsure of his role in the conversation, Walker spent most of the night speaking to the pair about the Brooklyn Dodgers, his favorite team as a boy. Hours later, Dell showed up at Walker's house unannounced asking him to run his company.

"I turned him down flat," Walker told Michael Barnes. "I frequently don't do well at sizing up situations. I had zero idea of the company's potential. To me, though, the crazy baseball story is everything because that's what happened when I met Michael... Michael is good at many things, including getting help and listening to people to get help."

Walker had a change of heart, though, and agreed to work with Dell as his first senior executive and join the board. His decades-long experience in the Austin tech scene gave him access that would come in handy when a confidant shared that Dell's bank was at risk of going under. In one of his many important moves in those early years, Walker guided the company to financing, partnerships, and its IPO.

Walker saw his role as a mentor in the vein of Lakshmi Balachandra's research. He was an entrepreneur, who admittedly had numerous struggles in his early years, and later an investor.

One Meeting Away: Michael Dell, founder and CEO of Dell Computers

Right Person. Lee Walker, venture capitalist and Dell Computer's first president.

Right Ask. Would you interview a candidate to be the president of Dell?

Right Start. After initially rebuffing the offer, Walker considered it further, spoke to more individuals, and took the role, leading the company through its IPO with Dell.

Right Time. Dell leveraged mentors throughout the early days of Dell, and Walker was known throughout Texas as a straight shooter who Dell asked to help vet a candidate for a senior role. But Dell realized in that meeting that the candidate he needed at his company was Walker.

After Walker left the company for health reasons, Dell continued to elevate and surround himself with the right mentor for the stage of his own needs. Mort Topfer joined the company as its vice-chairman in 1994, bringing his experience as a former Motorola executive. He originally planned to stay for a few months to help steady things, but Dell was able to harness Topfer's guidance and coaching so that he ultimately spent a decade with the company.

Investor Super Mentors often provide entrepreneurs with the confidence to take the leap and start on their own.

Adam Saven and Reilly Davis had a similar experience with their Investor Super Mentor Steve Altman.

"We thought we had something good but weren't 100 percent sure."

So as every entrepreneur does, Adam and Reilly began having conversations with experts and investors. One of these connections led them to a casual conversation with Steve Altman, who had recently retired as President and Vice-Chairman of Qualcomm in San Diego.

"I connected with Steve through my high school network," Adam told me. "His son and I went to the same school. The fact that we could point to a tangible idea and project around helping young people access the right job opportunities personally interested him as a father of three."

<table>
<tr><td>One Meeting Away: Adam Saven and Reilly Davis, cofounders of PeopleGrove</td></tr>
</table>

Right Person. Steve Altman, venture capitalist and business leader.

Right Ask. Can I get your thoughts on a project we're thinking could be a startup idea?

Right Start. Deciding to leap and the steps during and after that leap are different. Saven and Davis leveraged these insights throughout the early stages of their business.

Right Time. Altman had just retired after a successful career as an executive at Qualcomm. His son went to school with Saven, and he was beginning to get more involved in supporting and investing in start-ups. Altman saw potential in Saven and Davis and was willing to be first in line for any idea they came up with.

It was clear from the start that Steve was the epitome of an Investor Super Mentor. "From Day one," Adam explained, "Steve invested in Reilly and me. He has remained incredibly supportive throughout the evolution of our company."

This Super Mentor convinced Reilly and Adam to take their leap of faith. "I told Steve I was struggling to leave my safe job to pursue the start-up dream," Adam confessed. "Steve guided me to weigh the pros and cons of going not only all in but also even committed to being the first investor regardless of the idea. He believed in us. I feel incredibly fortunate to have someone like Steve in my corner."

***

Investor Super Mentors are a unique class of mentors in that they are often critically important to both the success of the entrepreneur and the business, but their loyalties are potentially torn if the company struggles. For this reason, their impact can't be understated; it's clear that when millions of dollars are at stake, investors who are able to counsel their protégés through the ups and downs are rare.

17

SHARED STRUGGLES

There's an underlying tension in doing work to drive change. On the one hand, we believe changemakers in fields like nonprofits, social justice, or innovation *should* be more fulfilled because they are doing what they are passionate about. But on the other hand, driving that change is incredibly taxing on the changemakers.

That tension often results in people who need more support and guidance avoiding seeking help.

Unite surveyed nearly a thousand professionals employed by charities and NGOs about their mental well-being and found that 80 percent of respondents mentioned experiencing workplace stress in the last twelve months, while 42 percent of respondents believed their job was detrimental to their mental health.

Because of this intense stress, changemakers—such as Martin Luther King Jr., Nelson Mandela, and Gandhi—often view mentors as important voices in driving that change. We describe this mentorship as based on a shared struggle.

Driving change is a lonely proposition. We know changemakers are loners and outcasts who are doing something that "doesn't make sense"… until it does. Entrepreneurs and social changemakers often need mentors who can resonate and work with them by connecting over their shared struggles. That connection is the foundation of the shared struggle mentorship, and we see numerous examples occurring in the most successful entrepreneurs and social movement creators.

Researchers find that for emerging entrepreneurs, it's important that they see themselves as a changemaker and then develop the tools to act on it. Mentors with similar experiences nurture this self-perception and can serve as a guide through the struggles.

But this mental shift required of a changemaker can often be debilitating.

***

Dr. Martin Luther King Jr. needs no introduction. His bold and unapologetic acknowledgment of racial abuse faced by people of color and his advocacy for racial justice is well-known. He's often introduced in the same breath as changemakers like Nelson Mandela and Mahatma Gandhi, who were all subjects of intense hatred and vitriol but who found others who shared their struggle to serve as guides and supporters.

King Jr. was not alone in his reformative journey. Dr. Benjamin Mays not only served as a mentor to Dr. King but was himself a known American civil rights champion who laid the foundations for the civil rights movement.

Born in Epworth, South Carolina, to a family of enslaved people, Dr. Benjamin Mays relied on education to transform the lives of thousands like him in America. After attending high school at South Carolina State College, he went north to Bates College in Maine. He worked summers as a Pullman porter to help pay his way and graduated with honors in 1920. Dr. Mays received his MA from the University of Chicago in 1925 and then his doctorate in Christian theology and ethics from the same university in 1935.

During his years as an academic and the president of Morehouse College, Dr. Mays met a young Martin Luther King Jr. Mays and King had a similar background and shared many of the same struggles. Martin Luther King Jr. was born to Baptist parents in Atlanta, Georgia, in 1929. He faced racial segregation throughout his youth. Known for his oratory skills from a very young age, King, like Mays, took a keen interest in politics and theology. In addition to a similar past, this shared interest helped them bond in the years that followed.

When a young King enrolled in Morehouse College in 1944, Dr. Mays had been the college's president for about four years. Relying on Dr. Mays' leadership example, King began his journey as a civil rights activist. The two of them shared a vision to change the face of civil rights in modern-day America.

In his biography *Benjamin Elijah Mays: Schoolmaster of the Movement*, University of Kansas professor Randal Maurice Jelks describes King's reliance on Mays's leadership in his efforts as an activist: "[King] also needed Mays for spiritual support as he faced the burden of being perceived as the personification of black America's hopes and dreams. Mays held the job as King's consignee over the next fourteen years as the death threats against him grew more ominous and the public battles more dangerous." Dr. Mays began as King's teacher, but he became his spiritual leader, guide, father, and closest friend in the years that followed.

A mentor is not necessarily a dominant figure in our lives. A mentor shapes our ideas for the better. When there's a shared struggle, such as the one between Dr. Mays and Dr. King, the relationship between the mentor and a mentee is nurtured even more. There's a sense of belief in a cause and a comradeship in adversity. While the mentor may have started as a primary source of nurture for the mentee, the relationship levels when the mentee establishes a place and a vision parallel to that of the mentor. This type of relationship works particularly well when the mentor identifies in the mentee a charisma or social impact that complements their revolutionary qualities.

The relationship began when Martin Luther King Jr. was fifteen years old and continued until King's death in 1968 when he was thirty-nine years old. Before his passing, King often spoke about how Dr. Mays was his "spiritual mentor" and "intellectual father," the man behind his strength.

Dr. Mays's affection for his mentee was well-acknowledged, too, and best described in his eulogy at King's funeral.

"To be honored by being requested to give the eulogy at the funeral of Dr. Martin Luther King Jr. is like asking one to eulogize his deceased son—so close and so precious was he to me. Our friendship goes back to his student days at Morehouse. It is not an easy task; nevertheless, I accept it with a sad heart and with full knowledge of my inadequacy to do justice to this man. It was my desire that if I predeceased Dr. King, he would pay tribute to me on my final day. It was his wish that if he predeceased me, I would deliver the homily at his funeral. Fate has decreed that I eulogize him. I wish it might have been otherwise; for, after all, I am three score years and ten and Martin Luther is dead at thirty-nine."

One Meeting Away: Martin Luther King Jr.

Right Person. Dr. Benjamin Mays, President of Morehouse College

Right Ask. How do I navigate being the personification of black America's hopes and dreams?

Right Start. Mays worked with King Jr. behind-the-scenes, helping him balance the broader movement with his rising fame and its burdens.

Right Time. Few could understand King Jr.'s struggles as a leader and a public face in the civil rights movement, particularly given the growing risk of violence he faced. But Mays had spent his career navigating a transition from his birth to a family of enslaved people to a graduate of some of the country's more prestigious academic institutions.

What Dr. King and Dr. Mays had was something special—a relationship with empathy, faith, and belief in each other. This type of relationship can emerge out of any situation that demands common perseverance long enough to see the mentee emerge, picking up skills and values from their mentor to find a common ground on which to operate.

When both parties find this level ground, they develop a shared network, and the two find themselves benefiting equally from each other's skillset and values. The result of pushing through these shared struggles is a trail for many more people to follow.

***

They say birds of a feather flock together, and that is certainly the case in the mentoring relationships we observed in our research. Changemakers are drawn to other changemakers by a shared mental, emotional and physical taxation.

Jane Finette is the author of *Unlocked: How Empowered Women Empower Women* and the founder and executive director at The Coaching Fellowship. She's seen firsthand how women respond differently to feedback and coaching from other women as opposed to feedback by men.

"When you do a Google search for 'women standing behind women,' almost every result returned is about a woman standing behind her man," Jane shared with a sigh. "In a typical corporation, though, it's understandably harder to help at work where a paralyzing mix of not 'rocking the boat' or not even knowing a woman needed your support reign supreme. Furthermore, it turns out there is a proven disincentive to helping. According to a 2016 study published in the *Academy of Management Journal*, [researchers] found that senior-level women who try to help other women at work face more negative performance reviews than those who don't. So it's already hard to help, and when we do, we pay for it."

But despite all of that, she finds a unique bond is built when women support and empower one another. She continued, "Fighting for something, someone, we believe in is paramount to change." Identifying those shared struggles is often a key way Super Mentoring relationships are built. For example, changemakers are prone to depression and anxiety. Yet, researchers found that individuals with a "natural mentor experienced significant decreases in depression over time."

***

Michael Dumlao has long found himself as one of the "others," a self-described black sheep of the family who blends his corporate affairs executive role at consulting firm Booz Allen with life as a performer and entertainer as the queen of the Gay Men's Chorus of Washington, DC and his performance alter-ego named Nuancé who is a gender-creative, undocumented alien from outer space with multiple personalities.

"So much of the LGBTQ movement," he told me, "is about disrupting traditions and questioning the binary. And in particular, we have a long history of challenging established patterns in our families."

Many of his peers in the LGBTQ community had to struggle to break through the norm and establish new norms. As an immigrant, Dumlao found it particularly challenging for him to gain acceptance in the broader Filipino immigrant community. Still, once he found his footing, he was quick to counsel other black sheep who struggled to find support for the aspects of their lives that didn't conform to their family's expectations.

"I became this gay uncle that people would turn to for help, guidance, or connections," Dumlao revealed. "It was very much this mentor and protégé relationship that would be created."

In his book *Guncle*, he describes this principal role in the LGBTQ community. The guncle is a trusted gay mentor whose lived experience of the black sheep journey and openness turns them into a mentor and advisor. Others struggling with their own "nontraditional" choices—be it a career, education, or even sexuality—find nonjudgmental guidance in their guncles.

"I found that the gay community has empathy for anyone struggling against societal norms," Dumlao shared. "I've spoken to guncles who guide someone to become the first in their family to go to college or pursue a nontraditional career, a guncle who was a refugee from Venezuela to help someone become the first in their family to immigrate to the US, and even an incredible transgender, drag queen guncle who guided someone through the journey of coming out to their family. It's very much a shared struggle story. We've been there and, in many ways, are just more open about helping others who feel like the other."

Dumlao is right that empathy is a powerful bond that leads to richer mentoring relationships. Whether they are struggles, such as those within the LGBTQ community, racial struggles, or gender struggles, that shared, lived experience is a reason to run into mentoring relationships rather than from them.

***

The concept of sharing struggles doesn't just apply to acquiring merit or chasing success. Sometimes, it has more to do with sharing a space where two people—a mentor and a mentee, in this context—can reach into new territories, even beyond their skillsets.

Jack Dorsey met his mentor Ray Chambers through a New York acquaintance. Chambers made his fortune in a private equity firm called Wesray Capital Corp., which he cofounded in 1981. He's currently involved in philanthropy and serves as the UN Special Envoy of the Secretary-General for Malaria.

By then, Dorsey was already a success, having cofounded Twitter and the mobile payments service Square. But from Chambers, he gained something else—ideas and inspiration on how he could make a real difference in the world.

This was important for Dorsey. He knew how to set up a social media platform and could probably mentor others to do the same in their respective fields, but he did not know much about making a real, tangible difference in the world. He wanted philanthropy to be his second career and did not know where he could start.

Chambers became Dorsey's mentor, with the pair speaking for at least an hour every month for more than two years. They exchanged several ideas and advice on how they could use their wealth and influence to impact the world.

Dorsey and Chambers found themselves in a common space of giving more to the world. With Chambers being the more experienced one, it was easy for Dorsey to pick up on his cues and integrate his values.

"He's an amazing guy. I learned a lot from him, so it's great if I can provide the same for other people," Dorsey shared of Chambers in a Bloomberg interview. "He's the closest thing we have to a capitalist Buddha."

Dorsey understood the value of support and how the mentorship culture plays a crucial role in addressing some significant challenges of switching careers—even moving from a lucrative, earning position to a giving role. It can be hard to do so without that support, as there's only enough room for trial and error when the timeline is long enough, and things get even more complicated when competition is present in the field.

One Meeting Away: Jack Dorsey, cofounder and CEO of Twitter; cofounder and CEO of Square

Right Person. Ray Chambers, cofounder of Wesray Capital Corp. and United Nations Special Envoy for Malaria eradication

Right Ask. How do I make a successful transition into driving direct impact through philanthropy?

Right Start. Dorsey listened to Chambers and was patient. Today Dorsey has successfully championed the role of decentralized tools and systems such as blockchain and bitcoin as a way to create opportunities for others.

Right Time. Dorsey had seen others in the technology sector struggle to make a comparable impact on social causes and initiatives and looked to Chambers, who had balanced his presence as a capitalist and a driver of social good.

However, like many successful people, Dorsey didn't just limit himself to learning from one person. He had several ambitions and people to guide him through the process, one of which was Steve Jobs. He also said that he learned a lot about design from Jobs, particularly about making things simple and easy to use. In a 2011 speech, he referred to Jobs as his "mentor from afar." And it's not surprising when we look objectively at the design of Twitter and Macintosh that both products are neat and provide hefty features in an uncomplicated interface. Jobs mastered it, and Dorsey knew that well. There could be no better motivator to find a mentor than knowing what you want and having the confidence in your skills to go after it.

We can learn so much from the experience of Jack Dorsey. For example, he demonstrates that you do not have to just settle into a career or even life. Mentoring isn't just for when you're starting; it can help at any career stage. Dorsey was already highly successful when he met Chambers but still learned valuable lessons from his mentor that he applied in areas other than Twitter to make the world better.

The relationship between Dorsey and Chambers also explains that inspiration from a professional mentor can extend beyond workplace activities. Chambers and Dorsey shared commitment to philanthropic causes, and that shared interest brought them together. Without this shared commitment, the engagement would've never happened.

***

It's counterintuitive in some senses that seeking others who share our struggles and being vulnerable with those struggles leads to tighter bonds. Researchers from the University of Mannheim call this the "beautiful mess effect." While we often see our struggles and flaws as unfavorable, others see those same struggles and weaknesses as "alluring." And, in particular, these flaws and efforts *in pursuit of* something important only add to that connection.

18

LUMINARY

Can certain people supercharge our path with their mere support?

***

"Have you gotten to meet Stephen King," I asked best-selling horror writer Riley Sager.

"Oh my gosh—no," he stammered. "No, I do not want to meet him. I'd be terrified. Like, 'hello, you God of Letters.' I would make an ass out of myself."

Riley Sager's life was transformed because of a simple act by a man he remains terrified of meeting. "I sent copies of *Final Girls* to many people I admired, and Stephen King was one of those mailings. He read it six months before it came out. And then he tweeted to his like six million-plus followers. That was good. He called *Final Girls* the first great thriller of 2017. And so that tweet changed my life completely."

Final Girls was Riley's first novel and a national and international bestseller that has been published in more than two dozen countries and won the ITW Thriller Award for Best Hardcover Novel. Sager's subsequent novels, *The Last Time I Lied*, *Lock Every Door*, and *Home Before Dark*, which received the Crimson Scribe Award by *Suspense Magazine*, were *New York Times* bestsellers. You might be tempted to reply that Riley Sager is a gifted writer and storyteller who would have succeeded without King; perhaps, but Riley Sager is the pen name for Todd Ritter, who did not have that support for his first three published novels.

"I wrote three books under my real name. And they just didn't sell at all. It just was pitiful. I was at a crossroads. I had a publishing deal and then they just dropped me."

Desperate, he spent nine weeks writing a draft of *Final Girls*. He shared it with his agent. "My agent read it and said, 'You know, this is great. This has breakout potential. This could be pretty big. You should use a pen name.'"

Armed with a new book written under a pen name that combined his favorite gender-neutral baby name and his maternal grandmother's maiden name, he let his work speak for itself. What followed was a "tweet that changed [his] life completely."

One Meeting Away: Riley Sager, *New York Times* best-selling author of *Final Girls*

Right Person. Stephen King

Right Ask. I've been inspired by your books and wanted to send you a copy of my novel.

Right Start. Despite having never met King, he's known as one of the biggest supporters of up-and-coming writers, even coming to speak to my class based on my cold email.

Right Time. Sager had published three books that underperformed under his given name and decided to publish this book under a pen name without any track record. The book would succeed based on feedback from readers, and Stephen King's public endorsement of the book created a buzz that would propel it to the top of "must-read" lists across the literary industry.

Luminaries like Stephen King have an unbelievable power to transform our trajectories; they represent a powerful type of Super Mentor whose support can truly change our lives.

But harnessing that power can take a lifetime.

***

Game recognizes game, so the saying goes.

Luminaries appear to be driven by exceptional individuals and work products. There's often no way around the power of demonstrated excellence in earning their support and praise.

And today, trust is at the center of the Luminary relationship. The influencer economy has changed our relationship with trust. Pew Research finds our overall trust on the decline and "about half of Americans (49 percent) link the decline in interpersonal trust to a belief that people are not as reliable as they used to be. Many ascribe shrinking trust to a political culture they believe is broken, which spawns suspicion, even cynicism, about the ability of others to distinguish fact from fiction."

We have transitioned to the "sponsored" economy. Today, even small-scale influencers are being paid to dress a certain way, drink a certain drink, or support a particular product. Particular luminaries like Stephen King, Michael Jordan, and Oprah Winfrey have built carefully curated brands based on trust. So when Oprah's September 2005 Book Club author James Frey was accused of lying in *A Million Little Pieces*, his memoir about addiction and recovery, she was forced to confront Frey in a live broadcast in early 2006.

Trust remains the hallmark of Luminary Super Mentors.

***

Richard Branson is no stranger to the power of the brand.

Branson has curated a rebel persona, becoming the flamboyant leader of a Virgin Group empire that has more than four hundred companies in its portfolio. But before there was Sir Richard, there was the outspoken and bombastic airline pioneer Sir Freddie Laker.

In 1977, Laker created the "Skytrain," which became a pioneer of cheap air travel. Laker was part of the highly competitive airline market post-World War II when aviation became a mode of transport reserved solely for the rich. Laker introduced the idea of cheap air tickets by enabling people to queue up outside airports to purchase tickets. The "Skytrain" first took off in September 1977 from New York, and Laker pocketed profits exceeding a million pounds in his first year in business.

Unlike Branson, Laker's experience came from within the industry. "Laker was a first-class aircraft engineer and had seen and done it all in terms of aviation," writes Ania Grzesik, author of *Laker: The Glory Years of Sir Freddie Laker.* He recognized the opportunity to democratize air travel and used the power of media and persistence to win three court cases over six years to realize his vision for Skytrain.

The risks initially paid off, helping Skytrain become the fourth-largest transatlantic carrier by 1978 before forces outside of his control—the 1979 OPEC oil embargo and an American Airlines crash grounding DC-10s, including all of Skytrain's fleet—bankrupted the venture in 1982.

It made little sense for a small-time record executive to get into the aviation business. Still, Branson had seen through Laker the power of personality at play to transform the industry. Branson tested the idea for a new airline service by accident, or necessity, using Laker's technique of selling directly to offer thirty-nine-dollar one-way tickets to his fellow stranded passengers on their way to the Virgin Islands. Then, Branson chartered his own plane, praying the credit card he used wouldn't be declined. "[When] we arrived in the BVI, somebody said 'sharpen up your service a bit and you could be in the airline business,'" Branson recalled to CNBC's Karen Gilchrist.

Fresh off his battles with the airline industry, Laker was skeptical of the opportunity but realized Branson was no ordinary entrepreneur with an idea.

"He's a genius," shared Laker. "If there hadn't been a Richard to follow on from Freddie Laker, there would have been plenty more restrictions on the airlines."

Laker insisted that Branson not change his personality to cower to the buttoned-up industry. Laker felt that the showman in Branson was just what was needed to finish the job he'd started.

"At the time, I was running a little record company. I was about seventeen years old. The first time I met him was some years later. I was thinking about setting up my own airline. He gave me this advice: 'You'll never have the advertising power to outsell British Airways. You are going to have to get out there and use yourself. Make a fool of yourself. Otherwise, you won't survive.'"

The approach had worked in the brash record industry, but it was far from obvious in a regulated industry like air travel.

"I wouldn't have gotten anywhere in the airline industry without the mentorship of Sir Freddie Laker," Branson wrote in his tribute to Laker in *The Guardian*. "He helped shape our vision for high-quality service at competitive prices and was the first to bring my attention to how fiercely we would have to battle with other airlines to make a success of our airline. Now, I love mentoring young entrepreneurs."

Laker's battles and support helped cushion the business wars Richard Branson's Virgin Atlantic fought against British Airways during the nineties. And many of Laker's former employees joined Virgin Atlantic as Branson slowly gained momentum in the aviation industry and began adopting some of Laker's promotion tactics.

One Meeting Away: Richard Branson, founder and CEO of Virgin Group

Right Person. Freddie Laker, airline pioneer and founder of Skytrain

Right Ask. How should I adapt my music industry persona to the airline industry?

Right Start. Laker worked with Branson behind-the-scenes, guiding and supporting him to establish Virgin Atlantic as an upstart force in air travel.

Right Time. Branson had succeeded in building a name and a brand around his brash, bold personality. Still, as he attempted to take on the airline industry, he was advised he'd need to "professionalize" to make the transition. Laker had been the brash upstart in the industry before Branson but had eventually succumbed and shut down Skytrain. But Laker encouraged Branson to remain true to his brand and that his failure resulted from external forces rather than the outsider brand.

In 2018, Virgin Atlantic boasted revenues of 2.781 billion GBP while Virgin Australia added another 5.4 billion AUD. As Richard Branson wrote, "It's much easier to follow a pioneer than to be a pioneer."

***

Risk-taking ventures are more successful when the founders choose to surround themselves with mentors. CPA Practice Advisor finds that start-ups with mentors are 12 percent more likely to remain in business after one year than businesses without a mentor.

In some senses, this challenge is driven by structural obstacles of any new venture—convincing customers, partners, regulators, or investors is difficult for a newcomer.

Predating Sir Freddie and Sir Richard were fashion pioneers Christian Dior and Yves Saint Laurent, who both set the fashion world on notice. Dior was a prominent figure in the fashion industry in the 1940s and 1950s. His designs were popular among Europe's rich families, particularly women from the British royal family. In December 1946, Christian Dior founded the house of Dior as it's known today at 30 Avenue, Montaigne, Paris.

But it wasn't just women who were awe-struck by Dior's beautiful designs.

Saint Laurent's mother noticed Yves's inclination toward fashion and design and set up a meeting for him with *Vogue Paris* editor Michael de Brunhoff. But de Brunhoff decided to take the youngster under his wing, serving as his boss and mentor for a year before encouraging Saint Laurent to gain formal design instructions at renowned fashion institute Chambre Syndicale de la Couture.

De Brunhoff also introduced his nineteen-year-old protégé to French fashion giant Christian Dior.

"I couldn't speak in front of him," recalled Saint Laurent of that first meeting. "He taught me the basis of my art. Whatever was to happen next, I never forgot the years I spent at his side."

Their relationship rapidly accelerated, and Dior heaped greater and greater responsibility on the young upstart. Dior noted of his protégé, "Saint Laurent is the only one worthy to carry on after me." Tragically, that prognostication came to pass when Dior suffered a fatal heart attack in 1957, leaving a young Saint Laurent in charge of Dior. At the age of twenty-one, Saint Laurent became the youngest ever artistic couturier.

Saint Laurent wasted little time in building upon his mentor's legacy, revamping Dior's traditional label-look by removing shoulder pads and corsets and replacing these with a new line of dresses named "trapeze," which hung freely from the shoulders and received a dramatic response from the women of that time.

However, Dior without Christian became a different and more hostile place for Saint Laurent. Christian Dior's business partner replaced Yves with Marc Bohan. Bohan would champion a more traditional return to the Dior brand.

Saint Laurent rebounded, buoyed by a successful breach of contract suit and a payout of £48,000, and the support of some of Dior's best staff. He established his label named "YSL" and once again reclaimed his spot at the center of fashion. By the end of the 1960s, Saint Laurent was a fashion icon.

In 2007, Saint Laurent was appointed a grand officier of the Légion d'honneur by the president of France, Nicolas Sarkozy. Sadly, a few months later, Saint Laurent lost his fight with brain cancer and passed away at seventy-one. Dior and Saint Laurent are forever linked in their individual and shared contributions to modern-day fashion.

One Meeting Away: Yves Saint Laurent

Right Person. Christian Dior

Right Ask. Could you look at the portfolio of this talented nineteen-year-old?

Right Start. Dior took a risk and gave Saint Laurent freedom, a responsibility the young man didn't waste.

Right Time. Saint Laurent's talent was evident at an early age, but when Dior took him under his wing and anointed him as the artistic mind of his brand, Saint Laurent rocketed to the center of French fashion.

"I tried to show that fashion is an art," writes Saint Laurent. "For that, I followed the counsel of my master Christian Dior and the imperishable lesson of Mademoiselle Chanel. I created for my era, and I tried to foresee what tomorrow would be."

***

Whether entrepreneurs are disrupting new industries, fashion icons are changing what we wear, or authors and artists are sparking our imagination, Luminary Super Mentors hold outsized influence to accelerate the potential of their protégés. Yet, with that great power comes a heavy reliance on trust to wield it. There's a significant reliance on demonstration in these acts of Super Mentorship, and that demonstration forces protégés to hone their craft before securing their patrons.

Game recognizes game.

19

THE COLLECTOR

If Bowman (Bo) Fishback wasn't a start-up founder, he'd be the perfect evangelist preacher. Fishback has a knack for finding exceptional people and getting them to join him. I should know because Fishback convinced me to quit a dream start-up job I'd taken just five months earlier to cofound a start-up venture with him. I soon realized he was the ultimate secret weapon.

Fishback is a Collector.

At six feet and eight inches, Fishback starred as a high school basketball player in Georgia before his recruitment to play for Southern Methodist University. He quit after a single season once he realized, "I didn't have the cutthroat mentality you needed to win. I wanted to help the other guys, and you can't think that way at that level."

His "help-first" attitude gave him success in his early entrepreneurial ventures, eventually landing him a spot at Kauffman Foundation as its head of entrepreneurship. The start-up bug was always on his mind, and with the explosion of mobile devices, he found a reason to jump back into the start-up arena.

The beginning of the 2010s was an insane time in Silicon Valley. Smartphones were stirring up our ways of experiencing and interacting with the world. That period led to the founding of billion-dollar companies, including Uber, Airbnb, Square, Venmo, Pinterest, Groupon, and Slack.

Zaarly, our start-up company marketplace, featured a big vision and backing from investors, including Ashton Kutcher and Meg Whitman. While the company didn't quite achieve the heights of Uber or Airbnb, Fishback's legacy may be just as impressive for the collection of mentees and early employees he brought into the company. Ten years after the company's founding, Fishback boasted a collection of incredible success stories from the "first job" alums he had under his wings:

- Two *Forbes* 30 under 30 winners
- At least six venture capital firm partners
- Multiple entrepreneurs boasting seven-figure revenue businesses
- Two best-selling authors

What is amazing about these success stories was Fishback wasn't drawing these from a team of hundreds or thousands of employees. In fact, he employed less than forty people during this period. Fishback knew how to help each person he coached, mentored, and supported to see a version of themselves they may not have known was possible. He collected ambitious people with his vision, his deep empathy, and his presence that made you feel heard whenever you spent time with him.

In our research, we found a set of Super Mentors with extraordinary success in developing multiple highly successful protégés, and much like Fishback, they were known for extreme levels of empathy. Researchers have long associated this trait with the most transformational leaders, showing their followers that they care for their needs and achievement.

We see Collectors in greater numbers within certain creative fields—Leonard Nimoy, Jerome Liebling, Ralph Lauren, Alice Waters, and Lorne Michaels fall in this category. Additionally, the business and sports realms, which showcase strong executives and hierarchical management, have fostered Collectors, such as Larry Ellison,

Steve Jobs, Michael Milken, Julian Robertson, and Bill Walsh. These people all find themselves becoming collectors of exceptional people throughout their lives.

***

Collectors are unique in assessing and developing "fit." Their hires might not align with the current organization, but collectors have a way of seeing people as unique puzzle pieces. Most collectors hire exceptional talent and help them figure out the right role as they go.

In her job interview, former Google CEO Eric Schmidt shared with Sheryl Sandberg, "If you're offered a seat on a rocket ship, get on. Don't ask what seat. I tell people in their careers, look for growth. Look for the teams that are growing quickly. Look for the companies that are doing well. Look for a place where you feel that you can have a lot of impact."

Collectors are less focused on developing talent and more on collecting it. Mentors who assume the Collector persona take pride in surrounding themselves with young or upcoming talents and guide them rather than groom them. Collector mentors take extreme joy in helping other people achieve their potential by giving them freedom, responsibility, and autonomy and then letting their natural abilities thrive.

Lorne Michaels has a long history of hiring hidden gems who thrive in *Saturday Night Live's* unique environment. One of Michaels's gems was Bill Hader, who never dreamed of working on the powerhouse. "I moved out here to be a filmmaker, to make movies, and write movies," Hader told podcaster Sam Jones.

Michaels liked Hader enough to offer him a job.

It wasn't immediate smooth sailing, though. While Hader loved performing, his pre-performance anxiety was nearly debilitating.

"The first four years at SNL, I was like, 'I'm going to get fired at any moment,'" Hader recalled.

Michaels sensed his emerging star was struggling. Rather than help him with his anxiety or change his style, Michaels played it straight.

"You know you could work here as long as you want," Michaels told Hader after a *Saturday Night Live* taping. "Just relax."

After an eight-year run on the show, Hader got his shot at film and television as the creator, producer, writer, occasional director, and star of *Barry*, an HBO dark comedy series. After the show's first two seasons, he won two Emmy Awards and received nominations for three more. Not bad for a guy who kept expecting to get fired.

***

"Live long and prosper," was the signature phrase of Leonard Nimoy's Spock, the half-human, half Vulcan character in the *Star Trek* franchise from its pilot episode in 1964 to the last *Star Trek* movie released in 2013. Nimoy earned three Emmy Award nominations for the role.

But Nimoy could have used, "Live long and mentor," instead.

In many ways, Nimoy was a surprise fan favorite. Born to Jewish immigrants from Ukraine, NBC was concerned his character would turn off viewers.

Nimoy told the Toronto Sun, "Star Trek creator Gene Roddenberry said that somebody in the sales department had been concerned that people in the Bible Belt might be offended by the idea of a devilish-looking character coming into their homes on their TV screen and NBC was saying to him, 'Keep this guy in the background. We don't want too much of that character up front.'"

A gifted actor who had honed his craft on the Broadway stage, Nimoy played to the outcast and misfit in all of us.

"Of course, shortly after the series went on the air," he continued, "the mail started to tell them otherwise. Suddenly, it was, 'Give us more Spock.'"

Nimoy played an important role in welcoming dozens of young actors and actresses into the *Star Trek* universe, particularly those who matched his outcast personality. His role as an actor and director would give him the ears of many of the most powerful people in Hollywood. That's not to mention the litany of future stars who, though they only briefly shared the screen with Nimoy, credit him with support and guidance in accelerating their careers.

Nimoy directed Christopher Lloyd in *Star Trek III: The Search for Spock* before Lloyd starred as Doc Brown in the *Back to the Future* series. Emmy-winning *Cheers* actress Kirstie Alley credited her big break to Nimoy's support after appearing together in *Star Trek II*. Regular costars William Shatner and George Takei remembered Nimoy's guidance, with Takei celebrating Nimoy's long-standing support of LGBTQ causes. Even Zachary Quinto, who played Spock in a reboot of *Star Trek* was grateful for Nimoy's guidance in taking over the iconic character.

One of his most outspoken supporters is Kim Cattrall, best known for her role as Samantha in the TV series *Sex and the City*. Cattrall had struggled with being typecast before earning a role as Lt. Valeris in *Star Trek VI: The Undiscovered Country* alongside Nimoy. She credited that experience with empowering her career. Nimoy served as an on-set mentor and a positive advocate for roles after her first big-screen break.

On his passing, Cattrall, who won a Golden Globe for her work in *Sex and the City*, wrote of Nimoy quoting Shakespeare, "Oh such another sleep that I might see but such another man—my mentor, champion and friend."

***

Collectors like Nimoy, Michaels, and Fishback seem to particularly thrive in their roles of "breaking" new talent. We know these skills help them operate almost as talent hubs. As I found with my own Collector Super Mentor, Steve Blank, these mentors know how to cultivate protégés, and if you find yourself in their orbit, consider yourself lucky.

But make no mistake. *They* drive the relationship, unlike most of our other Super Mentor personas.

Collectors have a strong internal filter and compass, are quick to move and move on, and are supremely confident in their actions. Relationships are intense and then may quickly cool. Usually, Collectors possess a strong, pointed vision and can see the world as it will be, even if you can't. Your job is to get on the bandwagon and follow their lead.

NFL Hall of Fame head coach Bill Walsh was exceptional on the field, winning three Super Bowls and being named NFL Coach of the Year in 1981 and 1984. He popularized the West Coast offense, which spread through the NFL. Walsh believed in offensive principles, and if you wanted to benefit from his guidance, you'd better believe in them too.

Despite his incredible wins, his legacy may lie in his ability to cultivate future coaches. His "coaching tree" features thirty-two current and former head coaches following his footsteps. Teams ultimately trusted Walsh as an identifier and cultivator of talent.

And if you hired one of his protégés, you'd better be comfortable running the West Coast offense.

***

Jerome Liebling was an American photographer, filmmaker, and teacher.

Ken Burns, award-winning documentary filmmaker, Buddy Squires, the cinematographer behind Mr. Burns's works, and directors Amy Steckler, Karen Goodman, Kirk Simon, and Roger Sherman count Liebling as their mentors. They've become known as the Hampshire Mafia, as they nearly all attended Hampshire College, the experimental college in Amherst, Massachusetts. Emmy and Academy Award winners and nominations fill Liebling's "family" tree, including an unusual number of successful filmmakers and photographers.

Liebling has transformed the motion picture industry through his unique ability to blend photography and film. Libling worked closely with filmmaker Allen Downs at the University of Minnesota. The pair collaborated on award-winning films *Pow Wow, The Tree Is Dead,* and *The Old Men,* and they coproduced several award-winning documentaries. In 1969, Liebling joined Hampshire College to run the newly established film, photography, and video program, a unique program that enabled Liebling to coach, teach, and mentor differently because it was designed no have no grades or no tenure for its faculty. Hampshire would soon become known as the hub for the documentary filmmaker community. Hampshire was.

His willingness to teach, coach, and support through a blend of tough love and genuine care has made him the most sought-after mentor in film.

Ken Burns is perhaps his best-known protégé, having earned two Oscar nominations, two Grammy Awards, and fifteen Emmy Awards in his career for his films, including *The Civil War, Baseball, The War, Brooklyn's Bridge, The Statue of Liberty,* and dozens more.

"Jerry turned me and made me look inward," Burns shared with the *New York Times,* "and it was not always a comfortable thing. I changed as a result of it. It was like molting."

Liebling recognized that filmmaking played a central role in documenting history as film and television took an ever-increasing role as the medium of record. Yale historian Alan Trachtenberg wrote that Liebling was not exactly a social or documentary photographer but rather a "civic photographer" whose work brought about a deep awareness of the person in the political. We see that deep awareness throughout the Hampshire Mafia.

"He was so authentic, in a way that a lot of us had never experienced," said Burns. "You wanted to be like him. You wanted to tell the truth. You'd go out to take pictures with him, and we all saw the same things he did, and then we'd come back, and he'd put up his prints, and you'd put up yours, and you were devastated."

Burns described all of Liebling's devotees and mentees as "all of us coming within Jerry's radiational sphere."

***

All Collectors seem to have that same radiational sphere.

In many ways, that's why Collectors, those rare individuals who are both deeply committed to cultivating others and empowered to cultivate them, may represent the pinnacle of Super Mentors.

EPILOGUE:

BECOMING A SUPER MENTOR

It perhaps fits that the book's last section features a story about the person most referenced in our study of mentoring relationships—Steve Jobs.

Writing and researching this book was one of my most rewarding experiences. In some ways, I feel privileged to have learned, read, and told hundreds of the most inspiring stories I've ever heard. The only shame of the process was that I couldn't include every story.

While the book focuses on the untold role of mentees and protégés in developing these Super Mentoring relationships, the consistent generosity of the Super Mentors was inspiring and somewhat surprising, although maybe it shouldn't be. It takes two to tango, and while in most of the cases we studied, the protégé extended their hand and pulled their mentor dance partner onto the dance floor, the dance itself was something to behold from that point onward.

The book was particularly instructive because it changed how I began to operate as a mentor.

While the book begins with my story of eighty-one failures—mentees who failed to create feedback loops and follow up with me—it ends with a much more promising story of nearly two thousand successes. What wasn't shared was what almost happened after the experiment.

Nearly two-thirds of those eighty-one people were students or former students. After tracking the outcome of those interactions, I came away very disheartened, and I quit teaching.

Or better said... I *tried to* quit teaching.

By the time I'd decided to quit, Georgetown informed me it was too late, and I'd have to teach one more semester.

I realized what I was doing for my students wasn't working, and rather than repeating the same mistakes, I decided to take that last semester to try something different.

Fortunately, when I spoke to my Super Mentor, Steve Blank, he shared an important insight about his own experience becoming a great mentor. He said, "Teachers, coaches, and mentors are each something different. If you want to learn a specific subject, find a teacher. If you want to hone specific skills or reach an explicit goal, hire a coach."

Steve recognized in his own life that his teachers and coaches had all been important people in his life, but his mentors had transformed his life.

He said, "If you want to get smarter and better over your career, find someone who cares about you enough to be a mentor."

I took that to heart, transforming my class into something altogether different, built on some teaching, some coaching, and many mentorships that I now have shared with nearly two thousand people through Manuscripts, my social education venture.

Thank you to Steve. Once a mentor, always a mentor.

***

Steve Jobs was the single most-mentioned Super Mentor in our research—seven times by our count, if not more. Steve has had numerous things written about him as a mentor, a teacher, an inspiration, and a force for good. In 2005, he spoke to the graduating class of Stanford University.

"Your time is limited, so don't waste it living someone else's life. Don't be trapped by dogma—which is living with the results of other people's thinking. Don't let the noise of others' opinions drown out your own inner voice. And most important, have the courage to follow your heart and intuition. They somehow already know what you truly want to become. Everything else is secondary."

But Steve Jobs in 2005 was a very different man than he was two decades earlier. Fortunately for us, though Jobs was taken from the world too early, we could see this evolution to the man he became.

Perhaps that self-awareness led him to become such an incredible mentor to so many. Maybe no single story best captured Jobs's brilliance as a mentor than the relationship he built with Mark Zuckerberg. Thanks to their prodigious rises to the top of the technology world and their bristling personalities, the two have often been compared to one another. But Facebook and Apple were rivals. Jobs had opportunities to go after the upstart, make their journey more challenging, or push off outreaches from the young founder. That, perhaps, makes the story of their relationship even more powerful.

Zuckerberg found himself at a precarious point before Facebook's success was assured. He considered whether he should remain at the helm or sell the company. He turned to Jobs for guidance, and Steve appreciated the gesture, sharing his admiration for the Facebook founder and his company until his death.

Jobs knew Zuckerberg didn't need his direction or his advice.

"Steve said that to reconnect with what I believed was the mission of the company," said Zuckerberg. The advice is echoed in what he told the Stanford graduates: *Have the courage to follow your heart and intuition.*

Jobs also encouraged Zuckerberg to take the time to find that answer. Zuckerberg recalled Jobs saying: "I should go visit this temple in India that he had visited early in the evolution of Apple, when he was thinking about what he wanted his vision of the future to be."

Jobs rediscovered much of what guided his philosophy during his second tenure at Apple while visiting the Kainchi Dham Ashram in North India.

Zuckerberg spent a month visiting the temple at the height of a chaotic and challenging time for his company.

"I went and I traveled for almost a month, and seeing people, seeing how people connected, and having the opportunity to feel how much better the world could be if everyone has a strong ability to connect reinforced for me the importance of what we were doing and that is something I've always remembered over the last ten years as we've built Facebook."

Zuckerberg saw how people in India connected more than finding an answer, strengthening his sense of Facebook's mission.

"That reinforced to me the importance of what we were doing, and that is something I will always remember," Zuckerberg said.

When Jobs passed away following his battle with cancer, Zuckerberg took the loss hard and penned a short tribute: "Steve, thank you for being a mentor and a friend. Thanks for showing that what you build can change the world. I will miss you."

***

What Jobs teaches us about being a mentor is remembering that the person across from us was once us.

WHEN THEY ASK FOR ADVICE, GIVE THEM GUIDANCE.
WHEN THEY ASK FOR GUIDANCE, GIVE THEM COACHING.
AND WHEN THEY DON'T KNOW WHAT THEY NEED,
GIVE THEM OPPORTUNITIES AND ACCESS.

Find someone full of potential and "[care] about them enough to be a mentor."

Your future mentee or protégé may not do all the right things, may not say all the right things, may ask the wrong question, or ask for more than you've got to give. But if you help them find the courage to follow their hearts and intuition, they'll be exceptional.

And you will too.

ACKNOWLEDGMENTS

This book began with a simple question:

WHAT DOES IT TAKE TO BE A SUPER MENTOR?

Along our journey to answer the question, we received help, support, and guidance from people we'd describe as the book's own Super Mentors. True to form, we aimed high, asked small (usually), and repeated this again and again until the book became a reality.

That means we have a lot of very important people to thank!

The first true "aim high" moment of this book was getting Adam Saven and the entire PeopleGrove family involved. When you want to write a book that pushes a new paradigm in the ancient art of mentorship, you'd better have a deep bench of passionate, thoughtful, and innovative people involved in the book. And that starts with Adam, who, in every conversation in the past five years, has never hesitated to push the thinking forward, bigger, and crisper.

I knew Adam was going to be so valuable to this book when he told me his own mission for PeopleGrove was to ensure everyone had access to the kind of mentors he had. And this book is another step toward that ambitious mission. Adam and his cofounder Riley have been gracious with their time, insights, knowledge, data, and wisdom about modern mentorship. The PeopleGrove team, beyond its cofounders, brought an infectious energy to the project—a breath of fresh air to the work. The team's research and content guru Matt Kelly deserves a special mention for providing invaluable insight and perspective. Bryan Landaburu, Greg Anderson, Autumn d'Adesky, Nicole Jeske, and Dani de La Fuente also brought their creative energy to this project and were instrumental in bringing this work to life.

To make a book that can impact people for a long time, you need a group of people involved in crafting who are invested in the mission, the purpose, and the author. We've been so grateful for the New Degree Press team offering vision, editorial help, beautiful artistic support, keen insight, and ongoing support in bringing this book to life. Brian Bies and Ethan Turer have been the quarterbacks getting this book out, and without their dedicated and patient support, it would not be the book that it has become. ChandaElaine Spurlock, Amanda Brown, Linda Berardelli, and Venus Bradley each offered patience coaching, teaching, and editing to make the book read the way it does. And Gjorgji Pejkovski, Grzegorz Laszczyk, and Mateusz Cichosz helped make the book a work of art. The New Degree Press publishing team are amazing partners. Because of your effort and encouragement, others will get to learn a skills that can transform their lives.

We knew early on that the book needed to offer something new to an ancient field that already had hundreds of studies, surveys, and papers. That meant an extensive investment into our research project to identify Super Mentors. Terry Wambui, Nisha Ghatak, and Biju Dev, Ribhu Singh were all critical contributors helping me to comb through thousands of individuals to identify those who fit our criteria. The first versions of the book were admittedly rough, and I'm grateful for the thoughtful and pointed feedback from my brother Mark Koester, the bigger thinking from a dear friend Shane Mac, and the pointed insights of Vedrana Damjanovic. I'd like to thank Jeff Reid, the head of entrepreneurship, Dean Prashant Malavia, Dean Patricia Grant, and Provost Randy Bass for their constant support of my research and new endeavors to bring innovative teaching, coaching, and service to the many entrepreneurial students at Georgetown.

My own Super Mentors deserve recognition here, many of whom have already been mentioned or profiled in the book, but all of whom made me realize how fortunate I've been to have them on my path. Steve Blank, Dan Chellman, Nick Malden, Scott Case, Shane Mac, Todd Glass, Fred Lawrence, Lee Hoedl, Mike Welborn, my father Larry, and my mother Kathy all gave me guidance and opportunities that helped me on my journey. I'd like the thank the individuals who shared their stories with me, through our conversations, interview, and research. The book was a pleasure to write because I got to see the power of mentoring through your eyes.

And lastly, but certainly most importantly, is my wife, partner, and best friend Allison. She's my ultimate Super Mentor. Truly, if I could only have one mentor in my life, having her as mine is my unfair advantage. Plus, I had three future readers in mind as I wrote the book, Quinn, Parker, and Aven, and I hope one day your lives are made happier, better, and more exciting because of the mentors you have in your lives.

This book was a labor of love and we tried to aim high, ask small, and repeat again and again until the book not only became a reality but became something we hope helps others. Great books change you, and it most certainly has changed me.

Finally, I'd like to thank the hundreds of beta readers, college students, and recent graduates who were part of the research and early reading of the book. Your contributions have made this a better book. Jiwon Hur, Ari Levine, Aarchi Kothari, Aman Bedi, Abigail Ramokoena, Abu Zafar Md Nuruzzaman Abir, Achintya Gupta, Aarathi Garimella, Sanskriti Agarwal, Agharnan Gandhi, Aryaman Gulati, Akshay Bhamidipati, Cassandra Giulietta Alvarino, Amankwah Clinton, Angela Mu, Ajay Natarajan, Aparna, Aritra Saha, Arnav Jain, Arun Singh, Akshat Toshniwal, Adilene Valencia-Sanchez, Alexander Z. Wang, Azamat Atabayev, Nadezhda Bagretsova, Ben H., Bharat Sachdev, Cameron Chaney, Chris Wang, Claire Gao, Atticus Maloney, Collin McCloskey, Vanessa Silva, Shaily Dave, Ukeje Ukeje, Devansh, Devin Gupta, Devon Montgomery, Diksha

Singh, Eric Dillon, Devin Mui, Donald Gaylord, Debbie Vu, Dyuti Dave, Dejie Zhen, Eshaan Vakil, Eyas Zedayesh, JJ Foster, Fred Nam, Gabriela Kochanowski, Karan Gajwani, Harsha Agarwal, Howard Yong, Sydney Hunter, Brandon Chu, Isabella Ortiz, Emre Isbir, Ishani Narwankar, Jane Yao, Jacqueline Cai, James Arvan, Jeffrey Fabian, Jimmy Gao, Jimmy Yang, Jenny Li, Jared Faulk, Johnny Hill, Joy Aun, John R Herrick, Jian Weng, Kenneth Cabrera, King Jemison, Khawaja Mujeeb, Kevin Yang, Lam Pham, KV, Lily Wong, Lauren Evelyn Sotell, Matthew A. Anderson, Manikanta Mudara, Marco Davis, Kanasai M, Matthew Plonskier, Maya Ravichandran, Muhammad Alwan, Mehul Arora, Mahfuza Haque, Madison Mullis, Madelaine Santa, Mallika P., Murad Zaman, Myckland Matthew, Nadav Kempinski, Nazanin Azimi, Natalia Suska, Nick Lugo, Olly Akindele, Partho Adhikari, Pamela Nelson, Patrick Cordery, Pratiksha Malayil, Raghav Chaturvedi, Regina Morfin, Rehan Rupawalla, Rishabh Jain, Ava Ritchie, Rohan Sharma, Raisa Tasnim Raofa, Sahil S. Bolar, Sandeep Ramesh, Sandy Chen, Sarah Syed, Sashank Kaushik Sridhar, Shriya Boppana, Sevara Mallaboeva, Sushant Ghorpade, Shagufta Naaz, Amal Sharma, Shekhaa Hameed, Shreya Patel, Siddhant Chadha, Siddhika Didel, Sarah Hakala, Sneha Ashish Makhijani, Sanjana Pendharkar, Spencer Schwarz, Simran Bagdiya, Subash Lamichhane, Sufyan Farooq, Suryansh Gupta, Shreyas Venkatarathinam, Taran Suresh, Theron Mansilla, Arya Vardhan, Vibhav Yawalkar, Vigna Kumar, Vijaylaxmi Saxena, Victoria Steinhoff, Wei-Ting Yap, Sarah Williams, William Deng, Wendy Tang, Yaseen Syed, Yuelin Dang, and Zage Phillips.

APPENDIX

INTRODUCTION

Lux Capital, 25 Feb. 2022. https://luxcapital.com/.

MacColl, Margaux. "Gen Z VCS: Meet the Top 29 Up-and-Comers Changing the World of Venture Capital." *Business Insider*, Business Insider, 19 Feb. 2021. https://www.businessinsider.com/the-top-29-gen-z-vcs-changing-venture-capital-2021-2.

"Study Explores Professional Mentor-Mentee Relationships in 2019." *Olivet Nazarene University*. https://online.olivet.edu/research-statistics-on-professional-mentors.

CHAPTER 1

Katzenbach, Jon, and Ashley Harshak. "Stop Blaming Your Culture." *Strategy+Business*, 19 Jan. 2011. https://www.strategy-business.com/article/11108.

Kelly, Matt. "A Vision of the Future for Students—Peoplegrove: Enable Meaningful Connections throughout Every Learner's Journey." *PeopleGrove*, 6 Apr. 2022. https://www.peoplegrove.com/a-vision-of-the-future-for-students.

Qi, Christina. "No, I Don't Have a Mentor, and I'm Doing Just Fine." *LinkedIn*, LinkedIn, 6 Feb. 2021. https://www.linkedin.com/pulse/i-dont-have-mentor-im-doing-just-fine-christina-qi-caia/.

"Steve Blank Innovation and Entrepreneurship." *Steve Blank*, https://steve-blank.com/.

CHAPTER 2

Campbell, Joseph. *The Hero with a Thousand Faces*. New World Library, 2008.

CHAPTER 3

Entis, Laura. "5 Famous Business Leaders on the Power of Mentorship." *Entrepreneur*, Entrepreneur, 7 Aug. 2015, https://www.entrepreneur.com/slideshow/249233.

Grant, Adam. "Are You a Giver or a Taker?" *Adam Grant: Are You a Giver or a Taker? | TEDx Talk*, https://www.ted.com/talks/adam_grant_are_you_a_giver_or_a_taker.

Milkman, Katy. *How to Change: The Science of Getting from Where You Are to Where You Want to Be*. VERMILION, 2022.

Narcisse, Whitnie Low. "We Studied 100 Mentor-Mentee Matches—Here's What Makes Mentorship Work." *First Round Review*. https://review.firstround.com/we-studied-100-mentor-mentee-matches-heres-what-makes-mentorship-work.

"Study Explores Professional Mentor-Mentee Relationships in 2019." *Olivet Nazarene University*, https://online.olivet.edu/research-statistics-on-professional-mentors.

CHAPTER 4

Berrios, Frank, and Marta Dorado. *The Story of Lin-Manuel Miranda: A Biography Book for New Readers*. Rockridge Press, 2022.

Duval, Shelley, and Robert A. Wicklund. *A Theory of Objective Self-Awareness*. Academic Press, 1972.

Eurich, Tasha. "What Self-Awareness Really Is (and How to Cultivate It)." *Harvard Business Review*, 4 January, 2018. https://hbr.org/2018/01/what-self-awareness-really-is-and-how-to-cultivate-it.

Miranda, Lin-Manuel, and Seth Meyers. "Watch Late Night with Seth Meyers Interview: Lin-Manuel Miranda Reveals How He Sneak Tested

Hamilton at the Obama White House." *NBC*, https://www.nbc.com/
late-night-with-seth-meyers/video/linmanuel-miranda-reveals-how-he-
sneak-tested-hamilton-at-the-obama-white-house/3544404 (accessed
January 4, 2021).

CHAPTER 5

Clemons, Steve. "Sheryl Sandberg Proved Herself with Summers." *The
Atlantic*, Atlantic Media Company, 6 Feb. 2012. https://www.theatlantic.
com/business/archive/2012/02/sheryl-sandberg-proved-herself-with-
summers/252627/.

Dolar, Veronika. "The Gender Gap in Economics Is Huge—It's Even Worse
than Tech." *The Conversation*, 19 Apr. 2022, https://theconversation.com/
the-gender-gap-in-economics-is-huge-its-even-worse-than-tech-156275.

Lopez, Sean Seymour and Shane. "Big Six College Experiences Linked
to Life Preparedness." *Gallup.com*, Gallup, 15 Sept. 2021. https://news.
gallup.com/poll/182306/big-six-college-experiences-linked-life-pre-
paredness.aspx.

Nevins, Jake. "Ava DuVernay: I'm Not Getting John Wick 3, Even Though
I'd Love to Make It." *The Guardian*, Guardian News and Media, 29
May 2019. https://www.theguardian.com/tv-and-radio/2019/may/29/
ava-duvernay-interview-netflix-central-park-five.

Perlroth, Nicole, and Claire Cain Miller. "The $1.6 Billion Woman, Staying
on Message." *The New York Times*, The New York Times, 4 Feb. 2012.
https://www.nytimes.com/2012/02/05/business/sheryl-sandberg-of-
facebook-staying-on-message.html.

Rushe, Dominic. "Sheryl Sandberg: The First Lady of Facebook Takes the
World Stage." *The Guardian*, Guardian News and Media, 24 Jan. 2012.
https://www.theguardian.com/theguardian/2012/jan/24/sheryl-sand-
berg-facebook-davos.

Sandberg, Sheryl. "Larry Summers' True Record on Women." *HuffPost*,
HuffPost, 8 December 2008. https://www.huffpost.com/entry/what-
larry-summers-has-do_b_142126.

"Sheryl Sandberg: The HBR Interview." *Harvard Business Review*, 30 Mar.
2015. https://hbr.org/2013/03/sheryl-sandberg-the-hbr-interv.

CHAPTER 6

Barrett, Jamie. "Nike 'Failure' Michael Jordan AD 1997." *YouTube*, Nike, Jan. 1997, https://www.youtube.com/watch?v=nvrbQBI4ElI.

Clear, James. *Atomic Habits: An Easy & Proven Way to Build Good Habits & Break Bad Ones*. Avery, an Imprint of Penguin Random House, 2018.

Fowler, J H, Christakis N A. Dynamic spread of happiness in a large social network: longitudinal analysis over 20 years in the Framingham Heart Study BMJ 2008; 337.

Grant, Adam M. *Give and Take: A Revolutionary Approach to Success*. Phoenix, 2014.

Hamilton, Arlan, and Rachel L. Nelson. *It's about Damn Time: How to Turn Being Underestimated into Your Greatest Advantage*. Currency, 2022.

Jorgenson, Eric. *The Almanack of Naval Ravikant: A Guide to Wealth and Happiness*. Magrathea Publishing, 2020.

Klein, Howard J., et al. "The Role of Goal Specificity in the Goal-Setting Process." *Motivation and Emotion*, vol. 14, no. 3 (1990): 179–193. https://doi.org/10.1007/bf00995568.

Latham, Gary P. "The Motivational Benefits of Goal-Setting." *Academy of Management Perspectives*, vol. 18, no. 4 (2004): 126–129. https://doi.org/10.5465/ame.2004.15268727.

CHAPTER 7

Dunbar, R. I. "Coevolution of Neocortical Size, Group Size and Language in Humans." *Behavioral and Brain Sciences*, vol. 16, no. 4 (1993): 681–694. https://doi.org/10.1017/s0140525x00032325.

Moore, Wes. *The Other Wes Moore: One Name, Two Fates*. Spiegel & Grau Trade Paperbacks, 2011.

Nathoo, Kirsty. "Female Founders and Raising Money: Founder Stories, Women Founders: Y Combinator." *YC Startup Library*, 26 Feb. 2018. https://www.ycombinator.com/library/5q-female-founders-and-raising-money.

Reader, Ruth. "The Riveter, a Female-Centric Coworking Startup, Raises $20 Million." *Fast Company*, Fast Company, 10 Dec. 2018. https://www.fastcompany.com/90279108/the-riveter-a-female-centric-coworking-start-up-raises-20-million.

Shoenthal, Amy. "How the Riveter's Amy Nelson Built a More Inclusive Women's Coworking Space While Changing the Motherhood Narrative." *Forbes*, Forbes Magazine, 23 Sept. 2019. https://www.forbes.com/sites/amyschoenberger/2019/09/20/riveter-amy-nelson/?sh=635e08fe6993.

Wilson, Chris, and Bret Witter. *The Master Plan: My Journey from Life in Prison to a Life of Purpose*. G.P. Putnam's Sons, 2020.

CHAPTER 8

Burkus, David. "You're Not the Average of the Five People You Surround Yourself With." *Medium*, Mission.org, 7 June 2018. https://medium.com/the-mission/youre-not-the-average-of-the-five-people-you-surround-yourself-with-f21b817f6e69.

Clifford, Cat. "Ex Facebook Board Member: I Knew Twenty-Year-Old Mark Zuckerberg. He's Not a Bad Person." *CNBC*, CNBC, 12 Apr. 2018. https://www.cnbc.com/2018/04/12/former-facebook-board-member-don-graham-on-young-mark-zuckerberg.html.

Stewart, Christopher S., and Russell Adams. "When Zuckerberg Met Graham: A Facebook Love Story." *The Wall Street Journal*, Dow Jones & Company, 5 Jan. 2012. https://www.wsj.com/articles/SB10001424052970203686204577116631661990706.

Szalai, Georg. "Facebook CEO Mark Zuckerberg, Washington Post CEO Don Graham Mentor Each Other." *The Hollywood Reporter*, The Hollywood Reporter, 5 Jan. 2012. https://www.hollywoodreporter.com/business/digital/facebook-mark-zuckerberg-don-graham-mentor-278698/.

CHAPTER 9

Goetz, Thomas. "Harnessing the Power of Feedback Loops." *Wired*, Conde Nast, 19 June 2011. https://www.wired.com/2011/06/ff-feedbackloop/.

Kumar, Amit, and Nicholas Epley. "Undervaluing Gratitude: Expressers Misunderstand the Consequences of Showing Appreciation." *Psychological Science*, vol. 29, no. 9 (2018): 1423–1435. https://doi.org/10.1177/0956797618772506.

Markman, Art. "Giving Advice Creates a Sense of Power." *Psychology Today*, Sussex Publishers, 14 May 2018. https://www.psychologytoday.com/us/blog/ulterior-motives/201805/giving-advice-creates-sense-power.

Smith, Spencer. *IRC Sales Solutions*, IRC Sales Solutions, 11 June 2021. https://ircsalessolutions.com/insights/sales-follow-up-statistics.

Straus, Sharon E, et al. "Characteristics of Successful and Failed Mentoring Relationships: A Qualitative Study across Two Academic Health Centers." *Academic Medicine: Journal of the Association of American Medical Colleges*, US National Library of Medicine, Jan. 2013. https://www.ncbi.nlm.nih.gov/pmc/articles/PMC3665769/.

Vardi, Nathan. "Robert Smith's Road to Paying off Morehouse Graduates' Loans Started with His Own Graduation Speaker." *Forbes*, Forbes Magazine, 30 Sept. 2019. https://www.forbes.com/sites/nathan-vardi/2019/05/20/robert-smiths-road-to-paying-off-morehouse-graduates-loans-started-with-his-own-graduation-speaker/?sh=11c6de2de0cc.

CHAPTER 10

Boogaard, Kat. "What's Microproductivity? the Small Habit That Will Lead You to Big Wins." *A Blog for Teams by Trello*, 3 Jan. 2019. https://blog.trello.com/microproductivity-break-tasks-into-smaller-steps.

Breznican, Anthony. "Steven Spielberg Reveals Secrets of 'the Shining' Sequence in 'Ready Player One.'" *EW.com*, 3 July 2018. https://ew.com/movies/2018/07/03/steven-spielberg-the-shining-ready-player-one/.

Duckworth, Angela. *Grit: The Power of Passion and Perseverance*. Scribner, 2016.

Dweck, Carol. *Mindset—Updated Edition—Changing the Way You Think to Fulfill Your Potential*. Little, Brown Book Group, 2017.

"Entertainment | Spielberg to Wrap Kubrick Project." *BBC News*, BBC, 15 Mar. 2000. http://news.bbc.co.uk/2/hi/entertainment/678278.stm.

Fogg, B.J. *Tiny Habits: The Small Changes That Change Everything*. Thorndike Press, a Part of Gale, a Cengage Company, 2020.

Phillips-Jones, Linda. *Skills for Successful Mentoring: Competencies of Outstanding Mentors and Mentees*. CCC/The Mentoring Group, 2003.

Qi, Christina. "No, I Don't Have a Mentor, and I'm Doing Just Fine." *Linke-dIn*, LinkedIn, 6 Feb. 2021. https://www.linkedin.com/pulse/i-dont-have-mentor-im-doing-just-fine-christina-qi-caia/.

Rose, Steve. "Stanley Told Steven: You'd Be the Best Guy to Direct This Film." *The Guardian*, Guardian News and Media, 5 May 2000. https://www.theguardian.com/film/2000/may/05/1.

Sambunjak, Dario, et al. "A Systematic Review of Qualitative Research on the Meaning and Characteristics of Mentoring in Academic Medicine." *Journal of General Internal Medicine*, Springer-Verlag, Jan. 2010. https://www.ncbi.nlm.nih.gov/pmc/articles/PMC2811592/.

Taleb, Nassim Nicholas. *Antifragile: Things That Gain from Disorder*. Random House, 2016.

Thompson, Anne. "Ready Player One: Inside Steven Spielberg's Epic Tribute to Stanley Kubrick." *Yahoo! News*, Yahoo!, 4 Apr. 2018. https://www.yahoo.com/news/ready-player-one-inside-steven-143028502.html.

CHAPTER 11

Schafer, Jack, and Marvin Karlins. *The Like Switch: An Ex-FBI Agent's Guide to Influencing, Attracting, and Winning People Over*. Atria Paperback, an Imprint of Simon & Schuster Inc., 2019.

CHAPTER 12

Chilton, Martin. "Bob Dylan's 25 Musical Heroes, Including Guy Clark." *The Telegraph*, Telegraph Media Group, 28 Jan. 2016. https://www.telegraph.co.uk/music/artists/bob-dylans-20-musical-heroes/.

Dylan, Bob. *Chronicles: Volume One*. Simon & Schuster, 2004.

Guthrie, Woody. *Bound for Glory*. E.P. Dutton, 1943.

Hampton, Adam J., et al. "You're like Me and I like You: Mediators of the Similarity—Liking Link Assessed before and after a Getting-Acquainted Social Interaction." *Journal of Social and Personal Relationships*, vol. 36, no. 7 (2018): 2221–2244. https://doi.org/10.1177/0265407518790411.

Montoya, R. Matthew, et al. "Is Actual Similarity Necessary for Attraction? A Meta-Analysis of Actual and Perceived Similarity." *Journal of Social*

and Personal Relationships, vol. 25, no. 6, (2008): 889–922. https://doi.
   org/10.1177/0265407508096700.

Scaduto, Anthony. "Bob Dylan: An Intimate Biography, Part One." *Rolling
   Stone,* Rolling Stone, 20 May 2021. https://www.rollingstone.com/music/
   music-news/bob-dylan-an-intimate-biography-part-one-244147/.

Winfrey, Oprah. "Oprah Talks to Maya Angelou." *Oprah.com,* Oprah.com,
   15 Dec. 2000. https://www.oprah.com/omagazine/oprah-interviews-ma-
   ya-angelou.

Winfrey, Oprah. "Oprah Talks to Maya Angelou." *Oprah.com,* Oprah.com,
   21 May 2013. https://www.oprah.com/omagazine/maya-angelou-inter-
   viewed-by-oprah-in-2013.

"YouthBuild Mentors—Getting as Much as They Give: YouthBuild USA
   National Mentoring Alliance Community of Practice." *YouthBuild
   Mentors—Getting as Much as They Give | YouthBuild USA National
   Mentoring Alliance Community of Practice.* http://youthbuildmentor-
   ingalliance.org/for-mentors.

CHAPTER 13

Buffett, Warren. "Benjamin Graham." *Financial Analysts Journal,* 1976.
   https://www.tandfonline.com/toc/ufaj20/current.

Flaherty, Colleen. *Research Shows Professors Work Long Hours and Spend
   Much of Day in Meetings,* 9 Apr. 2014. https://www.insidehighered.com/
   news/2014/04/09/research-shows-professors-work-long-hours-and-
   spend-much-day-meetings.

Glanz, James. "Arthur Walker, Sixty-Four, Scientist and Mentor, Dies." *The
   New York Times,* The New York Times, 9 May 2001. https://www.nytimes.
   com/2001/05/09/us/arthur-walker-64-scientist-and-mentor-dies.html.

Lambert, Leo M. "The Importance of Helping Students Find Mentors in
   College." *Gallup.com,* Gallup, 29 Nov. 2018. https://news.gallup.com/
   opinion/gallup/245048/importance-helping-students-find-mentors-col-
   lege.aspx.

"Profile: Best-Connected Man in PR—a Rough Exterior, Dedication to His
   Students and a Powerful Network of Former Students-Turned-PR-
   Pros May Make Gerald Powers One of the Most Formidable Men on

the PR Scene." *PR Week*, PR Week Global, 5 July 1999. https://www.prweek.com/article/1232315/profile-best-connected-man-pr-rough-exterior-dedication-students-powerful-network-former-students-turned-pr-pros-may-gerald-powers-one-formidable-men.

Serene Schneider, Louisa. "Warren Buffett Video Interview—Learnings from Ben Graham, Father of Value Investing." *The Heilbrunn Center for Graham & Dodd Investing*, 21 Oct. 2019. https://www8.gsb.columbia.edu/valueinvesting/warrenbuffettvideointerview?nid%3A170=Warren-Buffett.

CHAPTER 14

Adler, Carlye. "The Fresh Prince of Software." *Fortune*, Cable News Network, 1 Mar. 2003. https://money.cnn.com/magazines/fsb/fsb_archive/2003/03/01/338759/index.htm.

Amabile, Teresa, and Steven Kramer. *The Progress Principle: Using Small Wins to Ignite Joy, Engagement, and Creativity at Work.* Harvard Business Review Press, 2011.

Benioff, Marc R., and Carlye Adler. *Behind the Cloud the Untold Story of How Salesforce.com Went from Idea to Billion-Dollar Company—and Revolutionized an Industry.* Jossey-Bass, 2010.

Bontaş, Raluca. "Human Capital Trends Report 2019." *Deloitte*, 7 June 2019. https://www2.deloitte.com/ro/en/pages/human-capital/articles/2019-deloitte-global-human-capital-trends.html.

Harter, Jim. "Percent Who Feel Employer Cares about Their Wellbeing Plummets." *Gallup.com*, Gallup, 21 Apr. 2022. https://www.gallup.com/workplace/390776/percent-feel-employer-cares-wellbeing-plummets.aspx.

Kim, Eugene. "The Epic Thirty-Year Bromance of Billionaire CEOS Larry Ellison and Marc Benioff." *Business Insider*, Business Insider, 12 Aug. 2015. https://www.businessinsider.com/larry-ellison-marc-benioff-relationship-2015-8.

Hoffman, Reid, et al. *The Alliance: Managing Talent in the Networked Age.* Harvard Business Review Press, 2014.

"Larry Ellison." *Biography.com*, A&E Networks Television, 15 Apr. 2019. https://www.biography.com/business-figure/larry-ellison.

Roth, Daniel. "The Big Benioff." Fortune, 13 Dec. 2004. https://archive. fortune.com/magazines/fortune/fortune_archive/2004/12/13/8214218/index.htm.

Thorton, S. "Quantitative Data about How Mentoring in the Workplace Improves Staff Retention, Productivity, Promotion & Development." *Wonder*, 11 Apr. 2017. https://askwonder.com/research/quantitative-data-mentoring-workplace-improves-staff-retention-productivity-1g08mzsef.

CHAPTER 15

Casnocha, Ben. "Six Habits of Highly Effective Mentees." *Ben Casnocha*, 15 Apr. 2008. https://casnocha.com/2008/04/six-habits-of-h.html.

Grimmer, Jordan. "Experts vs. Friends: The Definitive Guide to Who Influences Us and Why." Medium, 29 Sept. 2016. https://medium.com/bestcompany/experts-vs-friends-the-definitive-guide-to-who-influences-us-and-why-6a0aa609c8c0

Gross, Terry. "Quincy Jones: The Man behind the Music." *NPR*, NPR, 27 May 2013. https://www.npr.org/2013/05/27/186052477/quincy-jones-the-man-behind-the-music.

Jones, Quincy. *Quincy Jones on His Early Mentors*, 9 Aug. 2013. https://www.arts.gov/stories/jazz-moments/quincy-jones-his-early-mentors.

Kroll, Justin. "Bradley Cooper and Todd Phillips Form New Production Company (Exclusive)." *Variety*, Yahoo!, 16 May 2014. https://finance.yahoo.com/news/bradley-cooper-todd-phillips-form-production-company-exclusive-180042003.html.

Lange, Julian E. "Twenty-Seven Million Americans Are Starting or Running New Businesses." *Global Entrepreneurship Monitor United States Report*, Babson College. 9 Jan. 2019. https://www.prnewswire.com/news-releases/27-million-americans-are-starting-or-running-new-businesses-based-on-data-reported-in-latest-global-entrepreneurship-monitor-united-states-report-300775598.html.

Lassonde, Karla. "The Humility of Learning: A New Approach to the Process of Changing Knowledge." *Psych Learning Curve*, 17 Jan. 2020. http://psychlearningcurve.org/the-humility-of-learning-a-new-approach-to-the-process-of-changing-knowledge/.

Martin, Rachel. "Bradley Cooper on the Personal Story behind *A Star Is Born*." *NPR*, NPR, 14 Sept. 2018. https://www.npr.org/2018/09/14/647491779/bradley-cooper-on-the-personal-story-behind-a-star-is-born.

Michaels, Jillian. "LinkedIn on Mentorship #Thankyourmentor." *LinkedIn*, 5 Aug. 2015. https://www.slideshare.net/LinkedInPulse/linkedin-on-mentorship-thankyourmentor.

Orman, Suze. "I Didn't Become a Mentor to Make Others More like Me." *LinkedIn*, LinkedIn, 9 Aug. 2018. https://www.linkedin.com/pulse/mentor-who-shaped-me-i-didnt-become-make-others-more-like-suze-orman/.

Parker, Dylan. "The Truth about Casting *The Hangover*." *TheThings*, 12 Feb. 2021. https://www.thethings.com/the-truth-about-casting-the-hangover/.

"Ray Charles." *Who Mentored You*, 15 Jan. 2015. https://sites.sph.harvard.edu/wmy/celebrities/ray-charles/.

Spiegel, James S. "Open-Mindedness and Intellectual Humility." *Theory and Research in Education*, vol. 10, no. 1 (2012): 27–38. https://doi.org/10.1177/1477878512437472.

Stanovich, K. E., West, R. F., & Toplak, M. E. (2013). Myside bias, rational thinking, and intelligence. *Current Directions in Psychological Science, 22*(4): 259–264. https://doi.org/10.1177/0963721413480174

Wallace, Amy. "Quincy Jones Gives Us a Glimpse into the Life of a Musical Legend." *Los Angeles Magazine*, 2 Dec. 2016. https://www.lamag.com/l-a-icon/quincy-jones-gives-us-a-glimpse-into-the-life-of-a-musical-legend/.

CHAPTER 16

Balachandra, Lakshmi, et al. "Investor Mentor: Evaluating the Entrepreneur as Protege." *Academy of Management Proceedings*, vol. 2015, no. 1 (2015): 17605. https://doi.org/10.5465/ambpp.2015.17605abstract.

Barnes, Michael. "First President of Dell Shares the Power of Fate, Imagination and Hard Work in Memoir." *austin360*, Austin 360, 18 Dec. 2019. https://www.austin360.com/story/entertainment/books/2019/12/18/first-president-of-dell-shares-power-of-fate-imagination-and-hard-work-in-memoir/2059216007/.

Eesley, Charles E., and Yanbo Wang. "The Effects of Mentoring in Entrepreneurial Career Choice." *SSRN Electronic Journal*, 2014. https://doi.org/10.2139/ssrn.2387329.

Guglielmo, Connie. "Andreessen, Horowitz: Venture Capital's New Bad Boys." *Forbes*, Forbes Magazine, 12 Nov. 2012. https://www.forbes.com/sites/connieguglielmo/2012/05/02/andreessen-horowitz-venture-capitals-new-bad-boys/?sh=1dc402cb68c2.

Marinova, Polina. "Foursquare Cofounder Dennis Crowley on His Decision to Step down as CEO and What It Taught Him about Success." *Business Insider*, Business Insider, 18 Feb. 2021. https://markets.businessinsider.com/foursquare-cofounder-dennis-crowley-stepped-down-from-role-as-ceo-2021-2.

Morris, Rhett. "Mentors Are the Secret Weapons of Successful Startups." *TechCrunch*, TechCrunch, 23 Mar. 2015. https://techcrunch.com/2015/03/22/mentors-are-the-secret-weapons-of-successful-startups/.

Pompliano, Polina. "The Profile." *The Real Story Behind Why Foursquare's Dennis Crowley Stepped Down as CEO*, The Profile, 31 Jan. 2021. https://theprofile.substack.com/p/the-profile-the-teenage-day-trader-253?s=r.

Sanchez-Burks, Jeffrey, et al. "Mentoring in Startup Ecosystems." *SSRN Electronic Journal*, 2017, https://doi.org/10.2139/ssrn.3066168.

Schiller, Colin. "How to Turn $1,000 into $10 Billion: The Mentoring of Michael Dell." *Modern Workforce Blog, by Everwise*, 14 Feb. 2019. https://www.geteverwise.com/mentoring/how-to-turn-1000-into-10-billion-the-mentoring-of-michael-dell/.

University of Texas. "George Kozmetsky." The IC2 Institute. https://ic2.utexas.edu/george-kozmetsky/ (accessed May 5, 2022).

CHAPTER 17

Bruk, A., Scholl, S. G., & Bless, H. (2018). Beautiful mess effect: Self—other differences in evaluation of showing vulnerability. Journal of Personality and Social Psychology, 115(2): 192–205. https://doi.org/10.1037/pspa0000120

Finette, Jane. *Unlocked: How Empowered Women Empower Women*. New Degree Press, 2021.

Guynn, Jessica. "Jack Dorsey Emulates Steve Jobs, His Mentor from Afar." *Los Angeles Times*, Los Angeles Times, 20 Oct. 2011. https://latimesblogs.latimes.com/technology/2011/10/jack-dorsey-steve-jobs-mentor.html.

Huspeni, Andrea. "Meet behind-the-Scenes Mentors of Fifteen Top Tech Executives." *Business Insider*, Business Insider, 11 July 2012. https://www.businessinsider.com/meet-the-mentors-behind-the-visionaries-of-tech-2012-7.

Jelks, Randal Maurice, and Benjamin E. Mays. *Benjamin Elijah Mays, Schoolmaster of the Movement: A Biography*. University of North Carolina Press, 2014.

Kirkpatrick, David, et al. "Twitter Was Act One." *Vanity Fair*, 3 Mar. 2011. https://www.vanityfair.com/news/2011/04/jack-dorsey-201104.

Preston, Justin. "Mentors Can Spot Mental Health Troubles in Mentees." *The Chronicle of Evidence-Based Mentoring*, Justin Preston Https://Www.evidencebasedmentoring.org/Wp-Content/Uploads/2018/08/Chronicle-Logo-1.Png, 9 May 2017. https://www.evidencebasedmentoring.org/research-shows-mentors-can-spot-mental-health-troubles-mentees/.

Staff, TIME. "Martin Luther King Jr.'s Death: Read the Eulogy." *Time*, Time, 4 Apr. 2018. https://time.com/5224875/martin-luther-king-jr-eulogy/.

Sumner, Barckley. "Charity Workers Suffering an Epidemic of Mental Health Issues and Stress, Survey Reveals." *Trade Union, Unions UK, Workers Union—Unite the Union*, 20 May 2019. https://www.unitetheeunion.org/news-events/news/2019/may/charity-workers-suffering-an-epidemic-of-mental-health-issues-and-stress-survey-reveals/.

Warnick, Sophia. "The Capitalist Buddha Who Mentored Jack Dorsey." *Modern Workforce Blog, by Everwise*, 14 Feb. 2019. https://www.geteverwise.com/mentoring/the-capitalist-buddha-who-mentored-jack-dorsey/.

CHAPTER 18

Branson, Richard. *Losing My Virginity: How I Survived, Had Fun, and Made a Fortune Doing Business My Way.* Crown Business, 2011.

Branson, Richard. "'The Best Advice I Ever Got.'" *CNNMoney*, Cable News Network, 21 Mar. 2005. https://money.cnn.com/magazines/fortune/fortune_archive/2005/03/21/8254830/index.htm.

Gilchrist, Karen. "How Richard Branson Started Virgin Atlantic with a Blackboard Selling $39 Flights." *CNBC*, CNBC, 30 Dec. 2019. https://www.cnbc.com/2019/12/30/richard-branson-started-virgin-atlantic-with-a-board-and-39-flights.html.

Gregory, Martyn. *Dirty Tricks: British Airways' Secret War against Virgin Atlantic.* Virgin Digital, 2010.

Gzresik, Ania. *Laker: The Glory Years of Sir Freddie Laker.* Myrtle Pr, 2020.

Hernandez, Chino R. "The Cult of YSL: How Yves Saint Laurent Climbed His Way to the Top of Fashion." *Lifestyle Asia*, 3 Oct. 2018. https://lifestyleasia.onemega.com/the-cult-of-ysl-how-yves-saint-laurent-climbed-his-way-to-the-top-of-fashion/.

Holmes, Daniel. "Remembering a Fashion Pioneer—Yves Saint Laurent." *Cov Uni London News RSS*, 8 Feb. 2018. https://www.cusu.org/news/article/7858/Remembering-a-Fashion-Icon-Yves-Saint-Laurent/.

Janssen, Elsa. "The Dior Years." *Musée Yves Saint Laurent Paris.* https://museeyslparis.com/en/stories/les-annees-dior-1-1.

Keeter, Scott, et al. "Trust and Distrust in America." *Pew Research Center—US Politics & Policy*, Pew Research Center, 27 July 2021, https://www.pewresearch.org/politics/2019/07/22/trust-and-distrust-in-america/.

Nazarenus, Franziska. "Top Ten Yves Saint Laurent Zitate." *Parisian (Style) Guides*, 6 Dec. 2020. https://franziskanazarenus.com/2020/12/06/yves-saint-laurent-zitate/.

O'Connell, Dee. "What Happened Next?" *The Guardian*, Guardian News and Media, 13 Sept. 2003. https://www.theguardian.com/theobserver/2003/sep/14/features.magazine87.

Staff, CPA Practice Advisor. "Business Mentoring Increases Small Business Survival Rates." *CPA Practice Newsletter*, 4 June 2018. https://www.

cpapracticeadvisor.com/small-business/news/12415443/business-men-toring-increases-small-business-survival-rates.

CHAPTER 19

Alberts, Hana R. "Documenting Authentic, Everyday New York from the 1940s On." *Curbed NY*, Curbed NY, 28 Apr. 2015. https://ny.curbed.com/2015/4/28/9966280/documenting-authentic-everyday-new-york-from-the-1940s-on.

Corcoran, Kieran. "How Stars Have Prospered since Sharing the Screen with Leonard Nimoy." *Daily Mail Online*, Associated Newspapers, 2 Mar. 2015. https://www.dailymail.co.uk/news/article-2973626/Spock-mentor-stars-like-Kim-Cattrall-lived-long-prospered-sharing-stage-Leonard-Nimoy.html.

Finkelstein, Sydney. *Superbosses: How Exceptional Leaders Master the Flow of Talent*. Portfolio/Penguin, 2019.

"Jerome Liebling: MOMA." *The Museum of Modern Art*, https://www.moma.org/artists/3549.

Jones, Sam. "Bill Hader." *Off Camera*, 17 Sept. 2020, https://www.podchaser.com/podcasts/off-camera-with-sam-jones-65445/episodes/ep-138-bill-hader-74734326.

Kennedy, Randy. "Jerome Liebling, Socially Minded Photographer, Dies at Eighty-Seven." *The New York Times*, The New York Times, 29 July 2011. https://www.nytimes.com/2011/07/29/arts/design/jerome-liebling-pho-tographer-and-mentor-is-dead-at-87.html.

Kennedy, Randy. "The Still-Life Mentor to a Filmmaking Generation." *The New York Times*, The New York Times, 19 Oct. 2006. https://www.nytimes.com/2006/10/19/arts/design/19lieb.html.

Kim, Susanna. "The Best Advice I Ever Received." *ABC News*, ABC News Network, 12 Mar. 2013. https://abcnews.go.com/blogs/business/2013/03/the-best-advice-sheryl-sandberg-received.

Slotek, Jim. "Remembering 'Star Trek' Star Leonard Nimoy." *Torontosun*, Toronto Sun, 27 Feb. 2015. https://torontosun.com/2015/02/27/leonard-nimoy-spock-of-star-trek-dead-at-83.

EPILOGUE

Blank, Steve. "Mentors, Coaches and Teachers." *Medium*, Startup Grind, 7 Feb. 2017. https://medium.com/startup-grind/mentors-coaches-and-teachers-7025749174d3.

D'onfro, Jillian. "Mark Zuckerberg Says That Visiting an Indian Temple at the Urging of Steve Jobs Helped Him Stick to Facebook's Mission." *Business Insider*, 27 Sept. 2015. https://www.businessinsider.in/Mark-Zuckerberg-says-that-visiting-an-Indian-temple-at-the-urging-of-Steve-Jobs-helped-him-stick-to-Facebooks-mission/articleshow/49130605.cms.

Mochari, Ilan. "Steve Jobs's Early Advice to Mark Zuckerberg: Go East." *Inc.com*, Inc., 29 Sept. 2015. https://www.inc.com/ilan-mochari/visit-india-creativity.html.

Raice, Shayndi. "Zuckerberg: Thanks for Showing What You Can Build Can Change the World." *The Wall Street Journal*, Dow Jones & Company, 6 Oct. 2011. https://www.wsj.com/articles/BL-DGB-23253.

Shrinag. "A Story of the Mystic Neem Karoli Baba and How He Inspired Steve Jobs and Zuckerberg." *MetroSaga*, 3 Nov. 2018. https://metrosaga.com/mystic-neem-karoli-baba/.

Stanford University. "Text of Steve Jobs' Commencement Address (2005)." *Stanford News*, 12 June 2017." https://news.stanford.edu/2005/06/14/jobs-061505/.